The Northern Rebellion of 1569

Faith, Politics, and Protest in Elizabethan England

K.J. Kesselring

Associate Professor, Dalhousie University

palgrave
macmillan

First published in hardback 2007 and in paperback 2010 by
PALGRAVE MACMILLAN

Palgrave Macmillan in the UK is an imprint of Macmillan Publishers Limited, registered in England, company number 785998, of Houndmills, Basingstoke, Hampshire RG21 6XS.

Palgrave Macmillan in the US is a division of St Martin's Press LLC, 175 Fifth Avenue, New York, NY 10010.

Palgrave Macmillan is the global academic imprint of the above companies and has companies and representatives throughout the world.

Palgrave® and Macmillan® are registered trademarks in the United States, the United Kingdom, Europe and other countries.

ISBN-13: 978-0-230-55319-4 hardback
ISBN-13: 978-0-230-24889-2 paperback

This book is printed on paper suitable for recycling and made from fully managed and sustained forest sources. Logging, pulping and manufacturing processes are expected to conform to the environmental regulations of the country of origin.

A catalogue record for this book is available from the British Library.

A catalog record for this book is available from the Library of Congress.

10 9 8 7 6 5 4 3 2 1
19 18 17 16 15 14 13 12 11 10

Printed and bound in Great Britain by
CPI Antony Rowe, Chippenham and Eastbourne

The Northern Rebellion of 1569

Also by K.J. Kesselring

MERCY AND AUTHORITY IN THE TUDOR STATE

Contents

List of Maps and Illustrations

Maps

Illustrations

Preface

On November 17, 1570, the bells of Oxford's Lincoln College rang. The day had long commemorated the life of St. Hugh of Lincoln, but in more recent years had also marked the anniversary of Catholic Queen Mary's death and the accession of her Protestant sister Elizabeth. As the past year had witnessed a rebellion meant to restore the old faith, Oxford's mayor initially reacted with alarm to the tolling of the bells. He first assumed the sound to be a dirge for the late Catholic Queen, performed by the unregenerate traditionalists who dominated Lincoln College. When challenged, however, the men quickly replied that they rang the bells not as a lament for what was lost but as a celebration of the blessings brought by their current Queen. Thinking this a lovely idea indeed, the mayor then ordered all the town's bells rung with like intent.[1] Recorded only in 1610, the story may well be apocryphal; nonetheless, it nicely illustrates the ways in which an action can take on vastly different meanings, possibly quite different than those initially intended. It also hints at the cautious mood that prevailed in the wake of the dangerous but short-lived Northern Rebellion, the one and only domestic armed revolt against Elizabeth's Protestant establishment.

My interest in the Northern Rebellion of 1569 was first piqued when completing a project on the use of pardons in sixteenth-century law and politics. After most of the period's many rebellions, participants engaged in dramatic spectacles of humble submission and lordly clemency. A few leaders usually suffered execution, but parades of penitents, often wearing nooses about their necks, received pardons from the sovereign they had recently defied. After the rising in 1569, in contrast, Queen Elizabeth's agents dispatched hundreds of rebels in hasty proceedings conducted under martial law. The pardons for the remainder, when they finally came, consisted of cash transactions with only a little of the paternalist pageantry that had long adorned the resolution of earlier rebellions. What was different about this particular rebellion and its context?

My initial impression was that this uprising in defense of Catholicism, happening at a time of intensified religious conflict and polarization throughout Europe, ran up against a newly fervid anti-Catholicism at court. Yet this preliminary speculation clashed with prevailing scholarly interpretations of the rebellion, which depicted it as a "rising of the earls," the product of an elite political conspiracy and feudalism's death struggle. In such accounts, the bulk of participants remained in the shadows, supporting the rebellion because of "instinctive loyalty" to their lords rather than any heartfelt commitment to the old faith. Yet if this is all the rebellion was, why did Elizabeth exact such bloody vengeance? And what are we to make of published court records that seem to show participants both enraged and exuberant, deeply engaged rather than tepidly feigning support? What did motivate the 6000 or so men who formed the rebel army, or the women and youths who stayed behind in the villages and took the chance to restore traditional services?

This book attempts to answer these questions. It also tries to emulate aspects of some of the better works on medieval and early modern rebellions, such as the late R.R. Davies's study of the revolt of Owain Glyn Dŵr and Richard Hoyle's book on the Pilgrimage of Grace, in being written for both an academic and a general audience. After all, the rebellion occurred at a fascinating and dangerous time of change. In its day, it engaged the hopes and fears of many people, who argued heatedly about its character and meaning. To borrow the words of sociologist Philip Abrams, the rebellion of 1569 was an "event": that is, "not just a happening there to be narrated but a happening to which cultural significance has successfully been assigned...An event is a moment of becoming at which action and structure meet."[2] In looking at this transformation from episode to event – the allocation of meaning to action – we can throw light on the broader social, political, religious, and cultural history of the day. The rebellion marked a turning point in Elizabethan history, and to understand why, we must explain not the rebellion alone, but the rebellion as it acted on the minds of the Queen, her councilors, her members of parliament, and her subjects at large. Studying the rebellion can enhance our knowledge of popular politics, the formation of religious identities, and processes of cultural change. It is an event with a significance worth unpacking, but it is also an interesting story – one to which I hope I have done justice.

In writing this book, I have been fortunate to have the assistance of many people. In the UK, Diana Newton and Simon Healy provided encouragement, archival advice, and much hospitality. John Morrill, Richard Hoyle, Helen Good, and Jane Dawson supplied useful counsel at key stages in the research. On this side of the Atlantic, Bob Tittler and Norman Jones offered valuable suggestions at the project's inception. Mark Fissel not only gave advice on military matters but also provided free copies of his books. Lisa McClain shared an unpublished paper on Catholicism in the border region. My colleagues Cynthia Neville and Gregory Hanlon gave generously of their time, Cynthia in reading through the entire manuscript and acting as a source for all things Scottish, and Greg in translating a set of Italian correspondence. A series of student research assistants including Amani Whitfield, Karen Peddle, James Flemming, Anne Cummings, and Heather Ward helped in a variety of ways; Heather's work on the maps that accompany this book was especially invaluable. Participants in a variety of seminars and conferences asked good questions and gave good advice. The staff people at many libraries and record offices dealt patiently and generously with my numerous requests. Jane Anderson, the archivist at Glamis Castle, went well above and beyond any reasonable expectation of aid, altering her schedule to fit the needs of a transatlantic researcher and even offering drives on rainy days. So, too, were the volunteers at the Bowes Museum library and the staff at the Durham Dean and Chapter and University libraries particularly accommodating. Dalhousie University's Document Delivery office, as usual, provided prompt and patient responses to a host of requests. To all these, and to more unnamed, I offer heartfelt thanks.

I am grateful, too, for the financial support from the Social Sciences and Humanities Research Council of Canada that funded the research upon which this book is based. I thank the Marquess of Salisbury and the Duke of Northumberland for permission to consult and cite the microfilmed copies of their papers at the British Library, and the Earl of Strathmore for permission to use documents in his possession at Glamis Castle. I am indebted as well to the University of Chicago Press and Blackwell Publishing for permission to reprint in altered form materials that first appeared in the following articles: " 'A Cold Pye for Papistes': Constructing and Containing the Northern Rising of 1569," *Journal of British Studies*, 43 (2004), 417–43; "Mercy and Liberality: The Aftermath of the 1569 Northern Rebellion," *History* 90 (2005), 213–35; and "Deference and Dissent: Reflections on Sixteenth-Century Protest," *History Compass* 3 (June 2005), 1–16.

Above all, I need to thank Todd McCallum for his patience and encouragement. His comments on the many drafts presented to him were often merciless but always helpful, and have made this a much better book than it would otherwise be.

K.J. Kesselring
Halifax, 2007

Abbreviations

BIHR	Borthwick Institute of Historical Research
BL	British Library
CPR	Calendar of the Patent Rolls
CSP	Calendar of State Papers
DDCL	Durham Dean and Chapter Library
DUL	Durham University Library
HMC	Historical Manuscripts Commission
STC	Short Title Catalogue
TRP	Tudor Royal Proclamations

Spelling and punctuation in all quotations have been modernized. All manuscript references are to The National Archives, Public Record Office unless otherwise noted and are quoted by the call numbers in use at each repository (see the bibliography for the class designations). When dates are given, the year is taken to have begun on January 1. For parliamentary acts, the *Statutes of the Realm*, ed. A. Luders et al., 11 vols (London, 1810–28) has been used, but citations are made by regnal year and chapter.

Introduction

In late November 1569, Elizabeth Watson went to mass at Durham, something she had not been able to do for over a decade. Soon after Queen Elizabeth had come to the English throne in 1558, Protestant services had replaced the Catholic mass only just recently reinstated by Queen Mary, after a turbulent few decades of religious change first begun by King Henry VIII. We tend to remember Queen Elizabeth as "Gloriana," the Virgin Queen who steered England safely and successfully through the shoals of the sixteenth-century reformation; Elizabeth Watson and her ilk we tend to remember rarely at all. Watson does not seem to have previously offered any overt resistance to the changes around her. But now in the north, a rebellion had begun in the name of the old faith and Watson, like many others, seized the opportunity to attend a Catholic service. In fact, so many people attended that she could not fight her way through the throng and had to sit at the edge of the crowd to say her rosary. Of course, not all welcomed the rebellion and its changes: Watson encountered one disconsolate Protestant woman, to whom she dismissively sneered, "the devil weep with you."[1]

Two northern noblemen initiated this rebellion. On November 14, 1569, the earls of Northumberland and Westmorland gathered their immediate followers and stormed Durham Cathedral. With the aid of those assembled, they ripped apart all Protestant books, overturned the communion table, and celebrated a Catholic mass. The earls declared themselves ready to remove those "disordered and evil disposed persons" about the Queen who subverted the true Catholic faith, the ancient nobility, and the rightful succession.[2] Momentum built from there. Within days, some 6000 armed men answered the earls' call. They marched under time-hallowed banners bearing the Five Wounds of Christ and the motto "God Speed the Plow."[3] One group successfully

1

besieged Barnard Castle, while another took the port of Hartlepool. Those who remained at home in the parishes set about dismantling the instruments of the new faith and restoring those of the old. In Sedgefield, churchwarden Roland Hixson stoked a communal bonfire with Protestant service books. As he fanned the flames, he declared gleefully, "Lo, see how the homilies flee to the devil!"[4] Infants were baptized and marriages blessed by the old rites, as many in the north embraced the return of Catholicism. Some individuals no doubt participated out of fear, promise of pay, or the same spirit of conformity they had always shown to whoever might be in power at the time, but others clearly offered their aid willingly and with enthusiasm.

If participants' motives varied, so too did reactions throughout the country. John Welles, a Norfolk sawyer, recounted news of the rising and urged his audience to take this as encouragement to rise in turn: "There are two earls amongst others in the north who [have] been in great business and trouble, and except they be helped they be but undone, but if all men would do as I would, they should have help."[5] Elsewhere, officials sent fretful or frightened letters to court, warning of imminent trouble in their own areas. Queen Elizabeth and her Council prepared for the worst. They mustered a massive army of some 14,000 men to send north, and gathered a special reserve guard for the Queen's person. The London aldermen ordered the city gates and portcullises fixed and the guns put in readiness.[6] Northern clerics of the Protestant persuasion fled south, with Durham's Bishop Pilkington and Dean Whittingham among the first to seek safety. Worried Protestants published pamphlets that condemned the rebels for turning their backs on the true faith and for endangering the realm; these actions, they claimed, threatened to return England to the yoke of papal slavery. One Catholic cleric intoned to his rebellious flock that, like a horse once stuck in the mire, no more would they be trapped in the Queen's schismatical faith; Protestants with equal fervor denounced any return to the errors of the papal past.

Soon, however, Elizabeth Watson and many others appeared in court to apologize for their actions and bonfires celebrated the defeat of the rising. The two earls fled to Scotland as the Queen's forces arrived from the south. The rebellion revived in Scotland under an altered guise; yet, by late December, the conflict in England had come to an ignominious end. It was a failure, but one with significant consequences. Hundreds of rebels died on hastily erected gallows and northern society came more firmly under the control of new men suitably loyal to the crown. More broadly, the rebellion also tested and toughened

Queen Elizabeth's political and religious settlement. Together with Pope Pius V's excommunication of the Queen early in 1570, it was a central element of a crisis that stretched from 1568 to 1572, from the arrival of Mary Queen of Scots in England to the execution of the duke of Norfolk, implicated in the plot by the Scottish Queen and Italian banker Roberto di Ridolfi to overthrow Elizabeth. Like other political crises, this one provoked a hardening of attitudes and a stiffening of policy; the 1570s differed in important respects from the 1560s. Religious identities polarized. Treason laws tightened. Committed Catholics with the resources to do so went underground or overseas. Changes begun earlier in the 1560s accelerated; the rebellion they had helped to trigger ironically confirmed their necessity to the governors of Elizabethan England.

Despite the actions of people like Elizabeth Watson, the standard accounts of the rising depict the events of 1569 largely as the product of power struggles within the Tudor elite. Rachael Reid and Wallace MacCaffrey have deemed it, respectively, "the last baronial rising" and "a merely personal enterprise" of the earls. Insulted and injured by various royal policies, especially the promotion of "new men" in the north, the earls plotted to put on the throne Mary Queen of Scots, a monarch they believed to be more sensitive to noble privilege. Drawn from a dark, backwards corner of the realm, the participants answered the call of their feudal lords out of an "instinctive loyalty." Some of the best recent work on Tudor rebellions continues to endorse this view.[7] Yet such characterizations of the rising as the product of elite political intrigue and of the participants as dutiful tenants responding to feudal instincts obscure the significance of the popular component of the rebellion and risk doing the same for the religious.

While the earls did have reason to fear for their position in northern society, we need not adopt the view put forth in loyalist propaganda that their protestations of faith existed solely to conceal baser motives. For Northumberland and at least some of his close confederates, attacks on Catholicism and on noble power were synonymous. Furthermore, M.E. James long ago observed that the tenants of the earls did not comprise the bulk of the rebel army in 1569; he insisted that by the late sixteenth century, "there was no state of affairs in which tenants still proffered their landlord unquestioning 'faithfulness' or knew 'no Prince but a Percy'."[8] Due in part to the erosion of feudal power that contributed to the earls' motivation to rise, this rebellion could not rely on the unquestioning support of a feudal tenantry. Indeed, in her meticulously researched doctoral dissertation, Susan Taylor demonstrated that some

80 percent of the known rebels had no tenurial links to the earls and must therefore have found motivation beyond traditional loyalties.[9] These facts have been recognized in some recent works that mention the rising, but have not yet managed to revise our understanding of the events of 1569.

The historiography of the 1569 rebellion has some affinities with that of the biggest of all Tudor rebellions, the Pilgrimage of Grace. The Pilgrimage, a massive revolt that spread throughout the north in 1536, had long been described as a mass movement with support from all sorts, if perhaps for differing reasons. In 1979, G.R. Elton recast the rising as one driven by court faction and elite conspiracy.[10] Widely endorsed initially, this view soon came to be challenged. C.S.L. Davies accepted it in part, but insisted that any conspiracy could not completely account for how the rebellion began, let alone its subsequent shape and strength.[11] More recently, Richard Hoyle and G.W. Bernard have gone further in discounting the role of court intrigue altogether. Hoyle argues compellingly that the Pilgrimage was the spontaneous product of popular action, arising from people's fears of royal attacks on their parish churches and rumors of risings elsewhere, and not the premeditated result of a gentry conspiracy. In response to those who assumed independent political action by the common sort unthinkable, he demonstrates that the tenants coerced their lords into participation, rather than vice versa.[12] Certainly, a spate of recent work renders the dismissal of self-directed action from the common people difficult. Building on the foundations laid by such scholars as George Rudé and E.P. Thompson, a wide range of works have decisively challenged assumptions of a passive, pre-political popular culture, opening the Pilgrimage and also the 1569 revolt to a fresh reevaluation.[13]

In retrieving the popular aspect of the Pilgrimage, Davies, Hoyle, and Bernard have also revived its religious history. Bernard goes the furthest in this direction, depicting the events of 1536 as essentially religious popular risings directed first and foremost against the King's assault on the monasteries. He suggests, too, that historians who focus on political conspiracy might have been misled by the crown's own propaganda, and depicts the social grievances as merely "a perennial undertow," an enduring feature rather than a trigger for protest.[14] In contrast, while Davies refuses to treat the religious dimension merely as a cover for political or pragmatic economic objectives, he also declines to privilege one factor over others. "Historians," he suggests, "pull apart the various factors involved in a complex movement in the course of their analysis and set them in rank order; in the process they are inclined to forget that it is precisely the interaction and fusion of several grievances which make revolt possible."[15]

With Sir Thomas Wyatt's revolt against Queen Mary in 1554, we have no difficulty acknowledging the range of divergent motives: the political machinations of the elite plotters intent on replacing Catholic Mary with the Protestant pairing of the Princess Elizabeth and Edward Stafford, alongside the Protestantism or merely anti-Spanish sentiments of willing and otherwise loyal rebels who hoped to change their Queen's mind, not necessarily to replace her.[16] A similar multiplicity of motives, I suggest, shaped events in 1569. The treatment of Wyatt's rebellion also highlights another tendency of historical writing that has worked to the disservice of the 1569 rebels. Wyatt's force of some 4000 men had no more success than the 6000 or so who rose with the northern earls. Yet, unlike the Northern Rebellion, that of Wyatt's men has generally been seen as a demonstration of genuine and widespread discontent. The contrasting portraits of the significance of these two risings bear some resemblance to what Murray Pittock has labeled the "heads-I-win, tails-you-lose" version of history. In his study of the eighteenth-century Jacobite revolts, Pittock criticizes historians' assumptions that popular passivity denoted a lack of support for the Stewart cause, and notes by contrast that such assumptions are rarely made about the comparable passivity that greeted Henry Tudor's invasion in 1485 and William of Orange's arrival in 1688. He concludes that "if no change occurs, those who do not overtly align themselves with its failed forces are held to have been against it; on the contrary, in cases where attempts at change are successful, the equal inactivity of the majority is held to show their consent to the change."[17] According to this version of history, Wyatt's hardy few opposed the Catholic and "Bloody" Queen Mary and represented the future; their northern counterparts fought the Protestant Gloriana and thus represented the failed past.

Comparisons with previous revolts and their historiographies highlight problematic assumptions and suggest possible avenues of approach, but do not themselves prove anything about the events of 1569. For that we must turn to the records. Several remarkably full correspondence collections survive. The voluminous papers of William Cecil, Elizabeth's chief councilor, are spread between the "official" state paper collections and those saved at Hatfield House by his heirs; as for so many other aspects of Elizabethan England, they offer a rich source of information for this rebellion. So too do the papers of Sir Ralph Sadler. Sadler was a long-time fixture in Tudor politics, serving variously as a diplomat, councilor, and treasurer, and in 1569 as the man Elizabeth sent north to reassure herself of the loyalty of the earl of Sussex, her northern lieutenant. Sir George Bowes, a northern gentleman of some stature who served on the Council in the North, also left a wealth of papers. Bowes carefully documented his work as provost martial in the aftermath of the revolt, as well as his losses at the hands of the rebels in hopes of suing the survivors for compensation. Sadler's papers are at the British Library; Bowes's are divided among the British Library, Glamis Castle, and several county Durham repositories. Selections from both Sadler's and Bowes's papers have also been published, the latter in a particularly valuable book by the notable northern antiquary, Sir Cuthbert Sharp.[18]

Thus, in some respects, this rising is well documented. In other areas, however, this rebellion has left frustratingly few records. The letters and records that survive are overwhelmingly those produced by the Queen's side. For other rebellions, historians have been able to get a step closer to the words and thoughts of the rebels themselves through court depositions. A few church court records do survive from both York and Durham, but relevant secular court records are few. Proceedings at martial law left no lengthy transcripts of rebel justifications. The bulk of the rebels who underwent common law trials were heard not at Westminster but before the Council of the North; unfortunately, its records fell foul of a later and larger conflict, the seventeenth-century civil wars. Nor do the records of the Privy Council survive for these months. Thus, the records are patchy and overwhelmingly those of the victors.

Historians have long known of these records; an extensive search through various archives has produced only a few fresh items. The receipts for the Queen's armies, the inventories of convicted rebels' lands, and other such documents add detail to the story, but few things that are wholly new have come to light. Yet enough remains to tell much of the tale, and the old can be brought together in a new and more complete way. The question is how to read the remnants, as selective quotations can seem to support almost any point of view. The set of court records that tells the tale of Elizabeth Watson and other enthusiastic participants in the restoration of Catholic services also includes the protestations of some that they had done so only from fear. The letters of Elizabethan loyalists include some passages which suggest that coercion and cash accounted for rebel participation, and others that attribute it to religious ardor. Sir George Bowes sought to excuse his inability to raise loyal forces from Richmondshire with a report that the earls had promised to terrorize those who did not join their side. In another letter, however, he admitted that "daily the people flee from these parts to the earls" with no regard for his own "fair speech and bestowing of money." Such footmen as he had already mustered threatened to leave unless better paid, Bowes added.[19] The earl of Sussex and others of the Queen's agents in the north observed that most who joined the rebels did so because they "like so well their cause of religion."[20] Should one set of claims impress us more than the other? Surely, careful attention to context can allow us to read some such statements as self-interested, simply mistaken, or indeed, as signs of the range of reasons and reactions that existed.

In reasserting religion as a key source of some of these reasons and reactions, Davies's warning should be borne in mind: in rescuing religion as a factor in protest, one must be careful to avoid reifying the term or simply reordering a list of discrete, objective variables. As historians of the Pilgrimage of Grace and the Civil Wars have reminded us, the "religious" cannot be abstracted from the material, the political, and the social.[21] To focus on the way ideas, and not just interests, mattered is not to replace social with religious explanations but to show how closely the two were sometimes related. The surviving records allow little to be said of the texture of the rebels' religious beliefs. Did attendance at masses and use of the rosary emerge from a belief in the doctrinal inadequacies of Protestantism or from a fondness for customary and familiar ways? Did preference for Catholicism emerge from beliefs that it represented a surer path to salvation or from a sense that Protestantism had brought with it new social divisions, new financial demands, and new international dangers? Even the fullest records do not usually allow these motives to be disentangled; of necessity, they coexist here under the label of "religious." While the fine-grained complexity of the rebels' religious beliefs cannot be recreated, the records suggest that we can do better than treat religion merely as legitimizing propaganda used by the earls to manipulate popular support or as something extraneous to the "real" interests of the common man and woman. Rather, it emerges as a filter through which other grievances were understood and articulated and, above all, as a motive force for people of all degrees.

Most every rebellion of the medieval and early modern periods included the participation of people from all orders of society. Nevertheless, we often label them "aristocratic" or "popular" based on who initiated them. By this criterion, the events in 1569 might legitimately be deemed "aristocratic." This label can, however, occlude the willing and dynamic participation of the bulk of the rebel host and imply too deterministic a role for the elite leaders; as the earl of Essex discovered in

1601, noblemen can call for rebellion but need popular support for it to happen. Yes, this *was* an age in which hierarchy mattered. Access to land, food, and other resources depended on hierarchical social structures; cultural norms reflected and reinforced those structures. In their study of Tudor revolts, Anthony Fletcher and Diarmaid MacCulloch discuss the intense, intrinsic importance of status and note that "even in time of rebellion, the fundamental assumptions of Tudor society persisted: the commons expected the gentry to give the lead" – even if they had to demand that leadership through force.[22] As such, a conjecture that lordly leaders could count on hierarchical social structures and codes of conduct to find followers to further their own cause has a certain plausibility. In this particular case, however, it fails to fit the evidence. We might better understand the role of hierarchy in this rebellion not as determinative but as enabling and legitimating. The noblemen provided the material resources needed for revolt – much of the weaponry, money, and banners – and also the rationale required to defy one's sovereign. Study after study of premodern protest has shown that rebellion was not a simple reflex response to grievance or hardship; people needed a sense that change was possible and that their actions were just. In 1569, as in earlier risings, elite leadership helped to provide that sense.

In what follows, I hope to show that while elite political action triggered the rising, and helped enable and legitimate it in the eyes of the participants, the rebellion's popular and religious elements were integral to its causes, course, and consequences. The cultural filters that shaped people's perceptions of what happened around them were similarly crucial components of the event. In other words, in order to understand how this rebellion began and how it mattered, we must acknowledge the range of motives and needs to which it responded, and also the ways in which contemporaries invested it with meaning.

Accordingly, Chapter 1 surveys the context that allowed the rebellion to take shape. Starting with providential explanations of disturbing occurrences and ending with the Irish rebels who appealed to a Catholic King to free them from a grasping, Protestant Queen, it suggests some of the many ways in which "religion" cannot be understood as a discrete category of experience. Surveying local and international events, it also describes the range of challenges that would push commoners, lords, and Queen to act in the ways they did. Chapter 2 narrates the northern rebellion itself, highlighting along the way the evidence for its religious and popular components. Among the leaders' motives, economic grievances and a sense of diminishing power cannot be separated from their commitment to Catholicism; for Northumberland and his fellows, attacks on the old faith and the old ways were part and parcel of the same problem. The rebellion had elements of an attempted aristocratic coup, but also engaged the hopes and interests of many people who helped or hindered it for a variety of reasons of their own. Chapter 3 follows the rebel leaders on their flight across the border into Scotland, and shows how they revived their efforts with the aid of the borderers and Queen Mary's Scottish supporters. Chapter 4 returns to the domestic aftermath. By executing hundreds of people and seizing thousands of pounds worth of land, the Queen sought to punish and prevent such challenges to her rule. The repression had both material and ideological dimensions; the latter became most evident in the public conversations about the significance of the rebellion. Chapter 5 accordingly looks at the ways in which contemporaries and those who followed tried to shape interpretations and memories of the revolt. For in the end, the actions of the people who burned Protestant books and marched with the earls in this last great Tudor rebellion did not result in the restoration of Catholicism. Instead, their actions, and the narratives constructed about those actions, allowed a reinvigoration of royal power and a change in the ways opposition would thenceforth be expressed.

1

An Impending Crisis?

In January 1569, Agnes Bowker, a serving woman of Market Harborough in Leicestershire, maintained that she had given birth to a cat. Local investigators appealed for advice to Lord Hastings, William Cecil, and Bishop Grindal in turn. Bowker's story, notorious then, has been resurrected more recently by David Cressy, who sees in the attention it received evidence of the religious conflicts, political anxieties, and cultural tensions in the unsettled 1560s. The story became "a matter of public concern when people saw threatening portents in this apparent violation of nature, and when credulous Catholics gained ground by exploiting a dubious story."[1] Both Protestants and Catholics found much meaning in such monsters; both sought to use them to their advantage. William Bullein's *A Dialogue...Against the Fever Pestilence* made specific reference to Bowker's cat, discrediting the tale, and deriding it as "a pleasant practice of papistry, to bring the people to new wonders."[2] Bowker's cat was one of a lengthy list of such portents in recent years. The 1560s saw a surge in publications on the deformities found in nature and their analogues in society more generally. Pamphlet writers glossed the births of "monstrous children" in Northampton-shire in 1565, Buckinghamshire and Surrey in 1566, and Kent in 1568 as signs of trouble within the realm. The Kent broadsheet included a graphic rendering of the deformed infant and bore the ominous subtitle "A Warning to England." But a warning of what, specifically? "This monstrous shape to thee England, plain shows thy monstrous vice," including blasphemy and a turning away from truth, the oppressions of gorging, greedy men, and the unruliness of those who "do seek not to be led, but for to lead amiss."[3] Such vices would surely be punished. Some people proved skeptical of such readings and viewed the monsters merely as entertaining diversions or frauds. But even Bullein, who dismissed Bowker's cat as a contrivance manipulated by papists, allowed that real monsters existed, and that "after them do come great battles, pestilence, earthquakes, hunger and marvelous changes in common-wealths."

Monstrous births plagued the 1560s, but so too did the elements themselves manifest God's warnings. The providentially minded noted the fatal lightening storm that struck Covent Garden, widespread thunder and lightening storms that lasted eleven days without remit, and earthquakes in Lincolnshire and Northamptonshire in 1563. The following year, the Thames flooded, then froze, and in its thaw burst bridges and took lives. The next year saw unusual storms with hail and fire from heaven that destroyed hundreds of acres of crops. The sea, too, spewed forth its own providential signs. Fish up to twenty yards in length washed onto shore; in 1568, at Downham Bridge in Suffolk, some seventeen "monstrous fish" appeared. All this was done "by God, his mighty power and strength, to warn us of our sin."[4] After the 1569 rebellion, some saw the event as the fulfillment of such signs. William Woodwall realized in retrospect that the birth of a two-headed monster had signified the imminent rebellion of the two earls.[5] Inspired by the recent rising, the author of *A Marvelous Strange Deformed Swine* (1570) thought that the unfortunate beast in question was a particular warning to beware those, like the recent rebels, "who meant the ruin of our realm, as Traitors to our Queen" (Illustration 1.1).[6]

Before the rebellion, no one knew quite what such signs portended, but they had plenty of reasons to be concerned for their future. In some respects, the 1560s were relatively quiet years; other than the disastrous Newhaven expedition early in the decade, no major wars – foreign or domestic – taxed the realm, and the widespread fears of impending turmoil upon Queen Elizabeth's accession in 1558 had proven unfounded. Yet the final years of the decade saw a sense of crisis and a set of challenges that help explain both the rebellion and the responses to it. Disruptions in the cloth trade, poor harvests, and enclosures agitated some. A religious reformation that proceeded too slowly or too quickly, depending on one's point of view, troubled others. With their Queen thus far unmarried and without an heir to ensure a stable succession, concerns for an uncertain future grew. In Ireland and Scotland, tensions threatened to redound upon English interests. Both witnessed rebellions, battles, and sieges that had repercussions for English affairs. The arrival in 1568 of Mary Stewart, the ousted Queen of Scots, proved especially troubling. No one knew quite what to expect of the Catholic powers of France and Spain, the former a long-time

Illustration 1.1   A Providential Wonder.

foe and the latter an increasingly uncertain ally. The papacy did both too little and too much to allow any in England to feel secure. It gave scant comfort or counsel to embattled English Catholics, yet courted conspirators and considered excommunicating the English Queen. As the interpretations of deformed births and unusual weather suggest, people did not take lightly the problems that surrounded them. Such tensions drove some people to contemplate rebellion; they also drove Elizabeth to decisions that both precipitated revolt and left her unusually well prepared to deal with it.

Riots and vagrancy

Manifestations of tension more credible to modern eyes than monstrous births may be found in the riots and disorders of the months preceding the November rebellion. Signs of popular rather than divine discontent, these tumults betokened and worsened an atmosphere of crisis. In Suffolk, authorities responded to a series of disorders and averted a more ambitious rising planned to begin at a fair in Beccles in the summer of 1569. According to a letter received by Sir James Croft, the arrest of vagrants had led to the discovery of a planned insurrection. Then, "by the apprehension of the principal parties before hand, the matter was wisely foreseen, and the head of a further and more general mischief cut off in time. Their color was against the multitude of strangers and foreign artificers, they said." Disruptions to the cloth trade had caused unemployment and grumbling in both Suffolk and Norfolk, and as so often happened in such cases, frustrations were directed at the "unjust" competition offered by foreign workers. The letter writer, however, feared the planned tumult had more ambitious aims: "But their intent was plainly, as the custom is, to have spoiled all the gentlemen and worthy personages that they might overtake . . . and so marching towards London, to have provoked with this example the whole realm to the like uproar."[7] Such fears were not simply the product of an overactive imagination. James Fuller, a Suffolk sawyer, confessed that he and others had planned to rebel for lack of work or money. Once they had rung the bells to gather men, they intended to "proceed and bring down [the] price of all things at our pleasure." He had pledged his fellow plotters that this time, "we will not be deceived as we were at the last rising, for then we were promised enough. But the more was a halter. But now we will appoint them that shall take the rich churls and set them on their horsebacks under a tree . . . and so let them hang."[8] The "last rising" of which Fuller spoke had been the 1549 peasant rebellions, in which commoners combined against their masters in staggering numbers and had suffered severely as a result. Memories of the 1549 rebellions apparently lived long in the minds of worried gentlemen and hungry workers alike.

In Derby, one persistent group of rioters made it well past the plotting stage. Reacting to the enclosure of their common lands at Chinley, within the duchy of Lancaster, they repeatedly destroyed hedges erected and reerected by one Geoffrey Bradshaw in the early months of 1569. Raising a common fund, arming themselves, and threatening to burn Bradshaw's home, they camped for a time on the disputed field. Already this posed more of a challenge than the usual enclosure riot. Bradshaw sought reinforcement of his authority to enclose the lands by obtaining a special warrant from the chancellor of the duchy, but it had no effect. Indeed, the rioters reassembled "in great companies... with unlawful weapons" to rescue one of their fellows previously arrested, defying the constable's order to keep the peace. Making the affair of special concern to the authorities was the report that some of the rioters circulated books of prophecy and consulted with one "Mr Bircles... concerning prophesies by noblemen."[9] The nature of these prophecies is unknown, but Keith Thomas raised an interesting possibility with his suggestion that this "Mr Bircles" was the John Birtles involved in a later conspiracy against the Queen, in which he was found to have "a certain old book of prophecy, wherein is great pictures."[10] Tudor authorities had long recognized and feared the radicalizing properties of prophecy in protest. While they relied on the sanction of the supernatural and had been known to use prophecies to their own advantage, the governors of Tudor England had specifically banned the use of political prophecy by others. Prophecies had contributed to the rebellions of 1536 and 1549, and to a host of smaller acts of disobedience. As with their providential interpretations of unusual events, people could find in prophecies novel, and for the authorities dangerous, ways to interpret the tensions about them.[11]

Nor was Derby the only county to experience an enclosure riot larger and more dangerous than usual. On June 24, local tenants gathered in the Westward Forest of county Cumberland to throw down enclosures recently erected. The forest, some twelve to thirteen miles in compass, had grazing fit for sheep, but most importantly, the woods had long served as "the great refuge of all the country for the preservation of their cattle against the Scots."[12] Reports variously identified the number of rioters as between three and four hundred or over a thousand. At either count, it was an impressive display. "Riotously or rather in the manner of rebellion," the gathering of men, women, and children set their cattle loose on the grain and grass. Sheriff Musgrave read a proclamation ordering the rioters to disperse, but to little avail. Efforts to forestall another demonstration on the commons the following day had more success and resulted in many arrests. Some two to three hundred people confessed to misdemeanor riot and paid fines, but the alarmed privy councilors insisted an example be set: "we think it good that no forbearing be used to convict as many of the offenders in this tumult upon felony... whereby more terror may grow." The earl of Sussex, then president of the Council in the North, singled out one of the instigators, a John Bawne, for special attention because of "his notorious abusing of the Queen's Majesty's name and authority." The resolution of the riot dragged on into early fall as officials did their best to dig to the root of the problem and find victims for the gallows.[13]

There is little evidence of direct links between these or other riots and the rebellion in the fall. In Norfolk, a few disaffected laborers would seek to combine action against foreign artificers with aid for the northern rebels in November, and later interrogations of Sir Thomas Fitzherbert of the Derbyshire Peak district suggest that the authorities suspected a tie between the earlier rioters and later rebels.[14] But no connections more substantial than these can be found between a summer of popular discontent and an autumn rebellion that offered no overt expressions of social or economic grievances. What the riots do show, however, is the presence of people not just capable of a critical consciousness, but also willing to respond to the tensions around them by engaging in direct action. They suggest an atmosphere of restlessness on which potential rebels would draw.

They also triggered action from the authorities to forestall a larger crisis, much of which focused on the wandering poor. As Paul Slack notes, "Vagabonds became the scapegoats for all social problems. They were carriers of rumor, sedition, and disease, and they infected others with their 'licentious liberty.'"[15] Wanderers spread news and ideas that the authorities thought best contained; stopping them would help stop the spread of crisis. Vagrants had not been immune from prosecution before. Indeed, at the beginning of Elizabeth's reign, some men in power had suggested reviving the notorious slavery act of 1547 against vagrants, and mass arrests began in Essex from 1564.[16] But now, such round-ups became more regular and more rigorous. From May 1569 to 1572, the Privy Council ordered monthly "secret searches" for vagrants, a campaign from which records survive for the arrest of some 1159 men and women. In June 1569, the Privy Council ordered London's common council to perform intensive searches for vagrants and to post a double set of trustworthy watchmen, lest "any levy or raising of people be made, as in some corners of the realm hath been lately attempted."[17]

Authorities also feared that the religiously disaffected hid among these masses; some of these "masterless men" might answer, in fact, to the Pope. And indeed the authorities did find a few such people. John Morwen, a former chaplain to Bishop Bonner, "wandereth in Staffordshire and Lancashire very seditiously" and on his travels spread a tract which argued that the lightening strike and fire at St. Paul's Cathedral were signs of divine displeasure at the official changes in religion.[18] A later round-up of rogues uncovered in Warwick a sawyer from Preston who refused to attend the new religious services "because his father and mother brought him up in the time of King Henry VIII and then there was other order and he mindeth to observe that order and to serve the Lord God above all things."[19] The clerics George Malton of Topcliffe and Thomas Bell of Thirsk found themselves similarly "moved in conscience and persuaded in opinion and belief that the religion now established in this realm is not the Catholic religion and true doctrine of Christ." They decided to "leave their ministry and orders and to go into the south part to serve as servingmen or to lead laymen's life, thinking there to live as men unknown." Arrested as vagrants in London, they managed to convince their questioners that they were wandering scholars from Oxford, but were later apprehended once more.[20] Yet such examples of religious dissidents caught lurking within the mass of Elizabethan vagrants were few and, one suspects, their danger not great. In fact, there had been little religious protest at all – much discontent and unruliness, but little overt protest in comparison to the more common grain and enclosure riots.

Religious tensions

Considering how traditional in their religious tastes historians have shown the majority of mid-sixteenth century people to have been, this paucity of forceful resistance to religious change is somewhat surprising. Numerous detailed studies of community responses to the reformation have shown the strong attachment of many to their saints, masses, and prayers for the dead. The reformation, in short, did not receive a wide, warm welcome. How, then, to reconcile this conservatism with the undoubted success of the Protestant revolution? Reasons other than the purely religious sometimes favored reform. The economic self-interest of those who acquired church property helped, as did the collaboration of those who found it useful in forwarding their own disputes to accept and employ the language of the authorities.[21] Pragmatism also played a part. Michael Sherbrook, a Yorkshire man writing in the late sixteenth century, recorded that when he asked his father how he could have participated in the spoil of the church he so loved, the latter replied: "What should I do, said he: might I not as well as other have some profit of the spoil of the Abbey? For I did see all would away; and therefore I did as others did." Sherbrook also noted the importance of simple fear in furthering change; clerics and members of parliament alike, men who he thought should have fought to preserve their church, showed more terror of the King of England than of the King of Heaven, "and so such ever turned but never burned."[22] If men with such political power feared the penalties for resisting religious change, it should come as no surprise that those with fewer resources did the same. As the humorist John Taylor later noted of one of his characters, the "Old, Old, Very Old Man," he "held it safest to be of the religion of the king or queen that were in being, for he knew that he came raw into the world, and accounted it no point of wisdom to be broiled out of it."[23]

According to recent studies, the main secret of the reformation's success lay in the gradual and adaptive nature of its changes. The new was grafted onto the old; the dramatic developments and destruction took place around a core of continuities. Late medieval popular piety had developed a Christocentrism, or focus on the passion of the Lord, which accommodated Protestant reform more easily than a single-minded focus on Mary or the saints might have done. The Protestant prayer book had enough in common with the old liturgy to ease its acceptance. Even Calvinist notions of providence – God's active intervention in human affairs – allowed room for vestiges of older views of the miraculous and magical. Lively tales of Protestant martyrs served at least some of the same functions as Catholic saints' stories.[24] Such examples of continuities and borrowings could be multiplied several times over. Norman Jones has drawn attention to the generational aspects of religious reformation; the young, raised in a progressively more Protestant environment, embraced or took for granted the changes, yet also respected and accommodated parents who did not.[25] In such ways did the new permeate, pervade, and finally replace the old in a manner far more peaceful than it had on much of the continent.

Jones also emphasizes the air of compromise, uncertainty, and "tolerant confusion" that prevailed in the years immediately following Elizabeth's coronation.[26] The reformation that had begun under her father had been enthusiastically extended under her brother Edward.

After his death, her elder sister Mary had restored Catholicism to the satisfaction of many and the fierce opposition of some. During Mary's reign, nearly 300 principled Protestants had suffered horribly at the stake and some others had sought safety in the havens of Protestant Europe. Upon Elizabeth's accession, few knew quite what she intended. Some sort of reformation seemed likely, but would it resemble more closely the church of Henry VIII, divided from Rome but otherwise only "halfly reformed," or that of Edward, more consciously Calvinist in doctrine and practice? The religious measures that Elizabeth introduced to her first parliament encountered significant hostility. The Act of Supremacy finally passed only after abandoning its attempt to name Elizabeth "Supreme Head" of the church in favor of the title "Supreme Governor," a change somewhat more palatable to those who thought the former an unwarrantable usurpation of the Pope's rights as well as to those who thought no woman capable of the sacramental duties attendant upon "headship."

Thus far, a reformation along Henrician lines still seemed possible. The Act of Uniformity, however, clarified that Elizabeth's church would look and sound more like her brother's. It mandated the use of a Prayer Book modeled closely on Edward's 1552 service book. This act faced even greater opposition than had the first, and ultimately passed by the narrowest of margins. Even this, however, did not settle all confusion. The act's provisions against those who refused to attend the new services were initially little enforced, and its statement on church ornament studiously vague. While teams of ecclesiastical visitors, or inspectors, set out about the realm to remove "abused" images and to ensure a minimum compliance to the new directives, Elizabeth herself retained a cross and candlesticks upon her communion table. This was a church that would continue to offend those Catholics who insisted upon papal supremacy, called papists or Romanists, and to displease those who returned from the purer Protestant air of Calvinist Geneva determined to effect a thorough purging of the church, sometimes known as puritans or precisians; yet, it might just be tolerable to the traditionalist majority. Lax enforcement meant that many had no immediate need to contemplate the importance of their disagreements with the newly established national church. So, too, did a sense that Elizabeth's reign and religious provisions, like those of her siblings, might be short-lived. After so many changes in so short a time, why rush precipitously either to accept or oppose those now presented?

Of course, one must avoid exaggerating the reformation's gradualism and the scarcity of resistance. Some people at the time were neither impressed with the former nor resigned to the latter. After Henry VIII's initial bout of reforms, thousands in the north embarked on the Pilgrimage of Grace, a massive and dangerous revolt in 1536. Edward's first Protestant prayer book prompted the rebellion of thousands in Devon and Cornwall in 1549. Smaller riots peppered the annals of the reformation: women in Exeter who armed themselves with pitchforks to resist the dismantling of a favorite shrine, parishioners in Seamer who physically ejected the commissioners who came to close their chantry, and revelers in Canterbury who blithely ignored a ban on their saint's day celebrations to light bonfires in the streets were among many who thought the changes sufficient to earn at least some opposition.[27] And, as Jones notes, the ambiguities of the Elizabethan reforms slowly came to be clarified. Although not passed into law until 1571, the convocation of the clergy issued its statement of doctrine in 1563, a set of thirty-nine articles based on those of Edward's Archbishop Cranmer and clearly Calvinist in tone. So, too, did the Catholics' Council of Trent clarify their doctrine and the impropriety of conformity under heretical regimes. The pace increased in the late 1560s. Arrests of those secretly hearing mass multiplied, as did the number of fines given those who refused to attend prayer book services. More and more Catholics went into exile, including such men as William Allen, a student of theology at Oxford whose conscience drove him to found a seminary at Douai in 1568 for others similarly troubled. The Privy Council turned its attentions to the Inns of Court in May 1569, naming suspected papists and ordering them barred from commons and court.[28] By the autumn, the Council extended the list of men from whom it demanded the oath of allegiance. The Ecclesiastical Court of High Commission and bishops' visitations also showed heightened vigor in detecting and correcting the recalcitrant.

In the parishes, much of this new energy focused on the physical reminders of the Catholic past. For traditionalists, images and art within the churches served a variety of functions: to focus attention on the divine, to beautify a holy space, or more pragmatically, to teach an illiterate audience or commemorate the donor. For reformers, however, most such imagery was idolatrous, presumptuous, and in violation of Holy Scripture. Despite iconoclastic purges from Elizabeth's earliest days, some communities had held out. The churchwardens of St. Mary the Great in Cambridge, for instance, waited until 1568 to sell their Catholic goods, wash the saints from their windows, and remove the "image of our lady which was taken of the blue velvet altar cloth by the commandment of the archdeacon."[29] Indeed, it was only in 1569 that Lambeth parish, in the archbishop of Canterbury's own backyard, sold its copes and purged the rood loft of its paintings.[30] Yet, over the 1560s, authorities more vigilantly pursued the lax. Diocesan returns and churchwardens' accounts show how successful this program was in the south; they record fewer and fewer parishes holding on to the remnants of their past as the decade progressed.[31] The north, however, was another matter altogether.

Bishop Best of Carlisle reported mixed success in his 1561 visitation. He said that the common people heard his sermons with "much rejoicing" and expressed regret that they had so long been deceived. On the other hand, some twelve or thirteen of his ministers refused to appear to take the oath of allegiance which recognized Elizabeth, rather than the Pope, as supreme governor of the faith. Under the protection of Lord Dacre, these "imps of antichrist" continued to say mass openly.[32] Real progress in Carlisle would not come until the 1570s, with Best's successor Bishop Barnes and the defeat of Leonard Dacre. Barnes found many of his parish churches still stuffed with the remnants of popery. In the diocese of Chester, which included portions of Richmondshire and Lancashire, the bishop at the time of Elizabeth's accession had been deprived for his intransigence. His successor, William Downham, was appointed in 1561 and proved only marginally better. Reluctant to antagonize his Catholic gentry neighbors, Downham generally left things alone. According to one critic, he skipped the planned visitation of 1561 "because he will not trouble the country nor put them to charge in calling them together." He did, in 1564, order the parishes to reform upon news that some still used holy water, allowed candle burning on Candlemas, and other such holdovers, but did little to enforce his own directives. So lackluster was his performance that in early 1568, he received a reprimand from the Privy Council, a consequence of "credible reports of disorders and contempts" to the uniformity of religion throughout his diocese.[33] Downham's was in some respects the exemplar of a gradual reformation characterized by tolerant confusion, but in 1568, the High Commission at York began to intervene and force the pace of change.[34]

Durham offered a marked contrast. At the time of Elizabeth's accession, Durham's Bishop Tunstall proved a stalwart opponent of her religious program. He lost his position in 1559, but was not replaced for some time, probably because Elizabeth hoped to benefit financially in the interim by collecting the rents of this wealthy diocese in which powers secular and religious resided in the incumbent. Finally, in May 1561, a new bishop arrived. James Pilkington had honed his

Protestantism to a fine point while in exile in Mary's reign. He returned to England determined to effect a thoroughgoing reformation, and took up his new duties with alacrity. He quickly surrounded himself with like-minded individuals to counterbalance the existing cathedral staff, some former monks and priors, who had survived the initial purge after Elizabeth's accession. Of these new men, William Whittingham stood out. Whittingham had worked in exile on the Geneva Bible, had succeeded the Scottish firebrand John Knox as pastor of the English community under the tutelage of John Calvin, and had married the latter's sister (or sister-in-law).[35] Whittingham had served for a time as chaplain to the English forces at Newhaven, where he earned a dressing down for eschewing the mandated prayer book in favor of a more rigorously Calvinist service. In 1563, he became dean of Durham cathedral. Together, Pilkington, Whittingham, and others of the "hotter sort of Protestant" sought to drag their diocese into the Protestant age, a task that left them sorely tested and much disliked. David Marcombe, who has written extensively on the reformation in Durham, suggests that Pilkington was probably the most radically Protestant of all the bishops appointed by Elizabeth and that he and his puritanical fellows showed more than usual indiscretion and abrasiveness in setting about their task.[36] Making matters worse, Pilkington combined his efforts at religious reform with a program to reendow the church with lands alienated by his predecessors and long in the hands of others, thus earning further enmity. He wrote of his flock that "I know not whether they like me worse or I they."[37]

Over the 1560s, the new establishment at Durham attacked the physical remnants of the old faith. Whittingham went even further than official directives allowed; whereas Elizabeth had specifically excluded funerary monuments from destruction, he broke up many tombs that bore images he found offensive and used the material for practical, mundane repairs around the cathedral. With equal insensitivity to local sentiment, his wife Katherine supervised the public burning of the ancient banner of St. Cuthbert. Cuthbert had been more than just a patron saint; he had come to symbolize Durham itself, and according to tradition, those who marched under his banner would suffer no defeat. As Marcombe notes, "if the Dean was hated for anything in Durham, it was surely for this."[38] In 1567, a concerted attack began on the images and altars remaining in the parishes. Churches that still retained altars instead of the mandated communion tables received orders to make the switch, and those that failed to act received visits from the bishop's representatives who did so themselves, in at least one case with the forceful opposition of the community.[39] "Our poor papists weep to see our churches so bare," Pilkington crowed, for "there is nothing in them to make curtsy unto, neither saints nor yet their old little god."[40]

Yet the bishop frequently complained of the problems he faced. Many newly arrived Scottish Catholic priests, fleeing their own reformation, "do more harm than other would or could in dissuading the people." Furthermore, "the parishes be great, the people many, the wage small, priests bad and very few to be had and fewer to be hoped for."[41] Of special concern to Pilkington were not just the recalcitrant traditionalists, but also an organized Catholic underground with its own ties to exile communities on the continent, particularly to the scholars and presses at Louvain. In 1564, he had warned Cecil about "the great number of scholars born hereabout now lying at Louvain without license and sending in books and letters which cause many times evil rumors to be spread and disquiet the people."[42] Making matters worse, at much the same time as the attacks on parish Catholicism, some of Pilkington's Protestant allies came under fire from the High Commission at York for their refusal to wear the legally mandated vestments, which they considered the "defiled robes of antichrist."[43] Durham saw extremes of both sides of the religious issue. A combination of the new puritanical establishment, the committed Catholics both abroad and at home, and the simply conservative minded in between made for an explosive situation.

The Durham clerical establishment may have been unusually abrasive, but the measures it undertook to purge the parishes of the remnants of popery from 1567 paralleled similar efforts elsewhere. For the archdiocese of York, more extensive records survive to allow a clearer image of the processes at work in the last years of the decade. York's Archbishop Heath had, like Durham's Tunstall, lost his position for opposing Elizabeth's settlement. Thomas Young replaced him. No Pilkington, Young nevertheless headed up a commission in 1567 ordering parishes that had not purchased the books and accessories needed for Protestant services to do so. Parishioners that had yet to destroy images or instruments that should have long since disappeared received strict command to remove them. In Preston, paintings of saints remained on the rood loft; in Welwick, a gilt tabernacle and image of St. John; in Burton Pidsea, a cope and banner cloths with saintly images in the needlework. Some churches still housed altars and holy water stocks.

In a few parishes, the offences were such that the ecclesiastical authorities thought public penance and burning of the images necessary. When the parishioners of Aysgarth in North Yorkshire were found to have retained "idolatrous" items, the commissioners ordered nine men to bring the images to church and to do penance. Wearing a sheet, bare of head, leg, and foot, each had to kneel throughout the service. At its end, they were ordered to recite aloud:

> Whereas we, good people, forgetting and neglecting our duties as well to almighty God as also to our sovereign lady the Queen and other her highness's officers, have through our negligence concealed and kept hid certain Idols and Images undefaced and likewise certain old papistical books in the Latin tongue which some time did belong to this parish church of Aysgarth to the high offence of almighty God, the breach of the most godly laws and wholesome ordinances of this realm, the great danger of our own souls, and the deceiving and snaring of the souls of the simple, for the which we are now most heartily sorry, humbly confessing our negligences and offences and instantly desiring almighty God for his dear son Jesus Christ's sake to have mercy upon us and forgive us for the same, not minding hereafter to fall into the like again and furthermore we do heartily desire all you whom we have herein offended to forgive us likewise and to take example... to avoid the like offences and also to assist us in our prayers to almighty God and say with us the Lord's prayers as he hath taught us, Our father which art in heaven &c.

This done, they were to gather outside the church doors to burn the offending objects in front of the assembled parishioners.[44] So much for ambiguity and tolerant confusion.

Not just *what* they were forced to abandon, but also *how*, must have caused resentment. Similar public burnings and public humiliations were ordered over the coming years as the authorities kept up the pressure on the parishes. In June 1569, the churchwardens and parishioners of Manfield, a parish some nine miles north of Richmond, were charged before the ecclesiastical commissioners for retaining "diverse and many monuments of Idolatry and superstition." The offending objects remained in the church, concealed but not defaced, by the "consent or knowledge" of the parishioners, "to the great offence of the laws of God and the statutes of this Realm and to the evil example of all good Christians." The vicar and one of the churchwardens had to do penance in the Richmond market place one Saturday in July, when the objects were publicly destroyed.[45]

In Ripon, the commissioners found even more intransigence. On the previous Hallowe'en, a group had processed from door to door begging money and candles which they then gave to the bell ringers, an old custom no longer deemed appropriate in Protestant England. For this, one man stood in the stocks. In addition, John Jackson still made communion wafers with the image of the crucifix. Nor was this simple ignorance on his part, as Jackson had previously been heard to "scoff and scorn at the Queen's proceedings in the state of religion." Banned images and books were hidden in homes and in dark corners of the church, including six alabaster depictions of saints and forty-nine Catholic devotional books. Altars remained in the Lady Loft and in the "old, abominable superstitious vault" that housed St. Wilfrid's Needle, a narrow passageway that survived from the church's earliest days and was popularly thought to serve as a test for virginity, for only the chaste could fit through the gap.[46] The Ripon conservatives presented enough difficulties that the authorities devoted a special commission to their reformation, one still working away into the summer of 1569.

Nor were the services themselves much better reformed than their physical environments. Several Yorkshire clerics performed communion for the dead and burials by the old Latin rites. Others refused or at least had neglected all this while to declare the Bishop of Rome's "usurped" power in their weekly prayers. Few provided the mandated quarterly sermons. Of course, some of the defects the commissioners encountered had no particular tie to the stubbornness of traditionalists but emerged from more enduring problems: ministers who mumbled their way incomprehensibly through services, one who allowed ale to be sold within the church precincts during service time, and another who dispensed with the middleman by using beer instead of wine for the communion. Some of the problems had only a hazy connection to the progress of Elizabethan reform. Parson William Allerton, for instance, was brought before the church court for living in sin with Margery Tailor. According to Tailor, her lover had promised to marry her "if this religion continued," since Elizabethan Protestantism allowed clerics to wed, in contrast to Catholic custom. Yet, in case the current settlement should change, "as he thought it would shortly," Allerton deemed it best to delay the nuptials. Other problems, however, clearly manifested opposition to reform. Edward Sandall, for example, a cleric and school-master, was accused of being not just a "misliker of the religion now established in this realm" who continued to advocate prayers to the saints, but also a "sower of seditious rumors amongst the Queen's people saying that he trusted to see the day when he shall have twenty of the heretics heads that now be in authority under his girdle."[47]

Thus, religious tensions, like the social, increased in the last years of the 1560s. The period of tolerant confusion came to an end. After the rebellion of 1569 galvanized the governors of Elizabethan England, there would be a clearer drawing of lines, tighter enforcement of existing laws, and passage of more onerous statutes. The process began, however, well before the rising. People who had not previously committed themselves one way or the other were now being forced to do so. Most chose conformity, but the reluctance with which many did so suggests that the right spark might move more into the ranks of the committed resisters. For committed opponents, the willingness and ability to wait on events was quickly dissipating. Some of them now actively sought a catalyst for action. Just as avidly, the defenders of the Elizabethan settlement sought to stamp out any fires.

Mary Queen of Scots

Elizabeth's chief minister, William Cecil, had little doubt where the spark might come from. An enigmatic blending of practical politics and conspiracy theories shaped Cecil's actions.[48] No stranger to providential and even apocalyptic modes of thought, he believed his daughter's fever in April of 1569 to be a divine punishment for his own sins, and worried that England as a whole might suffer God's wrath for failing to complete the religious reformation it had begun.[49] Like others, he weighed the signs both providential and pragmatic of trouble in the last years of the decade. In 1568 and 1569, Cecil penned a series of memos outlining the problems that plagued his country. For him, most challenges centered in some way on Mary Stewart, Queen of Scotland. Mary seemed Elizabeth's likeliest successor and was a Catholic. For those who thought the marriage of Elizabeth's parents illicit, moreover, Mary was the legitimate Queen of England. Cecil feared that her existence threatened to encourage "all papists and discontented persons...whereof the consequence is overdangerous to be mentioned."[50] The "helps" for Mary included "the secret and great numbers of discontented subjects in this realm, that gape and practice for a change by her means, to be rewarded by her." Interestingly, he also feared "the probable opinion of great multitude, both in Scotland and England, that have an earnest and as it were a natural instinction to have both these realms under one king or head, by means of the said Queen of Scots." Each problem bore on the others. "The imperfectness of the nation to make war offensive or defensive" grew from "the division of the people in every shire by diversity of opinions in the matter of religion." Ostensibly straightforward riots were "the cloaks or preparatives of rebellion." Nor were the problems Mary posed solely those of domestic turmoil. "The perils," he noted with alarm, "are many, great and imminent, great in respect of Persons and Matters." The Pope and the Kings of Spain and France uniformly sought Elizabeth's demise and saw Mary as "the Instrument whereby the matters shall be attempted against the Queen's Majesty." This league sought to restore Catholicism, and to do so by replacing Elizabeth with her cousin.[51]

Indeed, while France and Spain dwarfed England in resources both financial and demographic, it was the smaller neighbor to the north that presented the most pressing problems throughout the first decades of Elizabeth's reign. England and Scotland had been at war of one sort or another almost continuously from 1296. During these years, the Scots had formed close ties with the French, thus creating the possibility of dangerous Franco-Scots incursions across the border. Henry VII had followed up on attempts by Edward IV and Scots King James III to reach a concord by marrying his daughter Margaret to James IV and concluding a treaty of "Perpetual Peace" in 1502. The marriage had long-term significance, but the peace proved rather less than perpetual. The bellicose Henry VIII, inspired by the martial glories of his medieval predecessors, soon reopened conflict with the Scots. Just over ten years after her wedding, Margaret Tudor lost her husband to the armies of her brother at the battle of Flodden. During the sixteenth century, the Scottish throne too often passed to young children rather than adult heirs. The many years of rule by minors and their regencies aggravated factional politics in a realm that had a surfeit of ambitious noblemen. It also made the country seem easier prey to a monarch such as Henry VIII. James V, king at the tender age of seventeen months, later made effective alliances with the French; he married first the daughter of Francis I and then the formidable Mary of Guise, a member of one of the most powerful families in France. Yet James too died distressingly young in 1542, after another Scottish defeat at the hands of the English. He left as heir his week-old daughter, Mary.

From her earliest days, then, Mary Stewart became the center of innumerable fears and factions. The squabbles over her regency saw the religious divisions that plagued the rest of Europe first introduce themselves meaningfully into Scottish high politics. Appeals to the French or English for backing became intertwined with rival religious allegiances. Henry VIII, however, still thought primarily in dynastic terms and hoped to acquire Scotland through a marriage between the infant Queen and his son Edward. Despite the "Rough Wooing" that ensued under the armies of both Henry and then Edward's Protector Somerset, Mary passed into the control of the French with a betrothal to the dauphin Francis, son of Henry II. If anything, English efforts had merely driven the Scots more firmly into the French embrace. But the admixture of Protestantism with Scottish factionalism soon presented the English with another opportunity. Autumn of 1557 saw the first Band of the Lords of the Congregation, an agreement to pursue a Protestant settlement that included a few men we will encounter again: Lord James Stewart, the bastard half-brother of the Queen, and the powerful earls of Argyll and Morton. December of 1559 produced a larger and more effective Band. Whereas the Queen's mother and regent, Mary of Guise, had the backing of the French, the Protestant Lords of the Congregation turned to England for aid. After Cecil's urging, Elizabeth sent support. Combined with the death of Mary of Guise in June of 1560 and the weakness of the French after the death of Henry II the year before, this English aid promised a Protestant victory in Scotland. In July 1560, the Treaty of Edinburgh was sealed. Both the French and English withdrew their troops and in three short weeks the Scottish parliament effected a dramatic, thoroughgoing religious reformation. Mary's French husband died later that year. When she returned to the country of her birth in 1561, it was to a realm far different than the one she had left as a child, one that now had a faith at odds with her own and a group of noblemen who saw their interests more closely allied with the English than the French.

Assessments of Mary's political acumen differ widely. Jenny Wormald subtitled her examination of Mary's personal rule "a study in failure" and found her performance "dismal and dithering."[52] In their recent biographies, John Guy and Retha Warnicke offer more flattering verdicts.[53] In her first years at least, Mary adroitly avoided dangerous entanglements in the religious question, insisting only on Catholic practice in her own household. (Whether her refusal to risk war for the restoration of Catholicism came from principle, political pragmatism, or simple indifference is left to her biographers to argue.) She resisted English demands that she ratify the Treaty of Edinburgh, with its provision that she drop her claims to the throne of England, but otherwise cultivated friendly relations with her "sister Queen." She needed a good relationship with Elizabeth, and ideally recognition of her status as heir, if for no other reason than to keep her Protestant noblemen in check. While Cecil proved implacably suspicious of Mary, believing her to be part of an international Catholic and Guise conspiracy to undermine his Protestant Queen, Elizabeth was somewhat more receptive. She refused to acknowledge Mary or anyone openly as her successor, but did prefer her to other claimants. (The English heir presumptive, Katherine Grey, had incurred Elizabeth's wrath and a place in the Tower by marrying the earl of Hertford without permission.) Unlike her father, Elizabeth had no plans to subjugate Scotland; she seemed content with a policy of containment that kept other powers out of the country.[54] For her first years, then, Mary proved reasonably adept at managing her most important relationships, those with her Protestant nobles and her Protestant neighbor to the south.

Mary's first big mistake, and it is difficult to deem it anything other, was her marriage to Henry Lord Darnley in 1565. Elizabeth had wanted her to marry a safely English, Protestant lord. To this end, she had even suggested her own favorite, Robert Lord Dudley, as a possibility and created him earl of Leicester to make him more suitable to the honor. Elizabeth blundered, however, in refusing point-blank to recognize Mary's status as her successor at the same time as allowing the earl of Lennox and his family to return to Scotland.[55] Personally insulted and politically humiliated by Elizabeth's rejection, Mary soon proposed to Lennox's son Henry Lord Darnley. Tall, handsome, and flirtatious, Darnley was also at least nominally Catholic. More to the point, he had a sufficiently solid claim to the English throne to bolster Mary's own: through his mother, the daughter of Margaret Tudor's second marriage, Darnley was an English-born great-grandson of Henry VII. Unfortunately, his sudden elevation and apparent support for Catholicism drove some of Mary's most important counselors to rebel, most notably the earl of Argyll and her half-brother Lord James Stewart, now the earl of Moray. In what became known as the Chase-About Raid, Mary donned steel cap and pistol and drove Moray over the border into England. Darnley soon proved to be more than just divisive; he was also a drunken, violent lout. As relations between Darnley and Mary quickly worsened, he became convinced of tales of her infidelity with her secretary, David Rizzio. Bursting into her private apartments one Saturday night in March 1566, Darnley and his fellow conspirators murdered Rizzio before Mary's eyes. Remarkably cool and shrewd given the circumstances, Mary reconciled with her husband long enough to ensure her safety and to secure her greatest asset: the birth of her son James on June 19. With a male heir in hand, Mary again distanced herself from her murderous spouse. Others, too, came to see Darnley as a liability. In the early hours of February 10, 1567, Darnley was assassinated.

Mary has long been thought complicit in this killing, but John Guy has presented a fairly compelling case for her innocence. At the least, she and Elizabeth had nearly achieved the concord she had sought for so long. Mary had named Elizabeth the protector of her son, his guardian in case she should die young. In return, Elizabeth had decided to acknowledge Mary and James's status as her heirs, should she not marry and have children of her own, on the carefully worded proviso of a "reciprocal contract" in which both recognized the rights of the other as a lawful queen and pledged to do nothing to harm the other. But with Darnley's murder, this treaty also died. As Guy explains, this makes Mary's complicity in the murder plot improbable, for she would not have wanted to jeopardize such an agreement.[56] In one sense, however, her innocence or guilt is irrelevant, for enough of the people who mattered at the time thought her guilty or were able to depict her as such to ensure her downfall. Suspicions seemed confirmed by her decision to marry the man known to be at the center of the plot, James Hepburn, earl of Bothwell. Her lords brought forces against her. By June, she was imprisoned in the island fortress of Lochleven; by July, she had been forced to abdicate in favor of her infant son with Moray as regent. Not yet done, she escaped and rallied loyal troops for one last battle at Langside in May 1568. After suffering a crushing defeat, she made the fateful decision to flee to England.

Her arrival provoked a crisis. There had already been plots to put her on the English throne, most notably one in 1561 led by members of the Catholic and royally descended de la Pole family. What more might be done on her behalf now that she was in England itself?[57] A crisis it was, but one that might also present opportunities. It certainly represented a remarkable state of affairs. Mary wanted a personal meeting with Elizabeth, but the latter refused to entertain a person tainted by accusations of adultery and murder. Instead, Elizabeth and Cecil decided on a trial of Mary and Moray's competing claims about Darnley's murder as the best response. Long familiarity with this story has inured us to its novelty and significance. It was, as Cecil knew well, a dangerously unedifying spectacle to put a Queen to trial or to legitimize her opponents. Mary was, after all, "a queen and monarch, subject to none, nor yet bound by her laws to answer to her subjects."[58] Of equally grave import, as Stephen Alford has shown, was Cecil's justification for the trial. Cecil revived the notion of English suzerainty over Scottish affairs, insisting on the "superiority that of ancient right belongeth to the Crown of England in causes of Scotland."[59] Mary contested such a rationale, as well as any suggestion that she stood on par with her rebels, but had little choice but to comply.

The conference began at York in October. The earls of Sussex and Norfolk led the English party. Mary sent a contingent of representatives, and Moray came accompanied by his own counselors. Both sides made strong arguments. In pressing his depiction of Mary as an adulteress and murderer, Moray could count on Cecil's sympathy. He baulked at presenting his evidence, however, for fear that Elizabeth might restore Mary anyway and thus leave him open to reprisal. Mary's agents portrayed the whole affair as a contrivance and plot, not insignificantly happening in her twenty-fifth year, the age at which Scottish sovereigns traditionally revoked grants made in their minority. Fear of losing valuable property, they said, had moved Moray and his fellows to act.[60] The undoubted involvement of some of her accusers in the very murder of which she stood accused also made the English judges wary of Moray's claims. Cecil abruptly suspended the conference and moved it to Westminster, adding more judges to the panel. He did so partly out of fear about the widespread sympathy in the north for Mary, and also perhaps from a concern that his original judges were themselves becoming too sympathetic to the Scottish Queen for his liking.[61] Nonetheless, Elizabeth brought the proceedings to an inconclusive end in the final days of the year. In Scotland, Mary's supporters and detractors had observed a truce of sorts during the trial, but now prepared to wage battle. Mary remained in English captivity with no obvious solution to the problem in sight.

The proceedings had failed to achieve their intended goals, but they were not without fruit. Mary now entertained at least two different plans to secure her triumphant return to Scotland. One posed more obvious danger to Elizabeth than the other, but neither would have pleased her. In one, Mary would wed the duke of Norfolk, England's premier peer and one of the judges at York. According to Norfolk at least, this marriage would contain and control Mary, allowing her to be safely restored to her throne without danger to Elizabeth or to Scottish Protestants. The marriage would also solve the English succession problem, with Mary and Norfolk or their children standing next in line upon Elizabeth's death. Mary accepted this plan, but sought backups in case it should fail. She sent out feelers to the Catholic courts of Europe, cajoling their aid for her restoration to the Scottish throne with hints that she might also be the means to bring England back into the Catholic fold. When she had been in Scotland, she had carefully downplayed her Catholicism in an effort to placate her leading noblemen; now she presented herself as a faithful Catholic, woefully wronged by Protestants in both Scotland and England. She approached the French, as one would expect, but also the Spanish. To King Philip II of Spain she now described herself as "an obedient, submissive and devoted daughter of the holy Catholic and

Roman Church, in the faith of which I will live and die, without ever entertaining any other intention than this."[62]

Foreign foes

Such a posture came at a particularly tense time for English foreign relations, in which longstanding alliances had strained almost to the breaking point. Two major rivalries dominated European politics: one between Catholics and Protestants, and to confuse it, one between France and Spain, the two greatest Catholic powers. England had long found friendship with Spain a useful counterbalance to its enmity with France. From Henry VII's alliance with Spain in 1489 – cemented by the marriage to Catherine of Aragon of both his sons in turn – to Mary Tudor's union with Philip II, a loose partnership between the English and Spanish had stood against that of the French and Scots. During Elizabeth's reign, this longstanding arrangement fell apart. Nothing at the beginning of her years in power led inexorably to the famed crisis of 1588, in which Philip sent his armada to conquer England: at the outset, Philip had offered Elizabeth his hand in marriage and had held his nose at Elizabeth's religious policies in an attempt to keep her from the embrace of the French. Nor had Philip seemed overly fond of Mary Stewart; Catholic she might be, but she was also closely tied to France. Over the course of the 1560s, however, Anglo-Spanish relations strained. English intervention on the side of Protestants in Scotland in 1560 and in France in 1562 caused alarm, as did the prospect of English aid for the troublesome Calvinists in the Spanish-controlled Netherlands. Even if the English were not yet openly supporting Philip's Dutch rebels, they had offered many of them sanctuary and some trickled back into the battle zone suspiciously well-armed and supplied.[63] Spanish actions in the Netherlands in turn provoked fears in England, and not just among zealous Protestants concerned for the fate of their coreligionists. After the binge of Calvinist rioting and image breaking in 1566, the duke of Alba and the core of the Spanish army marched into Brussels to quell dissent. Such a force, stationed so near the Channel and North Sea, threatened English security and commerce. It also threatened each of the contending parties in France to varying degrees. As R.B. Wernham notes, having the most deadly army in Christendom garrisoned in the Netherlands "was one of the great turning points of early modern history."[64]

Philip's decision to expel the obnoxious English ambassador, Dr. John Man, in the summer of 1568 was justifiable but, in hindsight, poorly timed. (Among other failings, Man had reportedly called the Pope "a canting little monk" at a dinner party with Spanish guests – hardly language befitting a diplomat.[65]) Soon thereafter, the capable and conciliatory ambassador to England, Guzmán de Silva, asked to be recalled owing to poor health. His replacement, Don Guerau de Spes, unfortunately equaled Dr. Man in religious bigotry and diplomatic blundering. The unsuitability of de Spes, together with Elizabeth's failure to name a new man to the Spanish post, left both leaders without good conduits of information in the event of a crisis.[66] And the crisis was not long in coming. By the autumn of 1568, the duke of Alba found himself dangerously short of pay for his soldiers. Already overburdened by the Morisco revolt in Grenada and the Turks in the Mediterranean, Philip borrowed money from Genoese merchants. Five small ships set sail with the coin, but bad weather and French pirates drove them into English ports for safety. With some £80,000 officially in the chests of the Spanish pay ships, and perhaps another £40,000 of illicit funds, temptation mounted. Cecil and Elizabeth decided to seize the money.

Why risk such a dangerous affront to the Spanish? Presumably the motive was more than just the money, even for such a cash-strapped and parsimonious Queen, but rather a hope of hindering Alba's efforts.[67] Earlier that year, Cecil had spoken glowingly of the German palsgrave when he had seized Genoese gold on its way to Alba; in doing so, the palsgrave had shown himself "a plain maintainer of ... God's cause."[68] At any rate, the English insisted to the outraged Spanish that they had done nothing unjust, for the money still technically belonged to the Genoese lenders who were willing to let Elizabeth take over the contract for the loan. Upon the urging of de Spes, Alba and Philip responded by seizing English property in Spanish territory and shutting their markets to English goods. Elizabeth retaliated in kind. These actions had serious and potentially devastating economic consequences for the English merchant community and all whose livelihoods depended on it, as well as widening the diplomatic rift between the two crowns.

Adding insult to injury for Philip, the English also used the recent attack on John Hawkins's slave ships as a pretext for their seizure of the gold. Hawkins had been an annoyance to the Spanish for some years already. Hoping to steal a piece of the lucrative West Indian slave trade, Hawkins had sailed to the African coast in 1562. There, he captured and bought some 400 Africans whom he later sold in Hispaniola in defiance of Spanish prohibitions. Even though the Spanish seized two of his ships, he returned to England with enough profit to entice Elizabeth to invest in his next voyage. She lent him a ship and allowed him to fly the

Royal Standard. Again, he sold African slaves in Spanish territories, again angering Spanish authorities. Under diplomatic pressure, Elizabeth did not openly back the next fleet sent out, but in 1567, Hawkins again enjoyed her support. On this trip, however, his luck turned. When he put into the Mexican port of San Juan de Ulua for repairs, the Spanish attacked. Few of his men survived, and those who did spent much of the return voyage dining on rats and dogs. Upon receiving news of this disaster in December of 1568, John's brother, William Hawkins, urged vengeance.[69]

The English seizure of the Spanish pay chests may well have been legal, and no doubt struck some as a justifiable response to the attack on Hawkins. Vice-Admiral Champernown worried little about such pretexts, opining: "I am of the mind that anything taken from that wicked nation is both necessary and profitable to our commonwealth."[70] Others, however, expressed alarm at such unnecessary provocation of a powerful King. And the seizure did provoke a crisis in Anglo-Spanish relations. It drove Philip to reconsider his ambivalence about Mary Stewart's claim to the English throne. Early in 1569, after receiving the letter in which she maintained herself a devoted daughter of the church, he asked his ambassador in Paris to pass word to her that "I will treat her as a true sister, just as if we were children of the same mother, and as such I will help and assist her as much as lies within my power."[71] He began to talk of the need for force in dealing with such a woman as Elizabeth. What his biographer Geoffrey Parker has termed a "messianic element" appeared in his letters; a conviction of his duty to restore Catholicism to England grew stronger, especially since "God has already granted that by my intervention and my hand that kingdom has previously been restored to the Catholic church once."[72]

In the event, Philip did not end up aiding the northern rebels in 1569. He did write to Alba late in the year, noting his desire to send money to them, to encourage the Irish Catholics' rebellion, and to support Mary's claims to the English throne. Ambassador de Spes took his King's wavering as encouragement to plot in earnest; throughout 1569, he seems to have made lavish promises of aid to any opponents of Elizabeth he could find. However, Philip left the decision to his better-placed deputy, and Alba showed more pragmatism and wariness than his master. Alba stymied any plan that might disrupt the negotiations over the pay chests and disrupted trade.[73] Yet Elizabeth and Cecil were not to know of Alba's restraining hand, nor it seems did the rebel earls, who heard from their advisors throughout the affair that Spanish aid was imminent. In the months preceding the rising, the problems with

Spain, real and potential, fed the atmosphere of crisis that both drove Elizabeth to actions that precipitated the rebellion and gave her readier means to deal with it.

Compounding the fears of foreign aid for Mary in particular and for Catholics in general were the French and the papacy. Cecil feared the French less than the other international powers, as their own religious wars embroiled them too deeply to allow them an effective role in English affairs. He knew, though, that this might change in a moment. Henry II's death in 1559 had unleashed deadly forces in France. His eldest son Francis, Mary Stewart's husband, survived him by only seventeen months. Henry's widow, Catherine de Medici, then ruled as regent for their ten-year-old son, Charles IX. In these years, religious tensions between French Catholics and Calvinists, known as Huguenots, mixed with dynastic ambitions to produce conflicts that often engaged three parties: the Huguenots led by the Bourbon family; the royal party; and the powerful Guise faction, recently ousted from court and now using their claims as Catholic defenders in a bid to regain power. The second of the French religious wars had come to an end in March of 1568 with the uneasiest and shakiest of truces. In better circumstances, Mary could have expected aid from the French, both as widow of their former king and in furtherance of the centuries long alliance between her nation and France. Yet Catherine de Medici had her reasons for restraint; putting down plots in her own country kept her busy, she had no particular affection for her former daughter-in-law, and after English intervention in the first of the French wars, she had determined to maintain friendship with Elizabeth. The Guises, however, worked busily behind the scenes to further Mary's interests and those of English Catholics. The Guise Cardinal of Lorraine, in particular, proved an inveterate plotter and determined to aid his niece. If he and his family should regain their former dominance over French policy, whether through force or by means of aid to Catherine in fending off the Huguenots, support for Elizabeth's domestic foes would not be long in coming.

The Spanish and French, then, had their own internal problems and policy differences between key figures that might keep them out of English affairs. The papacy was another matter. Cecil was wrong about a grand Catholic conspiracy to conquer England led by the Bishop of Rome, but that this did not occur was not for want of trying on the part of Pope Pius V. The preceding Pope, Pius IV, had broached the topic of excommunicating Elizabeth, but on the whole had preferred conciliatory means. When Philip and the Holy Roman Emperor counseled him to hold back on such a drastic move, he had accepted their arguments rather than those of the English exiles at Louvain who pressed for such a clarification. Instead, he hoped that attempts to have Elizabeth accept a papal nuncio or a good Catholic husband might suffice to bring England back into the fold, a misguided hope that Elizabeth did her best to encourage.[74] In January 1566, however, a man of an entirely different sort succeeded him to the papal throne. A member of the Dominican order, Michele Ghislieri served for a time as Inquisitor-General under that most ardent of counter-reformation Popes, Paul IV. His background, then, did not dispose him to diplomacy. As Pope, he avidly hunted heretics, denounced any compromise by Catholics living within Protestant territories, and extolled the supremacy of the papacy over secular authorities. Already in 1566, he referred to Elizabeth as one "who presents herself as Queen." In the same year, he wrote to the Spanish and French to demand their help for the embattled Mary Stewart, whose claim to the English throne he far preferred to that of a heretic daughter of heretic parents. With Mary in English captivity, he wrote to Alba to promote an invasion of England with French and Spanish cooperation in March 1569. While urging armed support for English Catholics, he also sent a few priests to reconcile schismatics. Talk of an excommunication attracted him more than it had his predecessor. In the spring of 1569, Pius sent two priests, including Nicholas Morton, a former prebendary of York, to discover how such a measure might be received in England.[75] The Pope had not excommunicated Elizabeth before the rising, nor had he known of the rebellion in advance, let alone acted as its key mover, as Elizabethan propagandists later claimed. He was, however, more than willing to provide whatever support he might to English Catholics and more than receptive to Mary's pleas for help.

The Norfolk marriage plan

Mary's invocations of aid from the Catholic courts of Europe had been only one of two plans designed to secure her freedom. The other was the projected marriage to the duke of Norfolk. Norfolk's later execution for conspiring against Elizabeth, and the intervening rebellion with its ostensible ties to Norfolk's plans, have led historians to characterize the planning for the marriage as a "plot" or "conspiracy." Stephen Alford has recently demonstrated, however, that it was not a conspiracy in the dangerous, malevolent sense.[76] During Mary's trial at York, when trying to find an acceptable means to restore her with both the dignity attendant upon her royal status and the security demanded by the English, the marriage presented itself as one possible solution, one that promised, furthermore, to solve the English succession crisis and unite the two countries under a Protestant monarchy. Norfolk himself was Protestant, and while Mary carefully cultivated her Catholicism for an international audience, to others she left open the possibility of her conversion.[77] Norfolk later maintained his good intent: "I meant nothing, but that I thought by that means no papist prince should obtain her."[78]

While we might doubt his protestations of loyalty in light of later events, the earls of Leicester and Moray, both staunch Protestants, were among the initial proponents of the marriage. Nicholas Throgmorton, one of the most ardent advocates of Protestant internationalism, was another key supporter. He later explained the thinking behind the plan. As Elizabeth proposed to restore Mary but needed protections and assurances, "by this marriage her Majesty and the realm might take commodity." The duke had agreed to the marriage, somewhat reluctantly considering the possibility that Mary had violated her previous marriage vows with adultery and murder, but since it promised such utility for his Queen, "he could sacrifice himself."[79] Others involved concurred. The earl of Pembroke noted that Norfolk, Throgmorton, and Leicester had discussed the plans with him directly, and that he believed Moray and other leading Scots supported it. He had signed a letter to Mary, written by Leicester, which established the conditions to be met before they would approach Elizabeth to urge her consent: Mary would have to relinquish all immediate claims to the English throne, dissolve any leagues with France and make one with England instead, devise the government of Scotland in ways agreeable to Elizabeth, and keep the religious settlement in Scotland in line with the English.[80] And after all, when Elizabeth herself had earlier wanted Mary to wed a Protestant Englishman, Norfolk's name had appeared on the shortlist of candidates.

Two potential difficulties with Alford's characterization of the marriage project arise. One emerges from the context of Privy Council factionalism. Historians have long depicted Elizabeth's council and court as riven by bitter factional conflicts, and this plan as an attempt to overthrow Cecil. Councilors who did not want to antagonize foreign powers opposed Cecil when he proposed to help coreligionists abroad, and were sufficiently alarmed by his seizure of the Spanish pay chests that they plotted his removal. In recent years, however, evidence for such factionalism, at least prior to the 1590s, has melted away.[81] Alford is not alone in portraying the councilors' relationships as generally collegial and productive. His attempt to deny this particular instance of Council infighting in 1569, however, rests on shaky foundations.

He correctly notes that the strongest and most sensational "evidence" for such a conflict comes from ambassadors' accounts – rarely trustworthy for this sort of thing – and works written many years later, after factionalism had become an expected feature of politics.[82] Yet there is a pair of letters from the early summer of 1569 that attests some sort of division between Norfolk and Cecil. In one, sent May 15, the earl of Sussex expresses his regret that Cecil and Norfolk "stand on worse terms of amity" than previously; in a second, sent to Sussex on May 27, Cecil relates his "grief of mind, in that some had found power to move my L of Norfolk's grace to think otherwise of me than before." In a third letter, sent in early June to a friend in Ireland, Cecil notes that he had recently emerged "from some clouds or mists" that had resulted from strained relations at court.[83] The ambassadors may have exaggerated the gravity of the conflict, but a difference of some degree did exist. This need not, however, mean that Alford's portrayal of the marriage plan is wrong. Cecil and Norfolk had patched up their differences by early June, and while Cecil presumably continued to think poorly of the plan, he knew of it and did not attempt to impede its progress.

The other potential difficulty with Alford's characterization of the project is that none of the men involved told Elizabeth of their plans; their attempts at secrecy give it the color of a conspiracy. Yet their own subsequent explanations for their reticence are, in fact, quite plausible and should not be quickly discounted. Long experience of Elizabeth's angry responses to any who broached the topic of the succession made them want to present a united front, marshalling the support of all the leading men of the country before presenting her the plan. They also wanted one of the Scottish leaders, either William Maitland of Lethington or the earl of Moray, to raise the issue to give it greater weight. But Moray, who had initially backed the plan, changed his mind in the summer of 1569. He decided then that he could not tolerate Mary's return under any condition, and arrested Maitland, her somewhat more steadfast supporter. This posed a considerable problem for the plans, and weakened much of its rationale.

Rumors of the intended marriage leaked. When one of Norfolk's men talked of the project with the earls of Sussex, Westmorland, and Northumberland in July, the latter told him he had heard news of it already "in the country."[84] Another said that he had heard of the intended marriage "by common report" during the Queen's summer progress.[85] In early August, Lord Hunsdon wrote to Cecil from Berwick of "the common speech in Scotland and that daily comes from London and the court" about the planned union.[86] When the Queen dropped broad hints that she knew something of their intentions, Leicester sought to protect himself from her wrath and revealed all. When Elizabeth confronted Norfolk, he admitted the plan but insisted on his good meaning. Nonetheless, she was clearly angry, insulted, and worried. When Norfolk left the court without license on September 15, and left London for his estates soon after, her worst fears seemed confirmed. She ordered interrogations of all involved, save Leicester, and had Mary moved to more secure lodgings. Elizabeth had Lords Arundel, Lumley, and Pembroke detained and summoned Norfolk back.[87] After some hesitation and pleas that illness made travel dangerous, he finally complied. He threw himself on her mercy and by October 8 had landed in the Tower.

Like the secrecy in which the plan took shape, Elizabeth's response has shaped interpretations of the project as a conspiracy. Yet her anger only turned dangerous once Norfolk aggravated his offence by fleeing the court. The plan is often seen in a bad light because of the purported links between it and the earls' decision to rise later in the fall, but as shall be seen, the links between the two are neither as clear or direct as they are often assumed to be. Nonetheless, even if the plan was not the malevolent conspiracy it was once thought to be, it still grew from and contributed to a profound sense of insecurity in the waning years of the decade. Not knowing the extent and aims of the marriage plan after Norfolk's flight from court, Elizabeth demanded interviews with all who had knowledge of it. Her suspicions of any untoward act or rumor grew. Hearing reports of an intended or abortive rising in the north in October, she ordered the northern lords to explain themselves.[88] The northern earls, who had been busily plotting on their own, now feared for their very survival. They refused her summons and turned more intently to their plans for rebellion. Thus, while the Norfolk marriage plan cannot safely be treated as a direct cause of the rebellion, it very directly increased Elizabeth's fears and contributed to the more general sense of crisis that gave rise to the revolt.

Ireland

In the interim, however, the dangers of domestic discontent mixing with the possibility of foreign aid under the bond of religious solidarity were first revealed not in England, but in Elizabeth's other kingdom, Ireland. It was in Ireland that lords first professed to see links between an aggressively centralizing state and innovations in religion, with potential solutions in appeals to coreligionists abroad. The Anglo-Irish Butlers and Geraldines, kin of the earls of Ormond and Desmond respectively, set aside their longstanding feud to find common cause against the English. Together, they rallied sympathizers among the Gaelic lords in the north, especially among the O'Neills of Ulster and their own Scottish confederates. The series of loosely linked rebellions that began in the summer of 1569 both revealed the depth of the dangers facing Elizabeth and contributed to the growing sense of crisis within England itself. The broader "British" dimension, with links in all three of the island kingdoms, also served as a sign of things to come.

The English had laid claim to Ireland from 1190, when the Pope had granted Henry II the lordship of the island. Throughout the years that followed, various Kings had put varying degrees of effort into giving substance to such claims. At the beginning of the sixteenth century, the English crown had effective control of only a small region immediately surrounding Dublin, known as the Pale. Other areas, in the hands of Anglo-Irish lords descended from earlier English adventurers, offered nominal obedience. Others yet, still ruled by Gaelic chieftains, remained resolutely independent. Henry VIII determined to extend his authority, relying heavily on a policy known as "surrender and regrant": he invited Irish lords to surrender their lands and native titles, and to receive directly from him a new title and a regrant of their own lands. In return for pledges of protection and all the other things one could expect from a good feudal lord, the newly titled Irish also had to recognize the King as head of both church and state and agree to attendant cultural changes: they must substitute English law, customs, and manners for Irish. Aware of the incongruity of a claim to lordship based on papal grant after his break from Rome, Henry had himself declared King of Ireland in 1540. His successors continued his efforts to extend English control throughout the island.[89]

The first significant open rebellion under Elizabeth came from Shane O'Neill, who defiantly maintained himself to be the new leader of the O'Neills under Irish traditions of succession rather than the English rules of primogeniture his father had accepted when named earl of Tyrone. For a time, the English persisted in recognizing his elder brother and his heirs as the legitimate earls of Tyrone, but finally accepted claims of the senior branch's illegitimacy as a face-saving compromise. Nevertheless, Shane continued to bedevil efforts to extend English control into the north. The presence of Scottish Gaels in Ulster compounded English difficulties. At the beginning of Elizabeth's reign, she and Cecil had briefly flirted with accepting the Scottish presence and using it to their advantage. In the negotiations with the Scottish Protestant Lords of the Congregation in 1560, they adopted what Jane Dawson calls a "triangular British policy": in partial recompense for their aid, the earl of Argyll promised to use his force "to reduce the north parts of Ireland to the perfect obedience of England."[90] Probably the single most powerful lord in all three kingdoms and certainly the dominant power in the western Highlands and Isles, Argyll was both a Lowland peer and, as leader of Clan Campbell, chief of an extensive kin-based network. For centuries, Irish Gaelic lords had imported warriors from Scotland's western islands; the gallowglasses and their employers shared a common Gaelic language and culture. If anyone could halt the mercenary trade or tame O'Neill, it was Argyll.

The English wasted this opportunity, however, owing in part to the conviction of the earl of Sussex, the Irish lord lieutenant, that Scots of any sort – even if Protestant and friendly – had to be kept out of Ireland in order to secure English interests. By 1565, in fact, the situation had reversed itself, with O'Neill and Argyll on friendly terms. During the Chase-About Raid of that year, the anticipated English assistance for Argyll and his fellows failed to materialize, but Shane had offered his help. By the following year, Cecil expressed his fear that "O'Neill's boldness is fed out of Scotland."[91] This tie continued with Mary's encouragement after she reconciled with Argyll. Indeed, Argyll tried using his Irish connection to aid his Queen, warning the English that if they did not recognize Mary as Elizabeth's heir, then he would assist Shane in his rebellion.[92]

News of Shane's murder in 1567 at the hands of Scots he had previously betrayed received a jubilant welcome at the English court. Yet any hopes the English entertained for a new beginning in Ireland quickly died. A new and more dangerous situation developed in Ulster, based on new and more powerful ties to the Scots. The three major Ulster powers, the MacDonalds, O'Donnells, and O'Neills (now led by Tirlaugh Luineach), formed a coalition and turned to Argyll. In late 1567, the parties arranged two marriages to cement the new alliance. Lady Agnes, Argyll's aunt and the widow of James MacDonald, would marry Tirlaugh Luineach. Her daughter Finola would marry Hugh O'Donnell, and both would enjoy dowries of gallowglasses provided by Argyll. The English reacted with horror when the news leaked early in 1568. Mary's escape from Lochleven and last stand at Langside kept Argyll sufficiently busy to delay the weddings. In August 1569, despite the English ships sent to intercept the Scottish brides-to-be, Lady Agnes and her daughter arrived in Ulster with thirty-two ships and some 4000 men.[93]

In the interval before the weddings took place, Argyll had tried once more to use Ireland to wrest concessions for Mary. He sent a message to

Sir Henry Sidney, the new Irish lord deputy, promising that if Elizabeth helped Mary regain her throne, "he would minister from time to time all good and neighborly offices to this land: but if she would not, he would be in Ireland in person with 5000 men."[94] Yet as much as Cecil worried about Ireland, he worried more about English security. He feared, furthermore, that should Mary be restored to power, "Ireland shall be molested with the Scots more than it hath been."[95] Rather than negotiate, he contemplated plans to invade Scotland's western coast to curtail the supply of Scots mercenaries.[96] Like the Englishmen on the ground in Ireland, he believed that Tirlaugh Luineach and his Ulster confederates planned open rebellion once reinforced with the Scots.[97] In the event, Luineach held back, partly from caution and partly because he was recuperating after his jester had accidentally shot him. His rebellion and that of his fellows in the north diminished in importance before the onslaught of other, bloodier risings to the south led by the Butlers and James Fitzmaurice Fitzgerald.

Provocations there were in abundance. The council in Ireland had recently redoubled its efforts to ban coign and livery, a practice that allowed lords to billet and provision private armies at no cost to themselves. The English claimed that it brought disorder and depredation of the peasantry, whereas the lords thought it necessary for their dignity and defense. An Irish parliament in 1569 prepared to give statutory mandate to earlier proclamations against the practice. News spread of planned increases to the number of English plantations and of the establishment of regional presidencies. These offices were to be modeled on the existing councils in northern England and in the Welsh marches, which had done so much to extend royal authority into these regions. Such plans heightened the fears of some for their diminishing independence. The single most inflammatory act of the council was its response to the land claims of Peter Carew, an Englishman who sought to regain property that had last been in his family's possession some two hundred years before, a significant portion of which now lay in the hands of Edmund Butler. Rather than trying the claim in open court, Sidney and his fellows issued an order-in-council peremptorily giving the land to Carew.[98] Such aggressive centralization of government control and highhanded disregard for proprietors' rights sharpened oppositional solidarities.

In June, Edmund Butler and two of his brothers signaled their intent by humiliating an English gentleman who had wronged them: they dragged him about by a noose tied round his neck. They and their army quickly turned on Carew, destroying some seventy homes and thirteen people in the shadow of his fort at Leighlin. They killed the entire garrison at Ballyknocken castle and set fire to the surrounding area. Before long, the Butlers had devastated parts of counties Carlow, Kilkenny, and Wexford, among others. Their actions horrified their elder brother, Thomas, tenth earl of Ormond. Ormond had become a well-rewarded favorite of Elizabeth's; she had familial connections with the Butlers through her mother, and had grown fond of "Black Tom" during his many years at the English court. He returned to Ireland in August of 1569 to tame his brothers. The Butlers' local support, already shaky, dwindled upon the earl's arrival. By September 1, the brothers submitted to him, although it would take more than a year before they came fully to heel. Brother Edward proved a particular problem, running off to join Fitzmaurice soon after his short-lived surrender.

James Fitzmaurice Fitzgerald led the Desmond Geraldines in the absence of the earl, who was then imprisoned in England. Fitzmaurice had many of the same concerns over proprietorial rights as had the Butlers; his own centered on the acquisitions of Sir Warham St. Leger in county Kerry. But Fitzmaurice added a potentially more dangerous dimension to his revolt. Shane O'Neill had previously shown the way by portraying himself, at least briefly, as a Catholic crusader in an effort to find foreign support.[99] Fitzmaurice and his fellows now did the same. Early in 1569, they met secretly and agreed to offer the Irish crown to Philip of Spain. They sent the papally appointed archisbishop of Cashel, Maurice Fitzgibbon, to the Spanish court to plead their case. Fitzgibbon described to Philip the ardent wish of the Irish "to remain firm, constant, and unshakeable in the faith and unity of the Catholic Church, as also to persevere even to their last breath in their immemorial obedience and attachment to the Roman Pontiffs." As such, he proclaimed "the chief desire of the entire nobility and people of this kingdom to be taken under the patronage and protection of his Holiness and of the most benign and Catholic King of Spain."[100] Philip later noted to Alba that he had received the Irish messenger, who brought a promise to accept any leader he should name in return for his help in driving out the heretical English. He professed to like the idea in principle, but feared such intervention would put the French on their guard and hamper the continuing negotiations with the English for the return of the payship gold.[101] He continued to entertain the notion of striking at Elizabeth through Ireland, but apparently never seriously considered taking on the Irish as his own personal charge. Fitzgibbon and Fitzmaurice later tried finding Catholic aid elsewhere in Europe, but to little avail. One French captain sailed for Scotland with 500 men in June 1570, and later coordinated plans with Fitzmaurice for more men, but to no serious effect.[102]

Nevertheless, in Ireland rumors of impending Spanish aid circulated and Fitzmaurice infused his proclamations with protestations of Catholic piety. When he threatened Kilmallock, he listed as one of his demands that the townsmen "use no other divine service but the old divine service used by the church of Rome."[103] When besieging Cork, Fitzmaurice declared his enmity to the "heresy newly raised and invented" and denounced Elizabeth for forcing the Irish "to forsake the Catholic faith by God unto his church given and by the see of Rome hitherto prescribed to all Christian men."[104] Even if such statements brought no foreign aid, he perhaps hoped thereby to unite a larger Irish party behind him. Whether it was the religious dimension or the shared grievance with an English administration bent on accumulating ever more power and land, or some combination of the two, the various Irish rebels did at times link up. On occasion, the Butlers and Fitzgerald's men fought in concert, and both claimed to have a mutual defense pact with Tirlaugh Luineach.[105] Yet with the Butlers largely quiescent by early fall and Luineach hesitant, Fitzmaurice's Munster rebellion lost strength over the winter. More and more of his confederates submitted to the Queen's agents. Thanks in large part to the brutal methods of Sir Humphrey Gilbert, the worst was over by the end of 1570. Gilbert earned his knighthood in this service, which included such terror tactics as lining the path to his tent with the severed heads of rebels and the intentional slaughter of the women who raised and fed men of war.[106] Fitzmaurice himself fought on for a while longer, helped at one point by 500 Scottish reinforcements. In early 1571, Sidney reached an agreement with Luineach, and Sir John Perrot arrived to assume the Munster presidency. Perrot followed Gilbert's lead, and finally, in February 1573, he won Fitzmaurice's submission; the rebel had to lay prostrate on the floor of the ruined Kilmallock church with Perrot's sword point upon his heart before receiving his pardon.[107] In the meanwhile, the troubles in Ireland confirmed for English officials the dangers they faced at home and contributed to the sense of escalating crisis. In immediately practical terms, the need to raise and pay soldiers and to police them on their way to the point of embarkation posed difficulties and threatened to aggravate social unrest. More generally, the Irish rebellion spoke to the troubling potential of "British," religious, and even continental solidarities.

In order to deal with this sense of crisis and set of challenges, Elizabeth and her advisors ordered close searches for suspicious vagrants and investigated riots for hints of deeper aims. The threat posed by Mary and her Catholic admirers gave added impetus to the efforts to root out popery and papists; as Cecil believed, "the more the cause of religion be furthered and the tyranny and practices of Rome are abased, the less is the danger of the Queen of Scots."[108] By the spring of 1569, Elizabeth had ordered the collection of a forced loan to ensure sufficient funds and musters of men and weaponry should the Spanish retaliate for the seizure of their payships. By the summer, close searches took place not just for vagrants but also for Catholics in the Inns of Court. By the early fall, Cecil had prepared lists of gentlemen in each county, trustworthy and otherwise, and had ordered that all men in positions of power take the oath of supremacy. In October, 200 men from the English garrison at Berwick joined forces with the Scottish regent to tame the unruly borderers, whence aid for Mary was feared.[109]

Such was the soil from which the English revolt of 1569 grew. People across the country had accumulated a set and sense of grievances, be they classifiable as "social" or "religious" or as some mix of the two. They also had a rich store of tools for honing a critical conscious-ness, including normative principles derived from custom and faith, and warnings detected from providential or even prophetic texts. Their choices would shape those of their superiors. The social and religious tensions provided a populace sufficiently discontented to give the earls hope for followers and to give the Queen cause for alarm. Worsening relations with Spain, the plotting of the Guises, and the determination of a new Pope did not in the end produce the direct aid for the rebels that Elizabethan loyalists later claimed, but they created an atmosphere ripe for violent action and reaction and shaped the ways developments would be both interpreted and confronted.

2
The Rebellion in the North

Prophecies circulated in the north in the months preceding the rebellion. Some promised the arrival of better days, while others apparently threatened a turn for the worse if the Queen should put down the northern nobility. For this rising, like so many others, we have few words of the rebels themselves and have to rely on what outside, generally hostile, observers chose to tell us. The Protestant polemicists who responded to the revolt made repeated curt and dismissive allusions to the prophecies and their role. The *Ballad Against Rebellious and False Rumors*, for example, noted that

> Some sayth this year there shall be hapte,
> Much trouble in the land:
> Of prophecies they carp and clap,
> As they that have them scanned,
> Doth tell them so abroad.[1]

William Wharton, a conspiracy-minded Protestant who regularly sent missives warning Cecil of all sorts of nefarious Catholic deeds, later reported the circulation of a book of prophecies among the rebels in which "her Majesty's person and estate were dishonorably touched."[2] Others related "that it is concluded by astronomy that the Scottish damsel shall be Queen and the duke the husband," thus promising the success of plans to unite Mary Queen of Scots and the duke of Norfolk in marriage and have them succeed to the throne.[3] Some noted the role of predictions of a more purely religious focus in triggering the protest. John Phillips mocked those "rebellious papists that hope (as they term it) to have their Golden Day" and condemned that "secret, muttering sort" who talked of the Bull and Moon eclipsing the Sun.[4] The Moon referred to the heraldic device of the earl of Northumberland; the Bull to that of the earl of Westmorland. Thomas Norton, perhaps the most rabidly vociferous of the men who wrote against the rebels, included in one of his diatribes a prophecy that had recently circulated: "Alas the Moon shall be called in the house of enemies and prison, whereby is like to happen to us, especially to the common people, much adversity." Derisively, he depicted such prophecies as recent inventions intended only to deceive the common sort.[5]

How much currency such prophecies had among the people of the north will never be known. But Norton and the other polemicists correctly sought to explain not just the earls' decision to rise but also those of the many who joined them. This chapter narrates the rebellion itself, highlighting along the way reasons to deem it, in no small part, a religious rising with ardent popular support. Traditional ties to great lords continued to exert a powerful influence, but there no longer existed in the north a population that "knew no prince but a Percy." The Tudor years had produced at least equally powerful incentives for obedience and quiescence. Few people would enter rebellion lightly or merely at the whim of their local lords. Nor would the lords themselves find it easy to justify a move from grumbling complaint to forceful action. So what was it, what combination of factors beyond lordly ties, that convinced people to act?

From conspiracy to revolt

The main impetus moving the earls from conspiracy to revolt lay in the actions of the Queen, who feared their intentions. Admittedly, she had reasons aplenty to be suspicious of Thomas Percy, seventh earl of Northumberland. His family had a tradition of both loyal service and rebellion; the latter had most recently been exhibited by his father's participation in the Pilgrimage of Grace. Long a traditionalist, and deemed a "rank papist" in 1559, he became formally reconciled to the Catholic Church in late 1567 or early 1568 by Master Copley, a wandering priest. His wife, Anne, was a strong-minded woman who shared his religious views. His revived Catholicism sharpened his existing sense of grievance at the slights and insults he had received at Elizabeth's hands.

And insults he had received in abundance. To the detriment of his and other ancient families, the early Tudors had pursued the twinned projects of taming "overmighty subjects" and extending effective royal control into outlying regions. In furtherance of these goals, Henry VIII had promoted "new men" in northern society, often gentlemen rather than lords, who owed their status to him and served to diffuse power. Key offices that the crown had once bestowed upon the great northern lords as a matter of course, such as the wardenships of the northern marches or stewardships of royal estates, it now frequently gave to lesser but ostensibly more loyal men. The Percys had fared particularly poorly. After the death of the sixth earl and execution of his brother, the title had fallen into abeyance and the lands to the crown. Queen Mary had restored Thomas Percy to his uncle's title and most of his estates in 1557; the next year she named him to posts traditionally held within his family, the wardenships of the East and Middle Marches. Under Elizabeth, however, hard times returned. She revived her father's twinned projects and added to them an extortionate eye for an easy profit. Northumberland was soon forced to resign the wardenships to avoid being dismissed. He fared little better as High Steward of the Queen's lands in Richmond. When he supported the tenants' objections to an enclosure project, the Queen issued him a sharp rebuke and told her commissioners to ignore him. When he found valuable deposits of copper on his estates in 1566, the Queen claimed the mines as her own by virtue of the royal prerogative in precious metals. She even sued him for title to the water mill near his seat at Alnwick.[6]

Percy had only to look about him to find proof of his belief that assaults on the prestige of the ancient nobility and on the traditional faith were closely linked. Responding to the 1563 parliamentary discussions on a new "Test Act" that would require the oath of supremacy from many more people, in a parliament that heard heated rhetoric and calls that "maintainers of false religion ought to die by the sword," Northumberland reportedly warned of the dangerous implications of such a measure: "when they had beheaded the clergy they would claim to do the same to the lay nobles."[7] The following year, he was purged from the commissions of the peace because of his faith. His family's fortunes seemed to ebb and flow in response to changes in religion: disastrous under Henry VIII, good under Mary, poor again under Elizabeth. The "new men" now favored above him were not just inferiors, but Protestants as well. John Forster stood out among them: knighted and made warden of the Middle March, this Protestant parvenu had profited greatly at the expense of the Percys in the years before their restoration and continued to do so even after. Mary Stewart's arrival in the earl's lands in May 1568 may have seemed a sign; Elizabeth's refusal to let him host the distinguished guest certainly registered as yet another insult. Even before the Scottish Queen's arrival, he and his advisors had discussed rebellion, but with what seriousness is unclear. After her arrival, his plans took on a more determined aspect.

Less is known of the grievances that animated Charles Neville, sixth earl of Westmorland. He had become earl on his father's death in 1564, at the age of twenty-one or thereabouts. The fifth earl, an ardent supporter of Mary Tudor, had remained firmly committed to Catholicism and raised his children accordingly. On Elizabeth's urging, he had been prosecuted for marrying his dead wife's sister, admittedly a practice the Queen had special personal interest in condemning as a violation of divine law, yet humiliating for the earl nonetheless. With the principal family estates concentrated in Durham, he had had his problems with the aggressive new Protestant establishment in the bishopric. In one episode, Bishop Pilkington refused to pay the rent required for crossing Westmorland's land with coal from his mines; the earl ordered his tenants to stop all carts of coal, and only when the men leasing the pits complained did the bishop consent to pay.[8] Such problems continued between the clerical proprietors and the sixth earl. The Cathedral Chapter decided to halt the traditional annual fee paid to the earls of Westmorland for leading their tenants into battle. The lost revenue was small, but the insult grave. The earl's uncle, at least, declared himself "sore offended" by this slight.[9] Indeed, the young earl's uncles Cuthbert and especially Christopher Neville did much to hone his sense of grievance and sense of duty to faith and family.

Around these men existed a shifting group of similarly discontented Catholic gentlemen. Many had reason to share Northumberland's perception of the links between the new faith and the new ways, having lost lands and income to the recently promoted Protestants in their midst.[10] John Swinburne, for instance, had received a hefty fine for keeping a priest, and had problems with the bishop and chapter over tithes, rents, and titles; in one case, his servants and the bishop's came to blows over a coal dispute.[11] The group also included Thomas Markenfeld, who had returned from his self-imposed exile to the continent imbued with the zeal of Catholic counter-reform. Richard Norton of Norton Conyers, now in his seventies, together with his brother Thomas and several of his many sons, also dominated the disaffected. The head of a leading Yorkshire family, Richard managed to hold some official positions despite his Catholicism; at the time of the rebellion, in fact, he was High Sheriff of Yorkshire. Leonard Dacre, a notorious harborer of Catholic priests, had already lost to Elizabeth lands willed to him some twenty years earlier when a second case, in 1566, pushed him more firmly into opposition. The second son of the former Lord Dacre of Gillesland, Leonard launched a suit for portions of the estates in the hands of his young nephew, which he claimed were entailed to him. When pressure from the Queen helped turn the case against him, he began a regular correspondence with Mary Queen of Scots.[12] By 1569 Leonard's nephew George was, together with his sisters, a ward and stepchild of the duke of Norfolk. In March of that year, George died when his wooden vaulting horse fell upon him. Leonard Dacre began a new suit for the Dacre estates and title as heir male, only to find Norfolk busily arranging marriages for the Dacre girls with his own sons and defending their right to inherit.[13] Leonard would be in Westminster pursuing his claims when the rebellion began, but had spent years nursing his own and others' sense of injustice and contributing to their plots.

Much of the plotting had consisted of little more than consoling confederacies of complaint, and as few instances came formally to the attention of the authorities, few firm details survive. According to one subsequent and admittedly self-serving confession by Thomas Bishop, a man on the margins of the group, they had devised at least four prior plots with some degree of serious planning. In the third year of Elizabeth's reign, the fifth earl of Westmorland, with John Neville and several others, had tried to interest the earl of Northumberland in a plan to restore Catholicism by rising in support of the Lady Lennox and her son Darnley, Catholic descendants of Henry VII then resident in the north. After Darnley had married the Scottish Queen, Richard Norton went to the earl of Northumberland with promises of at least 700 of his own tenants and the assistance of the Scots should he rise. During Mary's trial at York, Richard and Francis Norton, together with Thomas Markenfeld and some others, hoped to kill the Scottish regent on his passage north and to have the earl of Northumberland raise the countryside. When Mary learned of the plan she warned them away, as she did for their next proposal, to free her on her move from Bolton to Tutbury in the early months of 1569 and use this as a signal for a general rising.[14] Yet another time, Leonard Dacre and Francis Norton rode to Tutbury on a tip from a man Dacre had in the household, but fearing their intentions to be known they returned empty handed.[15]

Plotting continued over the summer of 1569. Some talked of seizing Newcastle, York, and Hull; others talked of freeing Mary. Among the latter, some may have planned to replace Elizabeth with her Scottish cousin, while others hoped to use a freed Mary, restored to her throne and acknowledged as heir, to force Elizabeth into policies more to their tastes. The northern plotters may have seen the proposed marriage between Norfolk and Mary as an incentive for renewed scheming, even if they did not much like the marriage itself and had needed little such stimulus in the past. Yet, the evidence is surprisingly slim for the oft-repeated claim that the earls felt pressured to rise after Norfolk's arrest because of their complicity in his marriage plan; the links between the two are less direct than they initially appear. If anything, they felt pressured to rise after Norfolk's arrest not because of their complicity in his plan, but because they feared their own prior and concurrent plotting would thus come to light and that no other option for freeing Mary now remained. And the catalyst to convert talk to action, when it came, was not the duke's detention but the Queen's demand that they explain rumors of an intended October rising.

Most of the near-contemporary evidence for the coordination of the two schemes comes from later attempts to blacken Mary's name sufficiently to force her execution and can either be discarded or at least treated very cautiously. Evidence from nearer the rebellion itself comes primarily from the earl of Northumberland's subsequent confession. But Northumberland's confession, if read closely, provides little to support the conclusions usually drawn from it. Speaking days after Norfolk's execution, when no need to protect the duke remained, Northumberland insisted that no link between his rebellion and the marriage plan existed. He repeatedly noted his disdain for the marriage, and his preference that Mary wed a good Catholic, ideally the King of Spain himself. He said as much to the Spanish Ambassador and to Mary's messenger. Mary "sent to me (and I think to others too) to will us to seem contented, and to like of the match. Also Christopher Lassels came to my house, to Leckinfield, when the Queen of Scots lay at Bolton, at such time as I little thought of any match toward between her and the duke; and cast out such matter, how necessary and commodious a thing it might be to this realm, if the q. of s. should marry the duke." He made it clear that he was willing to offer any service for the sake of religion or to clarify the succession, but not for her marriage to a Protestant. The claims that Norfolk and the earls were planning a rising together rests on Northumberland's statement that the duke's servant visited Westmorland upon Norfolk's summons to court, telling him not to stir or Norfolk would lose his head.[16] While this is certainly suggestive, it is by no means conclusive; it can be read as nothing more than prudence on Norfolk's part, the product of concerns that his northern friends had more dangerous aims than his own.

The other evidence frequently cited for a connection between Norfolk and the earls are the contemporaneous dispatches of the Spanish ambassador. De Spes noted with some excitement that Norfolk and the earl of Arundel, Norfolk's Catholic father-in-law, kept in contact with him via "trusted messengers," one of whom, Roberto Ridolfi, we will encounter again. Through these messengers, both Norfolk and Arundel promised to find ways to bypass Cecil's influence with Elizabeth and ensure the return of the Spanish pay chests, while Arundel also promised to find some way to restore Catholicism, in return for a Spanish pension. De Spes acknowledged that Norfolk himself had given no indications of support for a Catholic restoration, but thought him prone to persuasion. Yet, all this time de Spes was under house arrest and closely watched, his access to information severely curtailed. Fearing a trap, Alba emphatically counseled him not to entertain any approaches from people purporting to oppose Elizabeth, and opined to both de Spes and the King that the covert negotiations were merely a delaying tactic or trick. When de Spes refused his advice, Alba wrote with some exasperation to the King that the ambassador's inexperience led him astray; he was being played the fool. And at any rate, when de Spes did learn of the marriage plan – not through Norfolk's messenger, but from Leonard Dacre – he expressed reservations much the same as the earl of Northumberland's. He was not so sure of Norfolk's support for Catholicism that he thought him a suitable partner for Mary, and like Northumberland, he preferred other candidates for her hand. De Spes had received visits from Northumberland himself – in disguise, at four o'clock in the morning – but nothing in his letters supports the notion of a link between Northumberland and Norfolk.[17]

According to the man who became Mary's closest advisor, John Leslie, bishop of Ross, the earl of Northumberland had offered Mary whatever service he might perform, including freeing her and returning her to Scotland with the help of Leonard Dacre. Leslie notes that when Mary asked Norfolk his advice, he thought the offer should be refused, for fear that Dacre and the earl in fact planned to stymie their marriage and secure her for another, more suitably Catholic candidate. Northumberland offered again, this time suggesting that he would bring both Mary and Norfolk safely to the north and see them married in "honorable conditions." But again, according to Leslie at least, Norfolk refused as he still hoped for Elizabeth's blessing.[18] Of course, Leslie was no disinterested reporter, and his claims must be viewed with as much caution as those later made by Walsingham and others against Mary and the duke. In one of his confessions after the exposure of the subsequent Ridolfi plot, furthermore, Leslie did allow that a link may have existed. He noted that Mary had pressed Norfolk over the late summer about his plans should Elizabeth forbid the marriage. Leslie said that although he had not seen any proof of this, the duke may have eventually agreed to effect the marriage by force if need be, perhaps in conjunction with the northern lords.[19]

It is possible that Norfolk had played a double game – selling the marriage as a Protestant solution for the succession crisis to some and as a Catholic solution for the religious problem to others – in an attempt to drum up as much support as possible for his own ambitions to wed a Queen. It is somewhat more likely that he began the project sharing the aims of his fellow Protestant planners, but became sufficiently committed and attracted to the marriage itself that when the plan threatened to fall apart in late summer, he turned to the northern earls. He seems at least to have known that the earls had discussed more forceful measures than had the original proponents of the marriage. What is certain is that the earls and their confederates had been plotting on their own well before the marriage plan's appearance and continued to do so even as it progressed, at times in opposition to its central aim. Westmorland may have liked the idea of a marriage between Mary and his brother-in-law, but Northumberland and Dacre emphatically did not. Treating the two plans as only tenuously connected, with links, if any, coming only at the end of the summer, allows us to make more sense of the Norfolk marriage plan and the broad support it had received.

Whatever the precise relationship between Norfolk's plans and those of the earls, the collapse of the marriage project in September did prove to be a factor in pushing the northern lords to their ill-timed, ill-planned revolt. When Norfolk fled to his estates in fear of Elizabeth's displeasure, Northumberland sent to him for advice and seems to have offered to rise in his protection. Norfolk waffled and decided instead to return to court to do his best with his angry Queen. He sent his message to Westmorland, urging his brother-in-law not to rise for fear it would mean his death. According to Northumberland's subsequent confession, when the messenger arrived, the earls were already locked in with their confederates discussing their options. Westmorland mulled over the message and said he would do whatever Northumberland and Dacre decided. These three leaders proved reluctant, reciting the inevitable dangers, but their companions were "so hot and earnest, that no way but they would stir." The group decided to rise the following week, on October 7. At this point, Westmorland intervened to ask what precisely the grounds of the quarrel would be. They had been talking of the succession and religion, and to a lesser extent of protecting the duke: which was it to be? When the others exclaimed it to be primarily for religion, Westmorland reportedly said: "No...those that seem to take that quarrel in other countries are accounted as rebels, and therefore I will never blot my house, which hath been this long preserved without staining." Northumberland later insisted that his younger confederate "was ever unwilling to the matter but only pressed and sore urged by others."[20] If Westmorland's intervention had been a ploy to delay, it worked. The men broke up and returned to their homes. Thinking the matter at an end, Dacre took off for London to pursue his property claims, not to be seen again until the rebellion was nearly at an end.

Within the week, however, Richard Norton, Thomas Markenfeld, and some of the others returned to the earl of Northumberland to try their hand once more. According to the earl's later recollection, they offered strong arguments. They described again the need to rise for religion, detailed the dangers to which they had already exposed themselves, and played on the earl's sense of duty to those who expected his leadership. They must rise, even without Westmorland's assistance:

> For so much as we have so often times assembled and talked together, we could not be able to answer it; and therefore, seeing our peril is so great, and our action so just, we must, of force, either to enter into the matter without the said earl and take such fortune as God should send, or else we must seek to depart out of the realm. The one would be a marvelous blot and discredit, most to you noblemen, and something to us, thus to depart and to leave off this godly enterprise that is so expected and looked for at our hands, throughout the body of the whole realm, who, no doubt, will in this case so readily assist as you will think it wondrous.[21]

The appeal of such arguments for Northumberland, and the depth of his religious commitment, should not be discounted. In his subsequent confession, he spoke of Thomas Harding, Nicholas Sander, and other authors of Louvain who had shown "how enormously" the Protestants did "misconstrue the word of God, and abuse and falsify the ancient writers." He referred specifically to two of Sander's publications, *The Supper of Our Lord* (1566) and *The Rock of the Church* (1567), which endorsed the papal supremacy over the church.[22] While we might wonder if Northumberland's religious commitment had grown during his intervening trials, Francis Norton's confession similarly painted the earl as a man moved by his faith. Norton told how the earl had reacted to the warnings of spiritual peril offered by Nicholas Morton, the papal emissary. Northumberland had "sent for my father, unto whom he brake his mind, declaring unto him (knowing my father to be a Catholic) the great grief he had, for that they all lived out of the law of the Catholic church; for the restitution whereof, he would willingly spend his life."[23] Richard Norton now reminded him of his earlier determination. Northumberland finally agreed to his and Markenfeld's pleas and told them to begin making precise plans.

They returned some days later fired with enthusiasm as men in Westmorland's coterie, presumably including uncles Cuthbert and Christopher, had promised to join notwithstanding their earl's qualms. Their zeal waned, however, upon receiving cold replies from other lords to whom they had written. Indeed, every missive for aid they had sent thus far received a negative response; Mary and even the Spanish ambassador had counseled them not to rise, at least not yet, while the earl of Derby, who had also entertained Nicholas Morton, refused even to respond. Northumberland at this point took fright yet again; without the guaranteed assistance of other noblemen, their attempt might end as soon as it started. They must, if nothing else, disable the Council in the North as this would allow time once the rising began for other noblemen to set aside their fears. The conspirators duly returned with a plan to seize most members of the council on a Sunday after church. Nevertheless, Northumberland thought this still insufficient and refused to act.

All this time, their activities had put the president of the northern council in a particularly difficult spot. Thomas Radcliffe, third earl of Sussex, had recently served as lord lieutenant in Ireland and only assumed his current position in July 1568, upon the death of Thomas Young, who had served as both archbishop and president of the council. Sussex considered Northumberland and Norfolk good friends. A moderate in religion and pragmatist in politics, he also had a strong loyalty to his Queen and desire for peace. He tried in these months to defuse the growing crisis. Having heard tales of trouble since Norfolk's flight to Kenninghall in late September, both at large and in admonitory letters from the Privy Council, Sussex dutifully enforced the orders to look carefully to rumors and "lewd speeches." He relayed reports of the intended stir on October 7, but omitted any reference to the earls of Northumberland and Westmorland in his letters to court. Upon news of Norfolk's arrest and plea not to rise, Sir William Ingleby and Francis Slingsby, two of the original conspirators, took fright and divorced themselves from the group. Thinking that the rising was still intended for October 7, they holed up with other local gentlemen in Knaresborough Castle. When local inhabitants saw their leaders run to the nearest castle with all their weapons and worldly goods, they understandably assumed something to be afoot. The action certainly lent substance to all the recent rumors. But in the event, nothing happened. Sussex called Northumberland and Westmorland before the northern council on October 9. He knew very well that they had participated in the plotting, but found encouragement from their dutiful appearance. When they pleaded ignorance and promised to help find the tale-tellers and suppress any commotion, and knowing of Norfolk's return to court, Sussex allowed himself to hope that matters had come to an end. He tried to calm the rampant rumors, even pursuing one poor coney-catcher whose talk of Christopher Neville's plans to rise had "unfairly" slandered a man better than he. Sussex's letters to the Queen and Privy Council urged patience and prudence. He insisted that the passage of time, and approach of winter, would see all troubles put to rest; as the season "will shortly cool hot humors," he asked the Queen to wait until "the time of the year avoids actions" before investigating further.[24]

Elizabeth, however, was having none of it. Famous for her usual prudence and ability to wait out a decision or crisis, in this case she wanted answers immediately. She had sources of information other than Sussex, ones that had not so delicately avoided implicating the northern earls. On October 24, she ordered Sussex to send the earls to court; he, in turn, reiterated his desire for patience. Sir Thomas Gargrave, another stalwart on the northern council, noted that all agreed with Sussex's determination, thinking it good to "nourish that quiet until further in winter, that the nights were longer and colder and the ways worse and the waters bigger to stop their passages, if any stir should be."[25] Nonetheless, they did Elizabeth's bidding. On October 30, they sent letters asking the earls to come to York for further instructions.

This helped provoke the final crisis. Sussex had somewhat moderated Elizabeth's demand, by requesting the earls' attendance at York rather than immediately at court, but to no avail. The conspirators had renewed their suit to Westmorland upon Northumberland's latest signs of reluctance. Now, they had proof of the dangers he faced even if he did not rebel. The two earls sent their apologies to York. When Sussex sent a firmer demand for their attendance on November 4 and received similar refusals, he tried one final time by sending pursuivants to each of the earls on November 9. He pleaded that they beware of bad advice and precipitate action: "take heed of the counsel of such as I have warned you would show you honey and deliver you poison...let not vain delusions abuse you with fear of your own shadow." The countess of Northumberland dispatched a servant to return with Sussex's man to explain that her husband had heard rumors that he and Westmorland would be sent to court as disguised captives. She, too, hoped that time would quell hasty action. Sussex's messenger left the earl's residence at Topcliffe to the ominous accompaniment of the ringing of the bells. When he asked his companion what it meant, the latter "sighed, and answered he was afraid it was to raise the country."[26]

Not just yet, but almost. On this false alarm, thinking that Sir Oswald Welstropp had arrived with a band of horse to arrest him, Northumberland fled to Brancepeth. There he found Westmorland ensconced with the Nortons, the brothers Neville, Markenfeld, Swinburne, and others. Westmorland was armed and ready to rise. Northumberland thought it "very strange" that Westmorland was "brought to that when all good hope was passed, and more fitted for us to seek to convey ourselves away."[27] The men talked for hours and finally agreed each to go his own way and make such shift as they could. But then, according to Northumberland at least, the countess of Westmorland interrupted their farewells with bitter tears and weeping. She exclaimed, "we and our country were shamed forever, that now in the end we should seek holes to creep into."[28]

Some of the men broke with the group and departed, but Northumberland heeded the pleas of the Nevilles and Nortons that if he left, they were all undone. His earlier waffling had, however, evoked their mistrust. When he said he must return briefly to his estates to gather men and equipment – or else ride under Westmorland's standard – the conspirators finally agreed but then sent a party to intercept him. Northumberland again explained his need to gather men and supplies, but one of his servants plucked him by the sleeve and whispered that he must return with the Nortons, as some in the party were "desperately bent" and meant him harm should he refuse. He acceded, and all returned to Brancepeth to begin their final deliberations.[29] On November 14, they rode into Durham with a few hundred men. Overturning the communion table and celebrating a Catholic mass, they began their rebellion.

Justifying rebellion

Such, then, were the grievances that pushed the earls and their confederates to conspire and the precipitants that pushed them from conspiracy to rebellion. The earls' links to the Norfolk marriage plan were tenuous at best, and despite the historiographical focus on them as the last defenders of a defunct feudal order, they clearly understood their grievances in terms of religion and were driven by others to act. But how did they now attempt to justify their actions to themselves and to others? How would they attempt to shape interpretations of their decision? There were, of course, traditions that allowed the baronial correction of a misguided monarch, just as there were traditions that enabled armed "petition" for redress by commoners. But the frequency of rebellion in this period should not blind us to the ideological and material hurdles that existed. Particularly in the Tudor years, a doctrine of unquestioning obedience had been tirelessly preached from the gallows and from the pulpits. As the *Homily on Obedience* baldly stated, "it is not lawful for inferiors and subjects in any case to resist the superior powers, for St. Paul's words be plain, that whosoever resisteth shall get to themselves damnation: for whosoever resisteth, resisteth the ordinance of God."[30] In such an intensely religious age, such strictures had a force that might now seem difficult to imagine.[31] Even the radical Protestant writers who suffered under Mary Tudor's Catholic regime had generally recognized a line between disobedience and active resistance. Most concluded that while they might justly disobey flawed laws, they must never take up arms against God's anointed.

The earls and at least some of their fellows wrestled with this issue. They discussed not just the practical impediments to rebellion – the material resources required to begin, and in event of failure, the forfeiture of lands and life, the latter with all the gruesome inventiveness of an earlier age – but also the intellectual. In at least one of their sessions, they debated whether God's law ever justified rebellion against an anointed, if misguided, ruler. Turning to learned men and poring over scripture, they found no firm answer. All agreed that rebellion became lawful if the Pope excommunicated the Queen. As head of the church and God's vicar on earth, the Pope had the power to free subjects from their bonds of obedience to a faithless sovereign. Unfortunately, he had not yet done so. But then one of the conspirators struck on a possible solution: had Elizabeth in effect already excommunicated herself? Nicholas Morton, a former prebendary of York Cathedral and then a special papal emissary, had talked with these men when in England earlier that year about the possibility of an excommunication. Thomas Markenfeld now reported Morton's opinion that when Elizabeth had earlier refused the papal envoy entry into England, she had for all intents sundered herself from the communion of the church. Northumberland later suggested that he and some of the others believed Markenfeld had lied in order "to advance the matter," especially as the two priests in attendance thought his justification insufficient. According to them, the excommunication had to be formal, and it had to be publicized. Guilt alone did not suffice; the Pope had to pass judgment. Upon this verdict, some of the conspirators departed. Nicholas Sander, a leading figure in the exile community at Louvain, later affirmed the seriousness with which the conspirators debated the issue:

> We can bear witness how eagerly the English nobles turned to us to know whether the Apostolic see had not yet issued some decree against the Queen, and further whether, even in the absence of any such decree, they might not with a clear conscience dare to take steps to free themselves from such tyranny. To the first question we made answer that, as far as we were aware, nothing of the kind had yet been made public, while as to the other question, the best theologians were not of one mind. Some had no doubt whatever that, even without any authority from the Roman See, it was lawful to defend the Catholic religion in those doctrines which are the common Christian inheritance, while others thought it necessary, or at any rate safer, to wait for a Papal decision.[32]

Belatedly, the earls wrote to the Pope for guidance on November 8. When he finally received their letter, he enthusiastically endorsed their actions, promised aid both divine and financial, and hastened to have Elizabeth formally declared a heretic.[33] His answer and his bull of excommunication, however, would not arrive for months.

With their fears of imminent arrest mounting, they did not have time to await Pius V's reply. The earls had to find other ways than a papal blessing to present and explain their actions to the people from whom they needed support. Unable to justify rebellion on the basis of the Queen's excommunication, they instead asserted that they were not rebels but loyal subjects. They reverted to the standard tropes of past rebel declarations and allied themselves to an older tradition that saw loyalty and protest as compatible. Their first proclamation made the restoration of the old faith their central rallying cry:

> We, Thomas earl of Northumberland and Charles earl of Westmorland, the Queen's true and faithful subjects: To all the same of the old and catholic faith. Know ye that with many other well disposed as well of the nobility as others have promised our faith to the furtherance of this our good meaning, forasmuch as diverse, disordered, and ill disposed persons about the Queen's majesty have by their crafty and subtle dealing to advance themselves overthrown

in this realm the true and catholic religion toward God, and by the same abuseth the Queen, disorder the realm, and now lastly seeketh to procure the destruction of these nobility. We therefore have gathered ourselves together to resist force by force and rather by the help of God and you good people to redress these things amiss with the restoring of all ancient customs and liberties to God's church and this noble realm. And lastly, if we should not do it ourselves we might be reformed by strangers to the great hazard of the state of this our country whereunto we are all bound. God save the Queen.[34]

Like previous rebels, they professed to act not against the Queen but against her evil councilors, and portrayed their action as one of justifiable self-defense.

Within a few days, they had refined their proclamation, repeating many of the same tropes but in more insistent, demanding language. They also added an intriguing reference to the reformation of religion in "these realms," perhaps referring to Ireland, then experiencing its own religiously inflected rebellion, but more likely to Scotland, whence they hoped for aid:

Thomas, earl of Northumberland and Charles, earl of Westmorland, the Queen's most true and lawful subjects, and to all her highness's people, sendeth greeting: Whereas diverse new set up nobles about the Queen's Majesty, have and do daily, not only go about to overthrow and put down the ancient nobility of this realm, but also have misused the Queen's Majesty's own person, and also have by the space of twelve years now past, set up and maintained a newfound religion and heresy, contrary to God's word. For the amending and redressing whereof, diverse foreign powers do purpose shortly to invade these realms, which will be to our utter destruction, if we do not ourselves speedily forfend the same. Wherefore we are now constrained at this time to go about to amend and redress it ourselves, which if we should not do and foreigners enter upon us we should be all made slaves and bondsmen to them. These are therefore to will and require you, and every of you, being above the age of sixteen years and not sixty, as your duty to God doth bind you, for the setting forth of His true and catholic religion; and as you tender the common wealth of your country, to come and resort unto us with all speed, with all such armor and furniture as you, or any of you have. This fail you not herein, as you will answer the contrary at your perils. God save the Queen.[35]

Their warning of foreign intervention lest they act first, elaborated in this second proclamation, initially seems somewhat odd. Yet, it may have been a strategy to make what they could from the lack of an excommunication; once the Pope excommunicated Elizabeth, not only could her subjects legitimately resist her, but foreign princes would also be expected to oppose her. How much better, then, to act first and forestall such a deadly outcome? Also and especially noteworthy was the complete silence in both public statements about the succession and Mary Queen of Scots. Mary's recognition as heir had been central to the rebels' objectives and inspiration. Perhaps they omitted her name for fear that the claims of a Scottish Queen prove a divisive rally point, but Cecil at least thought Mary dangerously and widely popular in the north. More likely, they omitted any reference to her for fear of putting her in greater danger of Elizabeth's vengeance or to maintain the posture of "loyal rebels": any mention of Mary, even as successor, raised the specter that this was a rebellion to replace, rather than correct, their Queen.

Their third proclamation clarified their intent to deal with the succession, while still avoiding Mary's name. Issued after Sussex and others had made proclamations of their own to brand the earls traitors to their Queen and liars to their followers, this third statement of their aims reemphasized the assault on the ancient nobility and their need to act in self-defense:

Whereas it hath been by the sinister and wicked report of sundry malicious persons, enemies both to God's word and the public estate of this commonwealth, devised and published that the assembly of these noble men, the earls of Northumberland and Westmorland, and sundry of the greatest worship and credit of this part of the realm, is and hath been to the overthrow of the commonwealth and the Crown; it is therefore thought good to the said earls and their counsel to signify to all and every the Queen's Majesty's subjects the true and sincere meaning of the said earls, their friends and allies. Know ye therefore, that where of late it hath been faithfully and deliberately considered and devised by the high and mighty prince, Thomas duke of Norfolk, Henry earl of Arundel, William earl of Pembroke, and the said earls of Northumberland and Westmorland, and diverse other of the ancient nobility of this realm, with a common consent of sundry of the principal favorers of God's word; and the same, as well for the avoidance of bloodshed and utter subversion of the commonwealth, as the reforming of certain disorders crept in by the abuse and malicious practice of sundry wicked and evil-disposed persons, to make known and understood to all manner of persons to whom of mere right the true succession of the Crown appertaineth, dangerously and uncertainly depending by reason of many titles and interest pretended to the same. The which godly and honorable meaning of the said nobility hath been sought by all manner of means to be prevented by certain common enemies of this realm, near about the Queen's majesty's person; by whose sinister and detestable counsel and practice, well known to us and the rest of the nobility, their lives and liberties are now endangered, and daily devices made to apprehend our bodies ... we have therefore, of just and faithful meaning of the Queen's Majesty, her common wealth, and the true successors of the same, assembled our selves to resist force by force; wherein we commit our selves, seeing no intercession will help, to the exceeding goodness of God and to all true favorers of this realm of England, resolved in our selves in this so just and godly an enterprise wholly to adventure our lives, lands, and goods, whereto we heartily crave the true aid and assistance of all the faithful favorers of the commonwealth, and the ancient nobility of the same.[36]

In this, as in the earlier proclamations, the earls professed the defensive, conservative, and loyal nature of their acts. Norfolk, Pembroke, and Arundel all heatedly denied their involvement, of course, but the northern earls still clearly believed the imprimatur of noble direction would help legitimize their efforts and gain support.

By such means the earls sought to justify their actions and to recruit aid for their cause. After their dramatic beginning in Durham, they marched to Darlington, Northallerton, and Ripon in succession, gathering men as they went. Unlike the crown, they had no access to the press to disperse their claims, but at each stop, they issued their proclamation and repeated the essentials of their religious display in Durham Cathedral by celebrating a Catholic mass. Thousands joined them; when they stopped in and around Ripon and Boroughbridge on November 18, they reportedly had roughly 6000 men in arms.

The rank and file

Who were these men, and why did so many join such a dangerous enterprise? Traditional narratives of the rebellion suggest that they were tenants of the earls moved by some mixture of feudal loyalties and coercion. This certainly accounts for some of the number. Yet, very few of the rebels were tenants of the earl of Northumberland. By report, some eighty to one hundred horsemen came from the Northumberland lordship of Langley.[37] Some of his household retainers joined the earl, but neither they nor he ever rode north to attempt to raise his tenantry. M.E. James argues that even if they had done so, feudal ties alone would have been insufficient motivation. In recent years, the Knight's Court of the barony of Alnwick – "the symbol and organizing centre of seigneurial authority in...the Percy heartland" – had fallen into disuse. According to the earl's own estate officer, the recent shift to copyhold and border tenure had caused tenants to see themselves as owing little more than rents to their lord. Furthermore, Sir John Forster and his kin had so effectively insinuated themselves into local society that their authority rivaled Northumberland's; with the Forsters' loyalty, added to the ostentatious obedience to the Queen of the earl's own brother, Percy's tenants might well have ignored any peremptory summons to rise.[38] At any rate, they were never called upon to make that choice. With the exception of the relatively few tenants and retainers noted above, the only rebels to come out of Northumberland were some 500 of the infamous Tynedale and Redesdale border reivers.[39]

As Map 2.1 indicates, the majority of rebels hailed from Durham and North Yorkshire. Some of these men did have ties to the earl of Westmorland or to other leading rebels. Christopher Neville set out for Kirby Moorside to raise his and his nephew's tenants in the area. Several of the gentry conspirators had holdings in rebel territory. When comparing the lists of the manors forfeited after the rebellion to the list of rebels' origins, the most significant overlap is with the estates of Thomas Markenfeld: men from at least ten of his manors participated in the rising. Thomas Hussey, Leonard Metcalf, Ralph Conyers, and Robert Lambert also held manors in key areas of rebel activity.[40] Yet, Susan Taylor's careful examination of the rebels' origins found that fewer than twenty percent had any feudal links with the rebel leaders.[41] Thus, there were pockets of men whose tenurial relationship with leading rebels presumably explains their ready appearance, but they comprised only a minority of the rebel army and were concentrated among the horsemen.

By all contemporary accounts, the rebel army consisted mostly of men who answered calls to muster, not demands to provide military service for their lords. Indeed, in 1569, as in the 1536 Pilgrimage of Grace, the main method of gathering troops was the use (or abuse) of the muster system.[42] Here, the earls had an advantage as they had served as commissioners for the Queen just months earlier. The crown ordered such surveys of able-bodied men and their weaponry haphazardly over

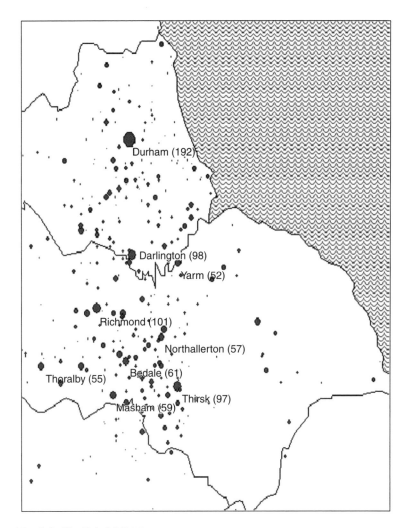

Durham (192)

Darlington (98)

Yarm (52)

Richmond (101)

Northallerton (57)

Thoralby (55)

Bedale (61)

Thirsk (97)

Masham (59)

Map 2.1 The Rebels' Origins

the years, usually when moved by rumors of domestic or foreign trouble. From March 1569, the crown had arranged such musters throughout the country, responding to both the tensions generated by Spanish threats of reprisal after the seizure of their payships and to the riots and rumors of worse that dominated the spring and summer months. The earls had participated in the northern musters, and thus had a good sense of the available forces readily at hand. Sir John Forster later complained that the muster books for the border region had been stolen during the rising, presumably for use by the rebels.[43] Now the earls issued commands to muster in the Queen's name, reading out their proclamation to those who appeared.

The musters occurred mostly along the main rebel route, but to build the rank and file and get better turnouts at the large musters, the earls also sent precepts to individual villages, charging each to produce a certain number of men furnished for battle. So, too, did they hijack some of the musters ordered by Sussex and his agents. Learning of the appointed places of assembly, the rebels sent bands of horsemen to lure the men away or at least despoil them of their weaponry and supplies.[44] At these gatherings, once their intentions became clear, the earls had to cajole or coerce the men to join their protest. As Sir George Bowes complained, "with fear, or fair speech, or offers of money they draw away the hearts of people."[45] Some men stayed only because forced. Rebel leaders occasionally followed past practice in their attempts to coerce local gentlemen to join their host. Francis Norton, for example, took one hundred horsemen to the home of John Sayers; unable to get Sayers's own participation, Norton took his son and armor. Nicholas Fairfax and a company of horse did much the same to Anthony Kittrick, forcing his two sons-in-law to join their army.[46] Once the men had gathered and agreed to participate, whether from coercion, promise of pay, or force of conviction, they took an oath of allegiance to the rebel aims.[47]

The size and membership of the rebel army fluctuated constantly, with men coming and going as they were needed or as they became disillusioned by insufficient pay or progress. In order to minimize their expenses, the earls told many of the men who had mustered and taken the oath to return to their villages and wait for subsequent orders. Others they foisted off on villages along their route.[48] Nor did the earls take all who appeared; according to Sussex, the rebels turned away great numbers who were insufficiently furnished. As with the Pilgrim leaders years before, they sought an effective, well-armed fighting force rather than sheer bulk.[49]

Despite the frequent characterizations of the rebels as the dregs of society, "the meaner and baser sort," the majority were yeomen; that is, relatively substantial farmers, heads of households, with security of tenure and middling status. Of the 2598 rebels whose status is known, 2191 were yeomen, 142 husbandmen, 66 laborers, and 63 gentlemen. The others were tradesmen, ranging from barbers to glovers to wheel-wrights. The preponderance of yeomen may have arisen as much from the earls' determination to keep only those men furnished with their own arms as from any special appeal of the rebel cause to men of yeomen status. At least seventy-one of these men were village constables and a few others bailiffs.[50] Generally men of moderate means and selected by members of their own communities, constables held an ancient and important office. To them fell such responsibilities as preventing and suppressing riots, removing vagrants, and apprehending serious criminals. Also, and of greatest relevance here, they assisted in the collection of taxes, including coat and conduct money and military levies in times of war.[51] These men were not, then, the degraded rabble that loyalists made them out to be; nor, presumably, were they sufficiently poor to trade security simply for the pittance on offer for service, at least not without some other contributing motivation.

The town of Richmond and the surrounding liberty of Richmondshire provided well over a thousand of the rebel soldiers and some evidence of the range of motives at play. Richmondshire formed a substantial part of the North Riding of Yorkshire, bounded by rivers on three sides: the Tees to the north, the Wiske to the east, and the Ure to the south. The liberty belonged to the Queen, but with Northumberland serving as her steward, tenurial ties of a sort did exist. Yet here, as elsewhere in the north, men acted on a variety of calculations. Sir George Bowes offered conflicting accounts of their decisions. In one letter just before the rising, he expressed doubts about the loyalty of the townspeople, and later complained that they had greeted the commissioner sent to levy loyal forces with manifest disrespect. In yet another he declared his belief that most in the liberty meant to be dutiful but hesitated to assemble out of fear.[52] Bowes had orders to muster the men of Richmondshire, and having failed miserably, he had cause to be frustrated and to explain away their defection. He described to Sussex how the earls had called a muster at Richmond, using the Queen's name to deceive and confuse the inhabitants, but also threatening force against those who did not appear ready and armed to fight. Two "of the substantialest men" of Richmond had told him how the earl of Northumberland "had required first by fair speech and after by offers of money and lastly by threat of burning and spoiling that they should give him aid of an hundred men." The two Richmond men offered Bowes a confused narrative, claiming they had initially refused to join the rebels, even in the face of threats, but then had consented to provide sixty unarmed men to accompany the earl to Allerton. He insisted on one hundred well-armed soldiers, whereupon they offered to all go with him a distance, but again unarmed. Three hundred townsmen accompanied the earl, but at the bounds of the town, he once again insisted that they come with armor and weaponry. Northumberland said he would return the next day, at which time he expected them to meet his original request for one hundred armed men. The Richmond representatives then maintained to Bowes that they were ready to muster for the Queen. Yet, Bowes also reported that when forced to chose upon news of his own approach, "sundry of the wealthiest sort of Richmond is departed towards the earls."[53] Whatever their intentions may have been, few men of the area ended up with Bowes.

Here, as elsewhere in the north, it seems likely that many men took the easiest and closest path, following whoever first offered them money and threatened force. Both rebel and loyal leaders sought men in the same way, and both found it effective to a point. (Indeed, Bowes maintained that many people hid in the forests to avoid the recruiters of both sides.)[54] Yet, the lists of those involved in the rising demonstrate rebel allegiances among the urban oligarchy, men of sufficient means and position that one would think them unlikely to fight simply for money. Of the forty-eight rebels known to have come from the town of Richmond, sixteen can be identified as burgesses, men who served as aldermen, bailiffs, or school governors over the 1560s and 70s.[55]

The school they governed had been a product of the troubled mix of finance and faith that had characterized much of the reformation so far, and that left many in Richmond doggedly favoring the old church or at least resentful of the impositions of the new. William Wharton, a Protestant who despaired at the impediments his recalcitrant neighbors threw in front of the new and legally established faith, wrote regular missives to Cecil complaining of first one, then another conspiring Catholic. In 1560, Wharton alerted Cecil that the town had concealed a number of chantries and their goods, keeping not just the land but also the chalices, vestments, and other items of superstition that should have been surrendered to royal visitors years before. When jurors who sat for the resulting commission of inquiry decided, against the odds, that the town had not violated the law, the burgesses recognized their luck and that it might not last. Accordingly, they used the chantry land to endow a new free grammar school.[56] Throughout the following years, the Richmond marketplace hosted a series of ritualized and demeaning public penances by those forced to bend to the Elizabethan settlement.[57] Such disputes and displays had not yet led the people of Richmond to adapt to the new church in any significant numbers. Nor was theirs simply a foot-dragging attachment to the old; at least two priests traveled the region, men whose practices Wharton later thought partly responsible for the numbers of people in the area who had "risen in this insurrection for recovery of their popish mass."[58] Indeed, the earls' call did reawaken the dormant sentiments of some. John Acrige, a one-time chantry priest, had continued to serve as an assistant curate in Richmond, a position to which the parishioners had apparently elected him. Upon hearing the rebel proclamation, Acrige repented "his so long continuance in schism and heresy." He sought reconciliation, and continued even after the rebellion to travel as a poor pilgrim, offering mass to his coreligionists until finally being apprehended on a visit to his sister in Richmond. On that occasion, when given the choice, he refused to abandon his faith and died in prison at York in 1585.[59]

The Richmond evidence, then, suggests the range of conflicting motives at work and lends some credence to claims by the earl of Sussex and others of the Queen's agents in the north that most who joined the earls did so because they "like so well their cause of religion."[60] While we can neither be sure of the motivations of each individual nor completely discount the lure of pay and fear of reprisals, we can surely move beyond talk of "instinctive" actions and assume the decisions were conscious and reasoned, and that the members of the rebel host had wills of their own. The earls and their close confederates grappled with a mix of motivations that included fear, faith, and a sense of responsibility; why should we assume the rank and file faced decisions any less complex?

The importance of religious beliefs and practices to the rebels' efforts is also suggested by their self-depictions and behavior. While we have few words of the rebels and their supporters, we do have accounts of their actions; for contemporaries, these actions seemed proof of their aims and motives. The men in arms declared their common identity and goals through symbolic displays that marked them not as rebels, but as participants in a long tradition of Christian soldiering. In addition to the heraldic ensigns of the earls, the men carried flags with the images of saints. They marched under time-hallowed banners that depicted the Five Wounds of Christ and the customary flag of those who fought to better the commonwealth, with its motto "God Speed the Plow."[61] One informant later identified people as participants because they had openly worn "the ensign of the order of these rebels": great crucifixes about the neck. Another reported that "all their force, both of horse and foot, wear red crosses, as well the priests as others."[62]

With these banners and badges the participants defined themselves and asserted their legitimacy. The religious ensigns linked their bearers with the potent ideology and rhetoric of the Crusades, a fusion of holy war and pilgrimage that continued to resonate in England as in the rest of Europe well into the late 1500s.[63] The red crosses worn in 1569 duplicated those worn by the Crusaders and called to mind the Christians' victories over the infidel. During an age in which clothing constituted identity much more directly than now, in which badges, liveries, and other such things invested rather than merely denoted status, the significance of such items for both wearers and observers should not be overlooked.[64] The banner of the Five Wounds of Christ and its inscription, "in this sign, victory," drew from a key episode in Christian history: when the Emperor Constantine fought under this banner, revealed to him in a dream, he won the promised victory over his foes and then in gratitude allowed Christian worship throughout his empire. The Prayer Book rebels of 1549 had marched under this banner in the more immediate past, as had the participants in the Pilgrimage of Grace. Thus, Constantine's banner of the Five Wounds had a history that linked it with Christian soldiering and with earlier moments of righteous protest against the faithless.[65] Such displays drew on shared cultural symbols. They served to unify the rebels behind common legitimizing claims, however disparate individual motivations may have been.

The nature and focus of the rebels' acts of violence also suggest motives rooted in the tensions that had built up around the Elizabethan religious reforms. The two main targets of violence represented recent, striking changes: married ministers and reformed church fittings. The rebels "raged" against married clerics and used violence against some of them. After the rebellion, Edward Otbye, parson of Terrington, complained to the York Court of High Commission that one Christopher Jackson had terrorized his wife Anna during the commotion time. Edward was away in Lincolnshire when the rebellion began. Hearing that parsons and their families had been attacked, Anna sent her own children away and hid in a neighbor's cellar. Whether the news she had heard was true or not, she remained convinced that "if she had been known to have been there, she would have received hurt of the rebels if they had come." Hidden in the cellar, she overheard Christopher Jackson's angry tirade against married ministers. From the various depositions, it seems that Jackson believed that the "uproar and rebellion began altogether of priests' wives." He swore "a vengeance upon all fuckbeggar priests and the errant whores their wives." His parson "had as good bedding as any in the parish" and at this rate, he complained, priests' children would soon be treated better than lords' children. His friend John Wingham marched with the rebels; if he could find Wingham, he would get him and his companions to put out the local parson and "carry the tykes away with them as well as they had in other places."[66]

The presence of married ministers and their families was an obvious, visible change that provoked many people, not just in the north. Earlier in 1569, John Smith, a New Romney tailor, declared loudly in both the alehouse and the street outside that his vicar was a knave and the vicar's wife an "errant whore." Furthermore, he said, "all the married priests in England are knaves, and their wives are very whores."[67] Years later, a parishioner of Ribchester declared that he would rather receive communion from the devil or a dog than from the hands of a married minister. Jane Scarisbrick received her license for midwifery only upon condition that she not refuse to attend the wives of ministers. Such examples could be multiplied many times over.[68] Queen Elizabeth herself thought poorly of this novelty. Although she continued to promote married clerics, she frequently expressed her distaste for clerical marriage and was for a time reluctant to enshrine the new practice in statute.[69] This animosity had numerous sources. Obviously, it came in part from the perceived immorality of the practice. Some apparently believed married clerics incapable of properly administering the sacraments. Elizabeth thought it detracted from the decorum and devotion one expected of clerical establishments. Others thought the families placed an intolerable burden on the communities that had to support them.[70] As Helen Parish has noted in her recent study of clerical marriage, those for whom the main point of contact with the church was a celibate priest may have found a married minister "an all too visible and unsettling sign of the rapid pace of change."[71] Some twenty-one priests of the northern province had been put out of their livings in 1559 for no other reason than to restore married Edwardian clerics who had been deprived at Mary's accession.[72] In 1569, the rebels took matters into their own hands, forcibly ejecting married ministers from their churches. How prevalent such actions were is unknown, but almost every chronicler and many letter-writers who commented on the rebellion noted the indignities offered to Protestant ministers in general and to married ones and their wives in particular as a defining feature of the protest.[73]

Another visible set of changes prompted action and reaction, and that, of course, was the recent purging of altars, images, and the traditional fabric of worship. The rebels' destruction of Protestant fittings and reerection of altars remains one of the better known features of the revolt, and has received at least passing mention even in accounts that minimize or dismiss the popular and religious aspects of the rising.

During the revolt, rebels and their sympathizers destroyed Protestant books in seventy-three Yorkshire churches and in at least twelve in county Durham; in the latter, the number may well have been higher, as other churches are known to have hosted religious services under the old rites.[74] (See Map 2.2.) This came, furthermore, after the concerted push by the authorities to rid the north of its idolatrous monuments of superstition in the late 1560s. When the rebels burned Protestant books, they reacted to recent changes, dramatically imposed.

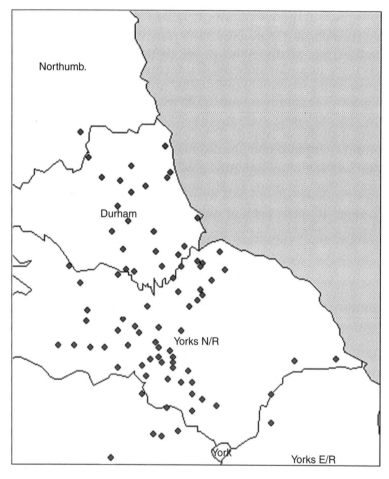

Map 2.2   Known Sites of Catholic Activity

Sedgefield offers some examples. In southern Durham, east of Darlington, Sedgefield had witnessed religious tensions of its own. So far as we know, the authorities had ordered no public burnings of Catholic items in the parish itself, but they had turned their attention to the recalcitrant parishioners who had failed to comply willingly with the bishop's various directives. The Ordinary arrived in September of 1567 to supervise the dismantling of the old altar and erection of a new communion table. One parishioner declared the Ordinary "a hinderer and no furtherer of God's service." Others took more direct action and within two months a group of the churchwardens "forcibly, contemptuously, and rashly" removed the new communion table. Other residents presented them to the bishop's officials, however, and the table was restored.[75] The religious changes had divided the community, but the people of Sedgefield seemed to come together during the revolt. In November of 1568, Brian Hedlam wore his cap during service and heckled the curate with lewd comments. Furious to find himself presented for this offence, he complained to his one of his accusers, churchwarden Thomas Watkin, that "in presenting me you have done to me as never was done to any of Sedgefield parish, for ever one of us have born with another."[76] Yet, Hedlam, Watkin, and at least one other of his accusers, Roland Hixson, later joined the rebellion; the latter we have already seen gleefully stoking a bonfire of Protestant books. The reformation of Sedgefield, like that of other parishes, divided its inhabitants but not along straightforward religious lines. Different kinds of conservatism coexisted: like Hixson, some people who had conservative religious sentiments found themselves enforcing the new provisions out of a respect for order.[77] Social and political conservatism often triumphed over the religious. But now, with the call to rise, some twenty-six men of the village and more from throughout the parish rode off to join the rebels. Those who stayed behind dismantled the communion table yet again. Hixson later noted that "one holy day after service the parish met together and consulted to set up the altar stone and the holy water stone." Some thirty people, young and old, gathered to winch the stones out of their hiding places and into the church. Women and youths helped carry the lime and sand, participating in the recovery and restoration. They also gathered up the Protestant service books to burn them at the cross in the town gate. According to several observers and participants, "a great multitude, and specially of youth" gathered for this and a second book burning. They attended mass offered by Richard Hartburn, who preached from the Sedgefield pulpit that just as they had freed the holy stones from the earth, so had they now extricated themselves from the Queen's erroneous faith.[78]

Similar scenes occurred throughout Yorkshire and Durham in these few weeks, as people attacked the books that symbolized and supported the new settlement, emulating the acts by which the authorities had destroyed the symbols and tools of the old. Of course, some of this participation was not offered freely. Of the 120 or so men and women brought before the Durham church court after the rising, many maintained that they had joined in the rites of burning only out of fear of the rebels or at their express command. It was not the devil, it seems, but Cuthbert Neville who made them do it.[79] Yet, given that claims of coercion would be expected from those facing punishment and that a few admitted to willing involvement, it seems safe to conclude that some of the violence offered to the symbols and instruments of the new faith reflected genuine popular grievances. Robert Hutcheson maintained he had only helped erect an altar after being thrown in the Durham castle dungeon; like others, Hutcheson told the court he acted "sore against his will." In contrast, while William Smith excused himself as a "simple man and easy to be seduced," he admitted that "at that time he was content and willing to do the things by him herein confessed." Similarly, Richard Fleatham volunteered to the court that he had helped erect an altar stone "unbidden or commanded of any man." Alice Wilkinson acknowledged her willing attendance at mass and use of the rosary, offering as her only defense that she merely did what "many thousand did."[80]

Nor was Sedgefield the only parish for which we have evidence of a communal meeting preceding the destruction. In Long Newton, several parishioners had been mustered to help Sir George Bowes defend Barnard Castle for the Queen, but the others met after church one day and agreed to pay the keep of four men sent to the rebels. Twenty men and six women contributed funds, and these Long Newton rebels would later convince their "loyal" fellows at Barnard Castle to join them. As in the rebellions of 1536 and 1549, even those not fighting offered direct support by financing the men selected to bear arms. Those still home in the parish had their own communal book burning, and a group of women helped rebuild the altar after others destroyed the communion table. Eighteen-year-old Isabella Mawer worked alongside Marjory Crawe, a seventy-five-year-old widow, carrying sand and mortar under the direction of Barbara Colling, one of the churchwardens' daughters. Richard Hartburn performed mass here, too.[81]

The willing participation of many in the violence and the targets they chose show the events of 1569 to have been, at least in part, a popular religious rising. In addition to their destruction of Protestant fittings, many northerners attended masses and other traditional services. When Elizabeth Rutter of St. Oswald's parish, Durham, gave birth to a daughter the day after the rebels rose, she asked her midwife to carry to the baby to Brancepeth to have her christened by the Catholic curate. Another woman went to William Smith, a canon at the Cathedral, to have him consecrate bread. When William Holmes performed mass he absolved his hearers of the sin of schism in the name of the Pope, having first asked those who did not want to be reconciled to leave. George Bowes's dismissive statement that John Swinburne forced people to mass is often quoted,[82] yet many of those brought before the Durham church court after the rebellion admitted to attending several masses. From the pulpit of Witton Gilbert, Sir John Brown repented of his former conformity; he confessed that he had led his parishioners astray these past eleven years and urged them now to follow his example in returning to the true, Catholic way. So, too, did the priest of Windleston apologize from the pulpit for having taught erroneous doctrine to his flock these past years. Roger Venis, the vicar of Mitford, reportedly ran off to join the rebels never to return.[83]

The rebellion offered many individuals the chance to demonstrate their resentment of the alterations in religion. The changes introduced to that point had not gone far enough to please the Protestant precisians, but from the perspective of those at the Richmond market place or Sedgefield gate, the changes had been visible, dramatic, and simply too much. One might wonder why, if there was such resentment, there had been so little overt opposition to the changes earlier. Indeed, this is a recurring issue in studies of the reformation; Robert Whiting and others have noted the seeming paradox that ran throughout the years of reform, with a widespread commitment to traditional devotional practices and yet a lack of overt resistance to their dismantling.[84] Here, we clearly have acts of overt resistance that provide some hint as to why there was not more. It is not just the focus of the violence in 1569 that stands out, but also its form; that is, its relative restraint. These were not mindless and random acts, nor were they frenzied, hate-filled orgies of destruction. Depositions make the burnings sound like fairly festive affairs; in Sedgefield, some women stopped stirring the flames long enough to pick up pages that they might take home as playthings for their children.[85] William Cooke of Bishop Auckland admitted to stomping the boards of the communion table under foot and tearing the books with his hands and teeth, but that was about as wild as it got.[86] Even the assaults on married ministers and their families seem to have been bloodless and designed to intimidate rather than kill. (Had any suffered death or serious physical harm, there would surely have been some mention of it in contemporary reports.)

Nothing in these events compares to the disorder in France, recounted so vividly by Natalie Zemon Davis, Denis Crouzet, and others: no vicars were strapped to plows and whipped to death; no Protestant worshippers were hacked to bits with butchers' cleavers.[87] The violence in 1569 resembles more closely that in earlier English protests. The Northern Rebellion parallels the enclosure riots that R.B. Manning and others have described as characterized by violence against property but rarely against persons. Manning, M.E. James, and others have argued that the controlled and calculated use of violence in these earlier protests derived from the protesters' need for a sense of legality and legitimacy.[88] The same may well be true here. Once led by two earls of ancient houses and marching under their traditional banners, they had their symbols and sense of legitimate authority. *Then* they adopted for themselves the magistrate's role, putting out married clerics and burning offensive books in an inverted emulation of official actions. Perhaps it was a need for a sense of legitimacy, a certain conservatism, that usually served to limit overt resistance to the acts of the crown; in 1569, this same need born of conservatism both allowed and directed violent opposition. The earls' call to rise enabled and legitimized people to express their opposition in particular ways. In explaining the usual paucity of resistance, the fear of punishment (and fear of futility) can never be discounted, nor should the respect for order. The earls wrestled with how to justify rebellion; presumably, others did too.

Planning and execution

At the least, enough evidence exists to allow that some of the people who participated in the rebellion did so willingly and some for reasons of religious conviction. They sought to justify and give meaning to their rebellion with the rhetoric and symbols of righteous religious warfare. But now, with their justifications and supporters marshaled, what did the earls and their advisors plan to do? The gathered men had to be fed and led. With these other two requirements for a successful rebellion – financing and planning – the earls had rather more difficulty, most disastrously with the latter.

The earls and their fellow conspirators used their own resources in the beginning, but these would not go far. Northumberland, in fact, had so little money on hand that in the days preceding the rebellion he sent a servant to York to pawn for sixty pounds the gold collar he had received when invested in the Order of the Garter.[89] Accordingly, the earls turned to a number of expedients. In his study of the Pilgrim hosts of 1536, Bush illustrates the traditional mechanics of protest, some of which reappeared in 1569. He notes that the Pilgrims financed their efforts in three ways: by confiscating the goods of gentlemen who refused to join them, by taxing the clergy, and by public subscription.[90] No evidence exists for the direct taxation of the clergy in 1569, but the rebels made ample use of the other two methods. Initial reports maintained that they allowed no spoil and paid for all they took. Quickly, however, they made a distinction between those who aided them and those who did not, allowing the latter, especially Protestant gentlemen, to be stripped of all that could be carried. (Indeed, Lord Latimer was stripped of much of his clothing as well, and in a ritual humiliation reminiscent of past protests, was paraded about on horseback wearing nothing save his hose and doublet.)[91] Bowes complained that the rebels emptied his mills and barns, drank the bishop's wine, and ate the dean's corn. They drove before them herds of fat cattle, once destined for the tables of loyal gentlemen but now to fill rebel stomachs.[92] The bulk of the rebels tried to limit the confiscations to their opponents, in order to ensure good will from friends and neighbors. Inevitably some, however, took the opportunity to enrich themselves at random. As Sussex reported in early December, the rebels "spoiled such in all places as they mislike, and specially Protestants; but their spoiling beginneth and of necessity will be general, as all rebels ever do."[93]

In addition to such impromptu "taxation" of their opponents and the unlucky, the rebels used the standard mechanics of the muster to gather resources as well as men. In their precepts they demanded not just troops but the weaponry and victuals that would normally accompany a muster for service. In one demand sent to the town of Richmond, for instance, the earls required the delivery of all men and armor as well as food for six days.[94] The villages that responded to the earls' written demands for men also contributed the equivalent to coat and conduct money. Various townships allocated money as well. Finally, the earls also appropriated for their own use existing taxes and levies. On December 12, the earls ordered the tenants of the "late supposed bishop of Durham" to make ready all such rents as were due at Martinmas, and to pay them into the palatinate exchequer as usual.[95] Such expedients never quite seemed sufficient, however, and by early December some of their men left in frustration at the lack of pay. Some who were promised but never paid wages reportedly returned to their homes "evil contented, saying that they will rather be hanged than serve the earls any more."[96]

Yet, as men continued to join the earls until the very end, the most serious deficiency emerged from their lack of clear objectives. The leaders had convened at Boroughbridge on November 20 to debate their options. Should they attack York and Newcastle, using them as barter? Or perhaps take York and winter there until more aid, either domestic or foreign, could be prepared for the spring? Maybe occupy Doncaster, to close off the main routes into the north, or head to Lancashire to join men from whom they expected aid? Or perhaps retreat northward to face the Queen's army in areas and with the people they knew best?

Their opponents feared they intended to capture Queen Mary. If so, they were in no hurry and eventually missed their chance. Mary had months before been moved from the north to the Midlands, as Cecil wanted her further from the borders and northern gentlemen of dubious loyalty, but yet not too near the southern ports with their possibilities for ready escape or rescue. She came under the guardianship of the earl of Shrewsbury first at Tutbury Castle and then at the more comfortable Wingfield Manor. Once Elizabeth learned of the Norfolk marriage plan, Mary's travels resumed. By September 22, Shrewsbury had moved Mary back to Tutbury and received the earl of Huntington and lord Hereford as reinforcements. They reduced her entourage, restricted her visitors, augmented her guard, and read all her mail before passing it on. When Norfolk went to his estates at Kenninghall, Elizabeth ordered even stricter security lest Mary escape. By the end of October, thinking the threats passed or exaggerated, Elizabeth indicated a somewhat lighter guard might do. But news of the rebellion soon forced another change. Shrewsbury acted first. On November 17, he reported that he had added one hundred guards, posted mounted scouts, strengthened Tutbury's fortifications, and ordered a search within a six-mile radius for caches of arms.[97] Orders from court were slow in coming. Only on November 22 did Elizabeth send word to move Mary farther from the rebels. She chose Coventry for its distance, its loyalty, and its walls. Arriving on November 25 with little warning, Shrewsbury and Huntington could find no other lodging for their prisoner than an inn, a choice Elizabeth found "most strange." They moved Mary into the inn late at night to avoid the "fond gazing" of the townsfolk for, as Shrewsbury complained, no matter where they took her, "I find that the more she is seen and acquainted, the greater is the danger."[98] With some 400 guards about the inn, Mary was not to see or be seen by the townspeople, was allowed no visitors, and had her companions reduced in number yet again. Tutbury had presented enough difficulties for the northern rebels; Coventry seemed out of the question.

Nor did York, Newcastle, or Doncaster seem likely possibilities. At the rebel council of November 20, they decided against trying York, but neither did they decide on what to do instead. Thomas Markenfeld took to sea to try for foreign aid, and in the meanwhile the rebels mustered, marched, and went to mass but did little else until the last days of the month. Each day of delay and uncertainty hurt their chances of success, for in the interim Sussex and his fellows had been busily preparing themselves.

The loyalist response

The lengthy lead up to the revolt had given Sussex time to begin planning, but throughout he remained hopeful that trouble could be averted or once begun, quickly ended. In the first days of the rebellion, Sussex continued to counsel prudence. He argued that a liberal display of mercy provided the best means of resolving the growing crisis. On November 15, he and four other members of the northern council wrote as much to the Queen: the earls "know their offences to be such as without your Majesty's pardon, they intend to do their uttermost which they affirm to be for the surety of their lives." Indeed, Northumberland had written to the Queen protesting his loyalty and desire to join her at court, if only he might receive assurance of her clemency.[99] In a second letter dated November 15, Sussex elaborated:

> It is for you to weigh whether it shall be greater surety for you to pardon those earls and their partakers their offences past, and to call the earls to attend at your court, where you may be sure from any practice, and to purge this winter this country and other parts of the realm of the ill-affected, and so to avoid the danger of foreign aid, and make all sure at home; or else to hazard battle against desperate men with soldiers that fight against their conscience...I find all the wisest Protestants affected that you should offer mercy before you try the sword.[100]

While Sussex urged the pragmatic use of mercy as a tool of statecraft, the Queen replied that since the beginning of her reign she had shown generous measures of mercy, perhaps too much so. Furthermore, pardon required a deferential display of repentance:

> in a matter that touches us so near, we can in no wise find it convenient to grant pardon or other show of favor unto those that do not humbly and earnestly sue for the same; yea, and though they should sue for it, ... it stands not with our honor to pardon the earls and their principal adherents without further deliberation by us to be had hereof, seeing they have so openly shown themselves rebels, and so grievously and arrogantly offended us and our laws.[101]

She did, however, authorize Sussex to offer pardon to the "meaner" sort. Accordingly, on November 19 the Lord President issued a proclamation assuring a full and free pardon to all who returned to their homes by November 22. This offer exempted the earls and seven additional named men: Richard and Francis Norton, Thomas Markenfeld, John Swinburne, and Robert Tempest, all key plotters, as well as Sussex's brother Egremont Radcliffe, and a shadowy figure who either was or soon became a government spy, Thomas Jenny.[102]

Such pardons offered at the outset constituted part of the usual response to rebellion; usually, in fact, they came sooner and more often. The effort may well have robbed the earls of some supporters who came to regret their initial enthusiasm. As Sussex realized, however, with the leaders given no incentive to cease, the rebellion was not to be ended so easily.[103] He wrote to Cecil, again expressing the wish that the Queen end the matter quickly, either by pardon or by force. Northumberland's earlier vacillation continued, and according to rumor only the constant support of his wife Anne – who rode daily with the rebels despite her pregnancy – kept him from an abject submission.[104] A timely offer of pardon might suffice to bring the matter to an end. Knowing the Queen's opposition to outright forgiveness for the leading rebels, however, he requested immediate support in men and money.

After her experiences of recent months, Elizabeth was not inclined to be merciful. Nor was she inclined to trust her northern lieutenant. His close ties with Norfolk, his sometimes overly discreet reports, and his constant calls for prudence made her suspicious; so, too, did the presence among the rebels of his half brother Egremont Radcliffe. She ordered north two of her most trusted advisors: her cousin, Lord Hunsdon and her long-time privy councilor, Sir Ralph Sadler. Although governor of Berwick since August of the previous year, Hunsdon had been at court when the rising began and now hurried north toward York. Sadler had been in royal service since the 1520s and had filled nearly every possible office, many of which had involved Scottish and northern affairs; he would now serve as Elizabeth's eyes and ears in the region. Her remaining councilors then ordered musters throughout the south for two massive armies: one, projected at 10,000 foot and 800 horse to safeguard the Queen, and the other, at 20,000 foot and 2500 horse to travel north.[105] The immensity of these planned armies indicates how serious a threat Elizabeth and her officials deemed the revolt. The earl of Pembroke, obviously forgiven for his part in the Norfolk marriage plan, would command the Queen's guard. Lord Admiral Edward Clinton and Ambrose Dudley, earl of Warwick and brother of Elizabeth's favorite, would lead the army intended for the north; both had experience against rebels, the former in 1536 and the latter in 1549. Whereas Sussex's commission to act as lieutenant general in the north had authorized him "to subdue, repress, and reform," the commission for Warwick and Clinton, penned some days later, urged them "to invade, resist, repress, subdue, slay, kill, and put to execution of death by all ways and means."[106] The army with which they were to effect these tasks never met the original projection, but ultimately amounted to an impressive force of some 14,215 men.[107]

While this army assembled slowly in the south, Sussex and others in the north made ready for battle. The governors of York hurriedly prepared their city for the expected assault. Even before the rising began, the mayor and aldermen responded to the mounting rumors and signs of trouble by ordering the repair of the city walls and gates. The city's ordnance received attention, as did the provisions for the watch. Handpicked representatives of "the most trusty citizens or honest men" reinforced and extended the watch, with ten men patrolling each ward by night and six by day. That the threat might just as easily come from within added to their burdens. The watchmen had orders to take note of the numbers and nature of the people entering and leaving through the main gates, and to prevent anyone from carrying armor, guns, or powder forth of the city. The council replaced initial orders to keep the posterns barred by declaring common work days, on which all had to carry earth to block the rear gates and gather stones to keep at the walls for defense. Supplies of pitch and tar were taken up and guarded. The aldermen readied a larger than usual supply of post horses to ensure speedy communications; on the other hand, they also worked to curtail news of a negative sort. Alehouse keepers received fresh injunctions to listen for rumormongers and suspicious words. Armorers and smiths responded to queries about recent orders they had filled. Inn holders gathered supplies of wheat, malt, and victuals. Once the rising began, the aldermen and council of twenty-four personally took shifts watching at the gates each night. Newly erected lanterns, lit from six o'clock each evening until daybreak, allowed more efficient surveillance of the streets. The council ordered all boats from the rivers Ouse and Fosse locked within the city walls, and urged that the ferryboat be either sunk or at least carefully guarded. Workmen scoured the suburbs for ladders, keeping them fast within the city walls. One order of November 21 intimates the tensions building within York as the rebellion continued: "at the commandment of the Lord Lieutenant it was now ordered that when so ever any alarm shall happen within this city, no manner of men, women nor children shall make any shouting, ringing or noise but to keep silent, and that the housekeepers to answer to the contrary hereof at their perils."

In addition to guarding the city against the rebels without and their potential sympathizers within, the council responded to the Queen's calls for troops. On November 14, they sought to muster all horsemen from the city and county and gathered one hundred foot. The constables brought all found fit to serve to St. Anthony's Hall and began musters in the Ainsty. Each recruit was promised 14s 4d per day in pay, as well as a dagger and sword, and clothing consisting of a long coat, boots, trousers, and cap of gray coarse wool. Those who demanded more pay or supplies other than those allotted risked committal to ward. The council documents suggest that the men facing muster were not the only ones expecting a profit from their efforts: smiths and inn holders received word not to raise their fees, and householders had orders not to charge more than a penny a piece for food and lodging for soldiers. And soldiers there were in abundance. York and the Ainsty together mustered 716 men; 980 men came from the East Riding and Cleveland to be billeted in the city; 1070 West Riding men were in Micklegate; 600 Ryedale men were in Bootham ward; and a further 200 came to the city from Birdforth.[108]

While York bore the brunt of preparations, the other major centers and castles in the region also received prompt attention. In response to the rumored October rising, Sussex had already appointed trusted men to assist in the defense of Hull and Pontefract should problems arise. In the event, Sir Thomas Gargrave repaired to Pontefract Castle, then a massive and imposing fortress, to guard the nearby passage across the river Aire at Ferrybridge, on the main route from London to York. Lord Darcy had intended to join Sussex at York with his men, but finding the way blocked by rebels, he turned to Doncaster. There, he alarmed the mayor by arguing that the bridge that afforded passage to the south should be destroyed, but settled for keeping some 400 soldiers to assist with its protection. Newcastle required special attention, both because its importance offered such a tempting target for the rebels and because of suspicious activities on the part of some of its inhabitants. Even before the rebellion began, Sussex and others responded to the rumors of trouble in the town by dispatching Sir Thomas Gower, an experienced captain and ordnance master, to attend to its watch and ward. The mayor requested aid from Berwick, whence Captain Carvell and fifty soldiers came to help with the defense. Sussex wrote to Sir Henry Percy, John Forster, and William Drury in the north to have a special regard to Newcastle's safekeeping. Some in Hull had also given cause for alarm – one of its customs officials had acted as a conduit of letters to and from the rebels and their friends at Louvain, for instance – but the town's extensive fortification in recent decades made it easy to secure. When Lord Hunsdon went to the town he pronounced his confidence in its preparations; indeed, the town was able to send eighty men, supplies, and a loan of £500 to assist Sussex in York.[109]

Defense, however, proved easier to arrange than offense. Hunsdon and Sadler arrived at York on November 24; at their appearance, Sussex "rejoiced not a little." Both did their best to allay Elizabeth's suspicions. Hunsdon noted that no man deserved more thanks than Sussex, without whose diligence the Queen would have neither York nor Yorkshire at that hour.[110] Yet, if the Queen continued to mistrust Sussex, that was in no small part because he had such reason to mistrust the men he did manage to muster. Sussex had serious difficulties recruiting trustworthy troops with which to face the rebels in the field. If rebels had had to make hard choices based on a variety of considerations, so too did the men who fought for the Queen. Just as unthinking, instinctive responses cannot be assumed on the part of the rebel force, nor should unthinking submissiveness or principled fidelity to the crown be assumed from the men in the Queen's northern army. As with the rebels, some loyal soldiers joined from necessity, some for pay, and some for tenurial loyalties. The young earl of Rutland was not the only one to note with pride that his tenants had answered his call to join him at York.[111] Nor was Bowes the only one to complain that lack of funds prohibited him from gaining more "loyal" troops. With the footmen he had managed to recruit threatening to leave unless better paid, he warned that "the country of Yorkshire never go to war but for wages."[112] Just as religious discontent cannot be assumed to have motivated the entirety of the rebel force, nor can Protestant ardor or principled political loyalty be assumed to have been behind the decisions of all the men who joined Sussex.

Certainly, the Protestant ardor was lacking. The Queen's officers on the scene continually fretted that their men's affinities for the old faith would ultimately trump their loyalties to the crown. Even those men who had answered the call of duty might change their minds or at the least fight poorly against coreligionists, friends, and family on the other side. Sussex complained that "he is a rare bird, that, by one means or other, hath not some of his with the two earls, or in his heart wisheth not well to the cause they pretend."[113] The reluctance of militiamen to fight their neighbors had posed a longstanding problem for the Tudor regime, one that had surfaced in all previous revolts to one degree or another. Here, the Queen's agents feared that a shared fondness for the old faith aggravated the usual reluctance to treat friends as foes. Sadler echoed Sussex's concerns. When the Queen queried the paucity of loyal local recruits, Sadler replied that "if it may please her Majesty to consider of it, it is easy to find the cause thereof, for there be not in all this country ten gentlemen that do favor and allow of her Majesty's proceedings in the cause of religion." And the common people felt the same. Even those already mustered for the Queen had dubious loyalties: "the common people are ignorant, superstitious, and altogether blinded with the old popish doctrine, and therefore so favor the cause which the rebels make the color of their rebellion, that, though their persons be here with us, I assure you their hearts, for the most part, be with the rebels." If shared religious convictions were not enough of a problem, then family ties also threatened to prompt loyal troops to fight poorly; the Queen's agents complained that if the father fought on the Queen's side, the son fought on the other, and while one brother might be in York, the other marched with the rebels.[114]

Sussex expended great efforts to disabuse his recruits of their liking for the rebel cause, and though he had some success, he remained reluctant to rely on these men in the field. He issued repeated proclamations that countered the earls' declarations point-by-point, and depicted the rebel leaders as men out for their own gain, not for religious reformation. Hunsdon later enthused that these efforts had borne fruit; gradually, Sussex had "brought the soldiers that liked well of the rebels to think very ill of them and to mislike their doings."[115] In Sussex's own words, "at the beginning of these matters, the people were so affected to these earls for the cause they had in hand, as it was gotten out of the flint that was had for the Queen's service, and those that came, saving a number of gentlemen, liked better of the other side." But now, having bestowed more money, made a show of strength, and offered many persuasions, he thought his men's fortitude improving.[116] In another letter, Sadler again voiced his suspicions of the "loyal" gentlemen of the north, but cautiously asserted that ultimately, "though most of them are well affected to the cause which the rebels make the color of their rebellion," the gentlemen were "willing to serve you against them." Nevertheless, he still thought it wisest to await the southern army, "which will the rather enforce them to serve truly, if they have any meaning to the contrary."[117]

On this latter point, the loyalist leaders agreed. Thomas Cecil bluntly told his father that "if these Yorkshire men be not backed with a stronger army of assured men from the south which may always command them, they will fight but with loose hearts."[118] No matter what the persuasions he offered, Sussex could neither secure enough well-armed men nor sufficient assurance of their fidelity to engage the rebels in the field until he had reinforcements from the south. Precipitate action had to be avoided, as the consequences of a loss on the field could be devastating in many ways, not least in the battle for public opinion. Forster warned that the people of Northumberland only rested neutral or favorable to the Queen as long as hers seemed the stronger party, and others made similar observations of their areas.[119] Bowes agreed on the dangers of failure, but pleaded for speedy action nonetheless, "lest delay of time might draw away the wandering minds of some such as yet do nothing."[120] In the troubled and divided north, the effects of the appearance of weakness – whether from a defeat or a delay – required careful consideration.

Sussex and Sadler, however, came to see some merit in the delays imposed by the need to await trustier recruits. The longer the rebels wandered the north, the more people resented their spoiling and foraging. So, too, did the rebels risk exhausting their meager resources. The harsh weather and dwindling pay sapped the strength of the rebel force. Make a virtue of necessity, the northern councilors argued. To the Queen's frustrated queries about the inactivity of her forces in the north, Sussex and the others excused themselves by explaining their position. They believed "that the rebels, the time of year considered, should in the meantime weary their company, decrease their force, grow to spoil and bring themselves into hatred; and therefore, better to protract the time with some expense of money, and to have a manifest appearance by all probable reasons of an assured victory, than by making of overmuch haste to adventure so great a matter with the smaller number, worse furnished, and perhaps not fully assured soldiers."[121]

While the wait might have merits, it must not last too long. While Sussex desperately needed troops from the south, he did not want the huge, lumbering army that was so slowly assembling. He asked repeatedly that a small, well-armed force be conveyed with all possible speed. Instead of the thousands of footmen gathering throughout the country, he hoped for 500 horsemen to rectify his main deficiency, as well as 500 armed pikemen and 500 harquebusiers. With such a force he believed he could "give the battle with the advantage, and with God's grace to have an easy victory. I fear not the force of a confused and disordered multitude, if either I were able to match them with horsemen, or had any shot and armed pikes by good direction to supply my lack other ways, but being always disfurnished saving of men's bodies, I am forced to tolerate for the time, because the matter is of so great importance."[122] Although his footmen still numbered only about half of the rebel force, he mainly needed the horse. Here the disparity was its greatest and most serious. His existing 500 did not allow him to prevent the rebels from doubling around behind any force he might put in the field. Rebel horse could also cross rivers that loyal footmen could not, giving the rebels an all too dangerous advantage of speed and mobility. Sadler reiterated Sussex's request largely verbatim – asking for 1000 horsemen rather than 500, but again, 500 each of pike and shot – noting that the expense and time of the southern army in preparation was largely unnecessary.[123] They simply had to fill in their main deficiencies sufficient to render their horse equivalent to the earls' and to have some contingent of trusty southerners to strengthen the resolve of northern troops with doubts or divided loyalties.

And it appeared they would have to wait for the southerners, as Sussex's pleas for aid from the wardens on the northern borders met with scant response. Sir John Forster on the Middle March professed himself unable to dispatch any men. The borders needed protection against the predations of the Scots, some of whom he thought in league with the earl of Northumberland. Threats to his own life made him leery of reducing his personal guard. And while none had yet risen in the region, he feared Northumberland's tenants would rise the moment any rebel leaders appeared to call them to action. He was busy enough warding off threats in his own area, believing that Northumberland had given "secret warning" to his servants and tenants to be ready at an hour's warning in defensible array. "I have served her Majesty in this office long," he grimly reported, "and yet did I never know this country in so great peril of disorder as it is now presently."[124] Berwick offered better prospects of aid, but not much. With its large and experienced garrison, the town might provide some of the well-armed and loyal men Sussex required. Initially, however, its commander in Hunsdon's absence, William Drury, proved reluctant. Having already dispatched fifty men to Newcastle, he refused to lessen his numbers any further for fear of the dubious loyalties and subversive activities of one of his captains. Rumors from Holy Island also made him nervous and required resources.[125] By early December, Drury sent some men and weaponry to Sussex, but not enough.

While the Queen's councilors both in York and the south grudgingly agreed with Forster's and Drury's decisions, they showed less understanding of the recalcitrance of the officials to the west. Lord Scrope in Carlisle warned that for a few days the area stood in great danger; efforts of servants and tenants of the earl of Northumberland threatened to raise rebellion there as well.[126] Furthermore, Leonard Dacre had returned to seize the disputed properties that the duke of Norfolk had recently won from him, giving further cause for alarm.[127] In response to the increasingly angry, pestering letters sent from the councilors in York, the Queen's agents in the northwest penned a missive justifying their lack of assistance. Lords Scrope and Wharton and the earl of Cumberland met on November 30 at Brougham Castle. Advised by the bishop of Carlisle and local gentlemen, they agreed to send no more men to supplement the poorly armed horsemen already dispatched. No more could be spared without incurring great danger on the borders, whether from the Scots themselves or from unions between Northumberland's tenants and the borderers. In response to this collective effort at justification, Sussex, Hunsdon, and Sadler scathingly declared themselves to be "nothing satisfied" and to "marvel" at its negligence. "Send the full number of 500 horsemen," they demanded, "for trifling spoil to be done by pilferers out of Scotland is not to be compared with the danger that may grow by toleration of these rebels."[128]

Hartlepool and Barnard Castle

And so the Queen's northern forces waited, dug in sufficiently to allow the rebels few easy options but unable to field a force against them. And the rebels, finally, took action of their own. On November 29, a contingent of 300 men under the command of Christopher Neville turned toward Hartlepool, a town about thirty miles to the south of Newcastle and long the main port of the palatinate. Northumberland had received a message, ostensibly from the Spanish ambassador, that urged him to make it a safe harbor to receive aid from Alba. (The earl and a few others did, however, suspect the message "was old Richard Norton's device to cheer us, to keep and continue together.")[129] Sussex had carefully ensured that the castles and fortresses of the north had loyal garrisons, but his plans for Hartlepool had fallen short. Messrs. Strangwish and Layton, two local and trusted Protestant gentlemen, failed to follow their orders to levy a force of 200 men for the port, possibly because the men of the area had already responded to the musters of the earls.[130] Whatever the reason for their failure, Neville had no difficulties claiming the town for the rebels. He left 200 foot behind and returned to the main rebel host with his horse.

Cecil and the Queen showed their alarm. The councilors in the north gingerly responded to Elizabeth's angry letters, apologizing for the unexplained failure in planning that had left her so "much grieved." She insisted they retake the port immediately, and dispatched ships and 500 harquebusiers to help them. On so many other matters she had procrastinated; not on this. Bowes had also urged Sussex to take immediate action before the rebels could fortify their prize, warning of the dangers if the ordnance at Brancepeth had time to arrive at Hartlepool (although, ironically enough, that ordnance was about to be used against him instead). Sussex, however, sought to convince the Queen that it could be easily recaptured at a later, safer time. He believed that the long neglected walls left the town difficult to defend, either for or against the Queen.[131] He did, nonetheless, send ships, some from Hull and some from Scarborough. While sailing from Scarborough to Tynmouth with Sir Henry Percy, the men of one ship exchanged fire with the rebels as they passed. As this had little effect, they attempted to return with a larger group, but bad weather drove two of the three ships into Flamborough Head. Trying to retrieve something of merit from this abortive attempt, they captured a small fishing cobble with its three poor fishermen and interrogated them about the rebel force. They did learn the comforting news that no vessels of any size were docked in the port, meaning that the rebels would not be able to use it as an avenue of escape.[132] On the other hand, if foreign troops did arrive, the north was left dangerously open.

Meanwhile, at the beginning of December the bulk of the rebel force turned upon Barnard Castle, a fortress located some twenty-five miles southwest of Durham on the River Tees. Sir George Bowes had been gathering men at the castle since before the rising, and had a complement of roughly 700 to 800 men. Some of these were loyal local gentlemen and their servants, and the others men Bowes had successfully mustered before the arrival of the earls. The siege of Barnard Castle became the main engagement of the rebellion and demonstrated the appeal of the rebel cause for many. Yet this, one of the rebels' only two successes, also marked the point at which their dangerous aimlessness became most evident.

The decision to turn on Barnard Castle came from no grand strategic vision of the earls. Rather, upon learning that their leaders had decided against the "enterprise of York," a contingent of the Durham rebels urged the earls to remove the threat Bowes posed to their flank. Worried about Bowes spoiling their homes in their absence, the rank and file "allured" the earls to Barnard Castle. While the earl of Northumberland seemed somewhat reluctant, Westmorland accepted the change of plans with alacrity.[133] The horsemen arrived first, on December 2. The footmen, now organized into bands and furnished with captains, bows and arrows, bills and jacks, arrived soon after. When Christopher Neville returned from his successes at Hartlepool to command the foot, Northumberland left for Durham with 500 horse. Backed up by some 1500 horsemen and 3200 foot, the earl of Westmorland summoned Bowes. The latter responded by shooting a gun above the messengers' heads and refused to let them speak.[134] Ruefully, he noted that the rebel horse stood within cannon shot of the castle walls, but with no ordnance on hand, volleys of useless harquebus fire remained the best he could do. In the meantime, the rebellion engulfed the surrounding area. The rebels heard mass performed in the village chapel, which must have pleased the local churchwardens who had two years earlier staged a sit in to protest the curate's disregard for traditional niceties.[135] The rebels fed their horses with Bowes's grain and looted the houses of the Protestant gentlemen now locked up within the castle. Turning on Barnard Castle allowed the rebels to protect their farms from Bowes's predations. It also offered the opportunity to act upon personal and religious animosities and make spoil of their own.

Sussex initially felt confident that such a strong castle would hold fast: it had three wards and a good complement of men, while the rebels' ordnance consisted of only three or four culverins and a cast iron falcon.[136] His optimism soon disappeared. For the first few days, the rebel bombardment had little effect, but by December 8, they had breached the outer wall, eleven yards high and nearly two yards thick, in two places.[137] By then, Sussex worried that perhaps Bowes had not stocked the castle with sufficient provisions for the number of men he had on hand. Nor could Sussex fulfill his promise of speedy relief until he acquired more force of his own. He dispatched a bevy of messengers in the hopes that one, at least, might get through to Bowes to relay the order to break his horse through the rebel camp at nightfall and join him at York.[138] Even this bleak command proved more than Bowes could manage. Each day more of his men went over to the enemy. Even with the two innermost wards still intact and food on hand, men defected daily. Four Long Newton rebels shouted over the walls to other men from their village; whatever they said convinced five of their neighbors to jump over and join them.[139] On Friday, December 9, some eighty men leapt over the castle walls to swell the rebel ranks. On Saturday, a further 150 or so did the same. In all, Bowes later recalled, 226 of his contingent joined the enemy. His only consolation came from the injuries they sustained in so doing: 35 of these deserters broke necks, legs, or arms in the leaping, accounting for the heaviest casualties to date.[140]

These injuries offered Bowes but cold comfort, however, as some who joined the rebels betrayed the castle's water supply. Another group, once thought to be "among the best disposed," opened the gate they had been specially detailed to guard. A skirmish began, in which the rebel guns injured 67 of the defenders. Five of Bowes's men perished.[141] At this, the rebels offered Bowes an honorable retreat: he left them the castle and its household stuff while departing unhindered with his armor, weaponry, and remaining men. Another brief skirmish followed, however, when the rebels discovered that some of Bowes's servants had smuggled out household items. A group laid chase, brought the men and the goods back to Barnard Castle, and then joined in the looting that would soon see the castle stripped bare. Some killed and quartered the livestock, while others absconded with feather beds and silver spoons.[142] Bowes joined Sussex at York with 300 horse and 100 foot, a welcome if tired addition to the loyal forces. He later complained that although the siege had imposed hardships – he had even been reduced to mixing water with his wine – he could have kept the castle if only his men had been true.

The rebellion's collapse

Any euphoria the rebel leaders might have felt upon the victories at Hartlepool and Barnard Castle quickly dissipated into desperation. Local support was not the problem, as they continued to find fresh recruits until the very end.[143] Furthermore, with Leonard Dacre recently returned to the north, the rebels hoped even more help was at hand. But the earl and countess of Northumberland's pleas to Dacre, sent first on December 8 and again on December 16, met with cold responses. On

December 13, the earls set out from Durham for Newcastle, but after a brief skirmish with loyal horsemen had to turn back. To make matters especially insulting, Forster and the earl's brother, Henry Percy, had led the band of loyal horse.[144] Spies within their camp persistently exaggerated loyalist strength in an effort to discourage them – one assured Sadler that he planned to "put such terror in their hearts as ... you may win the battle without stroke or shot" – and knowing that the rebels intercepted his letters, Clinton "made great boast of the number of men" he had available.[145] Edward Dacre's attempt to take Carlisle Castle for the rebels failed almost as soon as it began. Hearing that Scrope had departed and left the castle in the bishop's charge, Dacre had smuggled in some 200 soldiers in small groups on the night of December 13, and more the next morning under the pretext that they mustered for the Queen. Having received a warning, however, the bishop had strengthened the castle guard and so Dacre abandoned the attempt.[146]

Meanwhile, the bulk of the southern army had finally arrived. On December 13, a force of at least 12,000 men reached Wetherby with more expected shortly. Sussex set out from York, and on December 14 reported from Northallerton that he finally had enough horsemen – Scrope and the leaders in the northwest had at last filled his order – and enough trust in his foot to engage the earls.[147] Upon learning of Leonard Dacre's final refusal of aid, that Sussex had reached Darlington, and that the Queen's ships had arrived at Hartlepool, the earls gave up. On December 16, they abandoned their foot soldiers, took their horsemen, and fled past Hexham to Alnwick. They may have still hoped to find sufficient support in the heartland of Northumberland's estates to await foreign aid or the new year and fresh hope from home, but Forster again appeared with a band of loyal horse to force them back. They returned to Hexham, and then on to Brampton and Naworth. There, Leonard's brother Edward provided shelter and men; several hundred more horse, perhaps up to a thousand, joined them once in Cumberland. But the earls had given up hope for now, and decided their only safety lay across the border. Late at night on December 20, the earls, the countess of Northumberland, and roughly 100 horsemen fled into Scotland.[148]

The rebellion, so long in beginning, came quickly to an end. The thousands who had answered the earls' call to rise now found themselves leaderless and abandoned. As early as the first of December, one loyalist reported that the "common persons have conceived a mistrust towards the earls that they would steal away from them beyond the seas or out of the land and leave them in the briars."[149] Such fears in fact proved correct, as the irresolute earls proved unequal to the task they had set

. Those who had responded with such alacrity to the earls' restore the old faith, marching under Crusader banners, and ...,o ...nasses for the first time in over a decade, had their hopes quashed. All who joined now faced an uncertain future. The earls and their closest followers soon tried to revive their revolt from Scotland; the bulk of their men, however, now awaited the response of their offended Queen. The earls may have led the rebellion, but in her actions throughout its aftermath, the Queen demonstrated a recognition that it was the many men who answered the earls' calls, and the families and neighbors who supported them, that had made the revolt a danger to her regime.

3
The Rebels in Scotland

When Scotswoman Bessie Hamilton and Englishman John Hobkirke married, they committed treason. Like the many other cross-border couples, they perhaps did not know, but more likely did not care, that the laws of both realms forbade such unions as politically dangerous.[1] The borders were a region apart; not perhaps geographically, as numerous crossing points traversed the line formed by the waters of the Tweed and Solway, and enough rivers and passes ran north-to-south to complicate any simple division. Politics, rather than geography, gave the region its significance and such coherence as it had. Yet, centuries of effort from both Scottish and English authorities had failed to impress upon the borderers a due sense of the primacy of national loyalties. To be sure, many who ignored the border did so only long enough to rob and harry those on the other side, and then quickly claimed it as a shield from prosecution. The notorious groups of border reivers routinely found participants and victims from both countries. Sixteenth-century borderers have long suffered from a reputation for primitive violence, in ways either dangerous or romantic depending on the temporal distance of the judge.[2] Yet, ties other than reiving existed. In addition to cross-border trade, Scots and English frequently lived along the frontier as spouses and neighbors. Lord Hunsdon reported that some 2500 Scots resided in England's East March in 1569, in some areas in fact outnumbering the English, and few of them with the benefit of such formalities as letters of denization.[3] While the north was neither so dangerously backward nor violent as they sometimes claimed, border officials had ample reason to complain of a people "that will be Scottish when they will, and English at their pleasure."[4]

It was to the people of the border region that the rebel leaders turned in the final days of 1569.[5] Perhaps they fled to Scotland simply for safety in defeat, but some people at the time thought the rebels planned only to pass the winter before returning south in the spring. Nicholas Sander believed they awaited the pope's excommunication of Elizabeth; if Pius V would release her nobles from their obedience, and incidentally allow them to keep any church property they had acquired, then the rebels could renew their effort with overwhelming support.[6] But Scotland was not just to be a safe place to hide or wait: it also offered aid. Already during the rebellion the earl of Northumberland and at least one of the Scottish border lords, Alexander Hume, had discussed cooperation.[7] In some respects, the earls' flight to the north marked not the end of the rebellion, but the opening of a new phase. While the many followers they had abandoned in England now faced a marauding southern army and the vengeance of an angry Queen, the rebel leaders sought to revive their revolt in a new place and a new guise. In seeking to effect this cross-border confederacy, they drew aid from the borderers' longstanding ambivalence about the central feature of their political landscape, and also from Scottish lords who backed a "British" project of their own: the restoration of Mary Stewart to her throne, and her recognition at least as the heir to the English throne, if not as its rightful occupant.

Fight or flight?

The Scottish regent, James Stewart, earl of Moray, had certainly recognized the threats posed by the rising and by the prospect of the rebels' flight across the border. He had cultivated his own cross-border ties for reasons both principled and pragmatic: to preserve the nascent Protestant Kirk and his own tenuous hold on power. Since having engineered Queen Mary's abdication in 1567, the regent had desperately sought to assert his authority, rein in Mary's adherents, and maintain Elizabeth's support, now more necessary than ever. Over the past year, Moray had enjoyed a number of promising victories: the leaders of the Marian party had submitted or been incarcerated and he had made impressive judicial forays into the disordered borders and Highlands. Yet, he had angered Elizabeth by rejecting her proposals for Mary's return to Scotland. Elizabeth continued to make troubling signs of coming to an agreement with Mary, and had not exempted him from her suspicion upon learning of the Norfolk marriage plan, in which he had played an early part.[8] Thus, for his own security and to retain Elizabeth's support, Moray quickly offered his assistance against the northern rebels. He promised Elizabeth the whole power of his realm, noting that the affair touched not just the English but all those who professed the Gospel.[9] Reacting to rumors of Scottish help for the English rising, he issued proclamations prohibiting cross-border raids or aid for the rebels, warning that those who did either "shall be reputed and held as common enemies to our sovereign Lord, his authorities and common wealth of his realm." He patrolled the border with 2000 horse to give weight to his words. On December 8, he called on all men of military age south of the Forth to prepare for service against rebels who might cross into Scotland.[10]

He did not have long to wait. The earls, the countess of Northumberland, their personal attendants, and roughly 100 horsemen arrived in Scotland on December 20. Sussex and the Queen's agents in the north of England reported the rebellion safely ended. They expected to capture the rebel leaders and their beleaguered followers with the regent's help and without undue difficulty. Certainly, the rebels did not initially receive a warm welcome. Those to whom the earls first fled for safety urged them to leave for fear of Moray's wrath. The countess and two of her ladies had their horses and goods stolen; the earls wandered in disguise as ragged borderers. By December 25, the earl of Northumberland was in captivity. His supposed protector, Hector Armstrong of Harlaw, sold him to the regent. Moray lost one of his most trusted captains in a short skirmish that accompanied the handover, and Armstrong later became immortalized as a villain in border ballads, but the quick capture of the earl augured well for the forces of order. Elizabeth sent Sir Henry Gates to arrange for the earl's return to England, and ordered that watches be kept on the ports and coasts lest the remaining rebels try to flee overseas.[11]

But matters soon changed. By January 8, Sussex and Sadler began reporting that the rebels were being openly maintained and had gained fresh hope. Westmorland and his confederates now talked more explicitly of having deferred rather than abandoned their revolt, waiting for better weather and the stiffened resolve of fellow Catholics before renewing their efforts in the spring. More men had joined them, presumably fleeing the provost marshals who so busily exacted summary justice throughout northern England. The records, as usual, say little of men of lesser substance. Of the greater rebels, the records catalogued the Scottish border lords who now offered them hospitality. The earl of Westmorland stayed with Lord Ferniehurst; the Nortons with the sheriff of Teviotdale; Egremont Ratcliff, Sir John Neville, John Swinburne, and Thomas Markenfeld with the lord of Buccleuch at Branxholm Castle. Christopher and Cuthbert Neville, together with Robert Tempest and George Staffurth, were at Branxholm or thereabouts.

Robert Collingwood, Robert Carr, the countess of Northumberland, and others found shelter at Hume Castle. Others yet were at Bedrule with its lord.[12]

Not only were the rebels now openly maintained, but a broad cross-section of the Scots also deemed Moray's plan to return Northumberland to the English reprehensible. It seems that Moray initially intended to trade his captive for Mary, but the vehement opposition gave him pause.[13] Even the earl of Morton, a close and powerful supporter of the regent, did not think it just to deliver the captured rebels. The irony of the situation must not have been lost on Morton; both he and Moray had in the past relied on English protection after their own flights across the border, having taken refuge with the very man now at their mercy. Lord Hunsdon, back at his post in Berwick, warned that "the most part of the nobility of Scotland and especially on this side of Edinburgh think it a great reproach and ignominy to the whole country to deliver any banished man to the slaughter, accounting it a liberty and freedom evident to all nations to succor banished men."[14] From the Middle March, John Forster concurred with Hunsdon's evaluation. On January 21, he warned that the whole borders of Scotland prepared themselves to defend the refugees now in their care. One English spy, playing cards in a border household, was told that the regent would not be able to hand over the rebels, "for the like shame was never done in Scotland, and that he durst better eat his own luggs."[15] Moray would not find his task easy. In hopes of netting Westmorland and yet more rebels, he marched on Ferniehurst with some 800 horse and foot, only to have his company melt away as it approached. Left with fewer than 200 men, he prudently forbore. His judicial forays into the borders in the autumn of 1569 had apparently not sufficed to bring the borderers to heel.

Relatively little is known of the borderers' motivations. The bishop of Ross left an account of these people, in which he opined that of all the Scots, they always took the "greatest liberty and license." Due to the destruction and uncertainty caused by frequent raids and warfare, they lived in simple huts and cottages, easily rebuilt after a burning raid. A mighty race trained through much hardship, they scorned the armies brought to tame and police them. They knew well how to flee and live off the land, and returned to their homes only when the danger of the King's law had passed. They were not lawless, however. While some people whispered that the men of Annandale in the West March ate the flesh of their captives, Leslie insisted that the borderers for the most part abhorred the shedding of blood. They took seriously the law of God that forbade them to injure or kill gratuitously, but did not abstain from righteous blood feuds and revenge killings. They disdained to till the soil, knowing the harvest to be a ready target for predation, and instead sought their food through stealing and reiving. According to Leslie, they did not account this a crime: "they are persuaded that all the goods of all men in time of necessity, by the law of nature, are common to them and others." Exhibiting an equally marked disrespect for artificially imposed national boundaries and loyalties as for laws of property, the borderers cared little whether they stole from Scots or English. Leslie's account must be read with a large dose of skepticism; it resembles those ethnographic descriptions written contemporaneously about North American natives, replete with tales of exotic and barbarous practices, but also of habits and beliefs that might serve as an example to their more "civilized" observers. Nonetheless, despite its idealized qualities, two aspects of his account suggest possible motives for the borderers' assistance to the rebels. Leslie praised them for not having "vainly fallen from the faith of the Catholic Kirk, as many others have done." This attachment to the old faith may have played a part, but of even greater significance was their tradition of protecting outlaws. And their highest virtue, Leslie proclaimed, was their sense of honor. They always kept their word, even if given to an enemy: "insofar that one break his faith, nothing is thought more ungracious than he."[16]

The broad sympathy the borderers earned for their determination to protect the fugitives posed enough difficulties for Elizabeth's plans. Yet, to make matters worse, some Scots offered more than just the support traditionally owed to men seeking sanctuary. Some, including Lords Ferniehurst, Buccleuch, Johnston, and Hume, now openly supported the rebels in their earlier cause, seeing them as defenders of their own ousted Queen. On January 8, Sadler relayed rumors that the earls of Huntley and Argyll, along with other prominent Marians, planned to use this opportunity to renew their resistance. The Marian leaders who had submitted in the previous year now prepared new offensives: "Huntley and Argyll and all others of the Queen of Scot's faction are minded to revolt."[17] Contrary to earlier expectations that the rebels would flee by sea, they were staying to fight. Rather than simply waiting for the long expected English aid to materialize, they now had Scottish support. A localized revolt that had not been able to generate nationwide assistance now threatened to become international in scope. Papal representatives reportedly joined the English rebels and their Marian allies, who sent renewed entreaties to the Spanish and French. Foreign powers that had hesitated to offend Elizabeth by helping her domestic rebels might feel less compunction about helping this Scottish confederacy.

Hunsdon noted that while the rebels had been dismayed on their arrival in Scotland, they now thought themselves in a better position than they had been in Durham.[18]

Elizabeth and her councilors broadened their efforts to have the rebels returned. They increased the pressure on Moray, who had deemed it prudent to treat the earl of Northumberland less like a prisoner. He paid a small fortune to have more appropriate clothing made for his guest than the rags in which the earl had been captured, dressing him in satin, taffeta, and furs, and allowing him some freedom of movement.[19] Now Moray insisted that he could only consider returning the rebels on condition that their lives be spared. He would also expect something to make his trouble worth the while: the English must recognize young James as King and guarantee his possession of the throne. This and the hostility of the borderers did not bode well for Elizabeth. Sadler urged that troops be moved to the borders to intimidate and possibly to invade. For the time being, however, this advice went unheeded. Sadler turned to covert means. Robert Constable, a servant of the earl of Leicester and rather shady character, had already offered his services as a spy during the revolt itself. He had used his prior connections to the earl of Westmorland to insinuate himself among the rebels and report back on their doings. Once again he presented himself to Sadler.

This time he crossed the border to urge his erstwhile compatriots to turn themselves in, or at least to return to England in his care and plead for pardons from the security of his home. He tried convincing Richard Norton and his sons to cross back into England with the two outlaws who had served as his own guides. He urged them to hide with his wife, all the while planning to have them arrested. He offered similar speeches to the earl of Westmorland. The earl wept for his hard condition, but saw little hope in begging for mercy. Instead, he asked Constable to give the countess a ring as a token, apologizing for the grief he had caused her and their children. He hoped that the countess might send his "fairest gelding" and one of her best jewels to the Lord and Lady of Ferniehurst as compensation for the hospitality they had extended and also dispatch the ciphers once in his keeping.

After checking first with Sadler, Constable ventured off to Brancepeth to deliver his messages. Gaining an audience with the countess on the evening of February 14, Constable found her "passing joyful" to receive word from her husband. Obviously impressed by her, Constable reported that "for ripeness of wit, readiness of memory, and plain and pithy utterance of her words, I have talked with many, but never with her like."[20] She sent with him a diamond ring and several other pieces of jewelry for her husband and his hosts. The ciphers, however, had been buried by a servant now absent and could not immediately be retrieved. Constable then returned to Scotland, first explaining to Sadler his hope that "a golden hook" might persuade Ferniehurst to betray his guests, especially as he thought the Scot likely to weary at the great expense of hosting such a party and possibly to grow suspicious of the attentions Westmorland bestowed on the lady of the castle.[21] Failing that, Constable felt sure he could convince the chief rebels to return into England with him to sue for mercy. Once over the border, he could betray them to the warden and have them arrested in such a way that he might escape any appearance of complicity.[22]

New confederacies

In the end, nothing came of this scheme nor from the negotiations with the earl of Moray. Graver events intervened to render the situation even more unstable. On January 23, the regent was assassinated. Acting upon a prior and unrelated feud, James Hamilton of Bothwellhaugh shot and killed Moray as he passed through the high street of Linlithgow.[23] Moray's death ended any chance that the matter of the refugees might be quickly resolved and enabled the rebellion of the English earls to resume in an altered form by fanning the flames of Scottish factionalism. Some of the Marians had already had their hopes reawakened by the arrival of the English rebels. Others now joined them. Former Marians who had made their peace with Moray now broke from the King's side, expecting the regent's death to ease Mary's restoration. The presence of the English rebels made the situation especially volatile, as it gave Elizabeth a greater incentive and pretext to intervene.

Her incentive to act came not just from a desire to punish past offences, but also the need to ward off further threats. Soon, the earl of Westmorland and his men, together with the Scottish border lords, engaged in punitive raids into England and reconnected with rebels left behind.[24] Starting on January 26 and continuing almost nightly for a month, Ferniehurst, Buccleuch, Johnston, and Westmorland led forays into England. Failing to take Wark Castle, they nonetheless burned the corn and stole the sheep of its captain, Rowland Foster. On January 30, they rode as far as Morpeth, and on other nights were rumored to have reached Brancepeth, where both Christopher and Cuthbert Neville had been seen lurking. They targeted the tenants of Sir Thomas Grey and raided the area around Kirknewton, taking prisoners and even stripping a few victims of their clothes. On one worrying night they attacked Learmouth, which Hunsdon deemed the best manned and horsed town in the wardenry.[25] From Scotland, the English ambassador Thomas Randolph wrote that these skirmishes amounted to more than random retaliatory acts and had the active support of the Marian party.[26] Elizabeth and Cecil received conflicting reports about the state of the north; Bowes in one letter expressed his belief that all was safe except for the nightly raids, while in others he warned of an imminent reawakening of rebellion within England itself. Some of the clergy and "sundry others of the better sort" fled Durham once again and needed a stiff reminder of their duties to return. Hunsdon reported rumors that the people of Tynedale and Redesdale had assured the earl of their aid, and he feared that the people of the bishopric and Richmondshire would join, including some who had not participated in the first rising. Several loyalists in northern England warned Elizabeth that "whispering and mutiny have begun again."[27] A new rebellion threatened.

The English and Scots confederates first pinned their hopes on a fresh rising to be led by Leonard Dacre. The choice seemed unlikely. While Dacre had participated avidly in the early plotting of the northern conspirators, he had proven a fickle friend during the rebellion. In London at its outset, he did not return to the north until early December, and then forcibly to claim the Dacre estates as his own. When the earls had entreated him for aid, he waited to see how the situation would unfold and ultimately refused them.[28] His brother Edward had proven more helpful, sheltering the rebels at Naworth on December 19 and fleeing with them into Scotland. Leonard, in contrast, received commendations for his "honourable and diligent" service to the Queen.[29]

The confessions of arrested rebels soon confirmed Elizabeth's suspicions of this "foul and cankered traitor," however. She urged her wardens to seize him.[30] Lord Scrope knew the danger of such a move among people long loyal to the Dacre family and sought to have his prey come to Carlisle on false pretences. Leonard responded that a sore leg and "contagious ague" prevented him from traveling.[31] Whether from guilt due to his earlier betrayal or fears that his own arrest was imminent, Dacre sent a messenger to the rebels with apologies and promises that "he would show himself openly their friend."[32] His brother Edward replied that "my Lord of Westmorland, he hath assured me, upon his honor, by giving also his hand unto me, that if he might have the certainty of your handwriting, that you would maintain the ancient Catholic faith and the Queen of Scottish action, he would with like parts be yours, against all persons, til death."[33] Leonard began gathering forces from among both the English and Scots borderers. To queries from royal agents, he used the need to defend his tenants against the rebel raids as a pretext; to locals, he claimed that the Queen threatened to seize his rightful inheritance. Soon, he had 3000 men, Scots and English, at his side.

Fortunately for Elizabeth, her wardens arrived to arrest Dacre on February 20, just hours before Ferniehurst, Buccleuch, and a further 1500 Scots were due to appear. As Hunsdon and Forster approached Naworth late at night on February 19, they saw the beacons burning, and "every hill full of men, both horsemen and footmen, crying and shouting as they had been mad." Deeming Dacre's forces too strong for their own group of 1500, Hunsdon and Forster planned to march past and join with Lord Scrope. Dacre, however, rode out on the offensive. Hunsdon recounted that as his men attempted to cross a river, Dacre's footmen "gave the proudest charge upon my shot that ever I saw."[34] One chronicler added the intriguing but unsubstantiated detail that "there were among them many desperate women that gave the adventure of their lives and fought right stoutly."[35] If true, this suggests that Dacre commanded something other than a group motivated by just tenant loyalty or mustered for money. In any case, the battle was short but bloody. The wardens' forces defeated Dacre, killing some three to four hundred of his men on the field, seriously wounding many others, and capturing a further one hundred. They only narrowly missed taking Dacre himself, thanks to a last-minute rescue by a party of Scots.

This part of the plan for a cooperative rising between Scots and English to defend Mary's title and the old faith had failed miserably, but Dacre and a substantial remnant of his forces crossed the border to join the earlier group of English fugitives. Despite speedily offering full pardon to all those who would submit, Lord Scrope reported that only some 500 had come in. The others had gone to Scotland. On February 25, Scrope warned that roughly 2000 English rebels now wandered southern Scotland, openly maintained by Scotsmen bent on restoring Queen Mary.[36]

The leading English rebels joined the Marians at their conventions in Linlithgow in March and in Edinburgh the following month. The spring of 1570 marked the zenith of the Marians' power, while the King's faction, as yet without a new regent to replace Moray, continued to bleed support. As Jane Dawson has noted, by this time, "the newly consolidated Queen's party could plausibly represent the majority of Scottish opinion."[37] They were a diverse group; neither side in the Scottish conflict adhered to clear party lines. The Hamiltons, led by the duke of

Chatelhérault, had dynastic reasons to support Mary, as their chances for power and the succession improved with Mary rather than James on the throne. But few others had such clearly self-interested motives for their loyalties. One might expect the Marian faction to be composed of Catholics, with defenders of the reformation lining up to oppose them. As Ian Cowan notes, however, a variety of personal ties and considerations for legitimate, duly constituted political authority shaped party ties. Religious considerations were secondary.[38] The Catholic Lords Crawford and Cassilis appear to have favored the Queen for religious reasons, but at least a few of their brothers in the faith joined the King's faction. Lord Semphill, for example, followed his hatred of the Hamiltons rather than his Catholicism when choosing a side. Even less did Protestantism affect such decisions. Lords Herries, Hume, and Huntley, all proponents of the new faith, espoused the Queen's cause. Mary had, after all, tolerated Protestantism, whether from principle, opportunism, or indifference. Given the church lands transferred to the crown at the reformation, she also had a financial stake in the longevity of the Protestant Kirk. It was only as a consequence of her captivity in England, and her need to court continental opinion, that Mary assiduously presented herself as the faithful daughter of the holy mother church and only with the passage of time that she came to be seen as a Catholic martyr.[39] In 1570, her personal faith did not preclude Protestant support.

If religion offered no clear direction in the formation of factions, neither did international policy preferences. The King's party had no monopoly on defenders of the recent Anglo-Scots ties, and the Marians were by no means a party of Francophiles, nostalgic for the "Auld Alliance." One of the chief supporters of Mary's rights, William Maitland of Lethington, desperately pursued an Anglo-Scottish concord, and while he has been categorized as more *politique* than ardent Protestant, he was certainly not Catholic.[40] Another of Mary's mainstays, the earl of Argyll, had similar preferences in policy and faith. A staunch Protestant and key actor in the reformation of 1559/60, Argyll had long advocated a pro-English direction. In these earlier years, he had been a close friend of Moray. Together, they had opposed the Queen's decision to marry Darnley and the attendant weakening of ties with England. Her forced abdication a few years later was too much for him, however, and he broke ranks with Moray. Nor were such decisions left to the individual's conscience alone. Argyll's kindred and affinity, smarting from their lord's exclusion from political power and from the favors it brought, forced him to settle with Moray in 1569. Only with the revival of conflict after Moray's death did Argyll once again openly back his Queen.[41] As Gordon Donaldson has demonstrated at length, religious ties and concerns for rightful succession influenced such decisions, but both might also be "either channeled or diverted by familial and personal influences."[42] A complex bifurcation of loyalties resulted, producing a civil, rather than purely religious, war that was rendered even more complex by sudden switches of allegiance. Protestants who aspired to closer ties with England dominated both sides, but the Marians were prepared to take assistance where they could find it, whereas the King's faction knew their only help would come from England.

For a time, the fugitive rebels and some of their Scottish supporters may even have hoped to join forces with the Irish rebels. Argyll maintained his Irish contacts: in 1570, Tirlaugh Luineach sent his wife, Agnes Campbell, back to Scotland to negotiate for more assistance, and in April Argyll had with him some 300 Irish men.[43] Even more striking, in May, Fitzmaurice's men wrote to urge their representative at Philip's court to move more quickly in securing the King's aid, and noted that they had with them "two of the principal of those nobles who lately rose in England, seeking our friendship, and proposing things to which we cannot agree without first asking the king, to whom we have sworn fidelity."[44]

While nothing seems to have come from this overture to the Irish rebels, the Marians continued to offer their support. What they hoped to achieve by taking the English rebels into their counsel is unclear. Lord Herries later maintained that simple courtesy had constrained him to help men who arrived hungry and cold at his home. Lord Hume pledged that as a Dacre had kept his parents safe for three years, he would die a supporter of Leonard Dacre if need be.[45] Many seemed to think it a necessary and longstanding tradition to take in those who fled across the border for sanctuary. While such considerations of honor and custom cannot be ignored, neither do they seem sufficient to explain a decision so dangerous and so tenaciously defended. According to the anonymous author of a contemporary chronicle, Westmorland offered the Scottish lords not just men and money to help free Queen Mary, but also his assistance in bringing the northernmost counties of England – Northumberland, Cumberland, and Westmorland – under Scottish domination. At first glance, the existence of such a bold offer seems implausible, but not perhaps from Westmorland. In any event, even had he made it, his audience presumably viewed the acquisition of the counties as an implausible or irrelevant outcome, a medieval dream long since rendered all but unachievable.[46] The offers of men and money from other English lords must have presented a more attractive reason for the Scots to offer their protection. William Kirkaldy of Grange, who later became the backbone of the Marian party, initially opposed the decision of his godson, Ferniehurst, to join the rebels. Ferniehurst reportedly explained to him that if Elizabeth agreed to forget past wrongs and offer her support to Mary, then he and his party would enter into talks; if not, "they would follow forth the thing begun; for they were assured of the Queen's majesty's true subjects to assist them, and to have the assistance of the French soldiers." The Protestant William Maitland of Lethington purportedly declared that "Such as were fled from England had as honest and just a cause as ever had any banished men." When asked how he could speak so highly of men who had fought against the true Gospel, he explained his belief that the earls had made religion their rallying cry simply to gain popular support. Their true cause had been to secure the succession for Mary, the rightful heir.[47] Sussex surmised that the Marians surrounded themselves with English rebels when meeting with the French ambassador "to give some show of a faction in England" and thus increase their chances of obtaining support.[48] It seems that the Marians hoped to gain from the English rebels the manpower needed either to seize their Queen, to force an English invasion and thus provoke French aid, or, preferably, to encourage Elizabeth to deal with them on better terms.

Elizabeth's response

Their actions certainly put Elizabeth in a quandary, but one with both dangers and possibilities. By March, she recognized that no amount of diplomacy would get her rebels back. Nor was she yet ready to have one side or the other win. Early in 1570, Elizabeth outlined her four main policy goals for Scotland: the preservation of Protestantism, the safety of young James, the exclusion of French and Spanish power, and the retrieval of her rebels.[49] Whether she might best achieve these goals with the Queen's faction or the King's, she had not yet determined. While Cecil staunchly resisted returning Mary, Elizabeth possessed a much stronger respect for Mary's hereditary rights and greater concern with seeming to endorse the rebellion that had ousted her sister Queen. Leicester also favored restoration.[50] Elizabeth had wanted to return Mary late in 1569, and the earls' rebellion only confirmed the dangers of keeping Mary so close to hand. English aims in these months are unclear (assuming unitary "English" aims existed), but three main options presented themselves. First, Elizabeth and her councilors could seek to keep the King on the throne and his party in English thrall, but circumspectly, to avoid the very real threat of war from Mary's protectors, the French; Cecil almost certainly wanted this outcome. Secondly, they could return Mary to power, but on terms extraordinarily favorable to Elizabeth; to do so, the presence of a strong party for the King was necessary to force Mary and her adherents to accept the deal. It seems that Elizabeth seriously entertained this option. Or, thirdly, if the two Scottish factions remained roughly evenly matched, and equally dependant on English whims, a decision one way or the other could be deferred for the time being. In the months after Moray's death, members of the two factions met repeatedly in efforts to find a resolution.[51] For any of the three possible English aims to succeed, however, a Scottish-engineered solution was precisely what needed to be avoided. The rebels gave Elizabeth an excuse to intervene that might just placate the French. While she wanted the rebels returned, Elizabeth realized that their presence in Scotland had its benefits.

In these early months of 1570, Elizabeth received entreaties from both sides of the Scottish conflict. Morton, Mar, and Glencairn, the leaders of the embattled King's party, dispatched Richard Pitcairn, the Commendator of Dunfermline to plead their case. They needed her open declaration of support, and money, and in return promised to maintain Scotland to her devotion. The King's faction had the young prince, an advantage that could not be underestimated, and as they depended utterly on English aid, they would presumably be more malleable than the others. They urged her "not to think of this last commotion in her own realm as a matter ended."[52] Lethington wrote to Leicester and other friends in England to make the opposing case. He asserted, correctly, that the majority of the leading men of the country now opposed the King's faction. Some ardently supported Mary, and while others did not necessarily oppose the King, they did resent the "three or four of the meanest sort of earls" who purported to rule in his name. Lethington urged Elizabeth to favor the greater and better part, and threatened to turn to foreign aid if she did not: "If for the pleasure of a few she will send forces to suppress those whom they mislike and so consequently offend many, men be not so faint hearted but they have courage to provide for their own safety."[53] The Marian parliament that met in Edinburgh in April sent protestations that they wanted friendship with England and a bond to protect the true faith, but reiterated their willingness to turn to the French if need be.[54] The English rebels had sent messengers to Alba, and they and their Marian confederates received effusive promises of aid from the French. The English ambassador in France repeatedly warned of French preparations to aid the Scots, noting that if by chance Charles IX forbore, Mary's uncle, the Cardinal of Lorraine, would not.[55] Few of the scruples that kept the French from aiding English rebels at home applied to the Scottish case. Their own religious conflicts had distracted and divided the French, but for how long? Elizabeth had become the arbiter of Scottish affairs, but with one hand tightly bound by the threat of foreign opposition. The presence of her rebels north of the border was thus fortuitous in that it provided the pretext to intervene militarily. With all these considerations in mind, Elizabeth ordered the earl of Sussex to prepare an armed invasion of the northern kingdom.

When discussing Mary's fate in 1568, William Cecil had stated his view that the imperial nature of the English crown gave Elizabeth rights to adjudicate Scottish disputes. Based on the evidence of "records, examples, and precedents," he maintained that "It belongeth of very right to the Crown of England to give order to dissensions moved for the Crown of Scotland."[56] Although Cecil may have thought that Scotland's "junior" status and English suzerainty justified interference across the border, Elizabeth carefully portrayed her actions in the least antagonistic light possible. She had to placate the French and counter accusations of unprincipled interest from her enemies, and did not yet want to declare herself openly for one side over the other. Cecil had her first proclamation explaining her decision to send troops into Scotland hastily removed from the booksellers' stocks, presumably because he feared it might cause offence.[57] The subsequent proclamation, issued on April 10, 1570, carefully enumerated the "just, honorable, and necessary causes" that moved the Queen to dispatch her army, "with an assurance of her intention to continue the peace with the crown and quiet subjects of the said realm of Scotland." Elizabeth maintained herself justified by the laws of arms, God, and nature to pursue her rebels and their Scottish abettors, and insisted that previous treaties between the two realms authorized such intervention. Condemning those who "slander and falsely report her Majesty's intent," she rehearsed her past assistance to the Scots whereby she had delivered them from the yoke of foreign powers with no expectation of a return on her great charges. In contrast to Cecil's private jottings, the proclamation used no language that might imply a claim to overlordship, and protested that Elizabeth's actions emerged purely from "the natural love she beareth to that Realm, being to her own crown and dominions so near a neighbor by situation, blood, natural language, and other conjunctions meet for amity."[58] The ambassadors to France received frequent reminders to portray the incursions simply as forays to recapture rebels and punish their helpers, and not as intrusions intended to designate the Scottish crown. When the representatives of Queen Mary and the King of France each warned that, in their view, such action violated all the pertinent treaties, the English simply reiterated that their rebels' presence justified a limited incursion. Sussex was urged to tell everyone that he came to deal with people, not with titles, and to convince them that his only objective was the rebels. He should give hope to the King's party, but also explain that Elizabeth refused to support them openly because of their failure to hand over captured English rebels without condition. To the Marians, he should insist that his raids constituted lawful punishment of the rebels and their supporters, justified by treaty, not an intervention for one side over the other.[59]

Elizabeth was, however, interpreting the border treaties fairly freely. The most recent agreement authorized the pursuit of march traitors, not rebels in this sense, and then only in a "hot trod," which was supposed to take place within fifteen days of the offence in question. Nor did the treaty make any allowance for cross-border raids to punish the abettors of such traitors.[60] Yet, that was what Sussex and his men set out to do. In early March, Elizabeth had ordered Sussex to prepare an army; in April, she set him loose. He, Forster, Hunsdon, and Scrope decided to mount incursions simultaneously on each of the three marches to prevent the Scots from assembling together.

Scrope had been unsure of many of his men, worried in particular of their loyalties if required to fight the men of Lord Herries. Sussex accordingly had given him an extra supply of horsemen mustered from more southerly regions. While Scrope worried about the conflicting ties of borderers, Sussex himself had concerns about the reliability of northern men so recently involved in rebellion and had sought troops from further afield.[61] Thus reinforced, Scrope set out from Carlisle on April 18. He sent part of his force with Simon Musgrave, master of the horse, on a separate route. In the event, Musgrave and his men encountered more action than the main contingent under Scrope. After burning the towns of Heddon and most everything else on his way to Dumfries, Musgrave lost a skirmish with Lord Maxwell and the local inhabitants at Old Cockpole. Forced back to Blackshaw, the English again encountered Maxwell's force. There, an English cavalry charge led by the brothers Graeme put the Maxwells to flight and resulted in the taking of some 100 prisoners, including many of the burgesses and aldermen of Dumfries. Musgrave had little time to gloat over his victory, as Lords Maxwell, Johnston, and others regrouped with 400 horse and 600 foot to offer a spirited counterattack. Subjected to three hours of

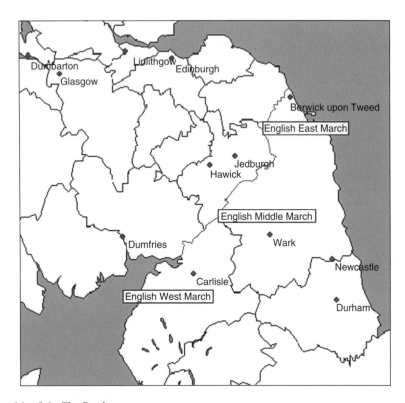

Map 3.1 The Borders

intense charges, Musgrave's men only put the Scots to flight after finally receiving reinforcements from Scrope. With cattle and more prisoners to their credit, Scrope's men returned to Carlisle (Map 3.1).[62]

To the east, meanwhile, the bulk of the English forces prepared their incursion. On the evening of April 17, Sussex, Hunsdon, and their men set out from Berwick. As dawn neared, they began burning their way through Teviotdale, leaving "neither castle, town, nor tower unburnt." They reached Jedworth (now Jedburgh), where the locals had desperately stored their possessions in Moss Tower for safekeeping. After a heated engagement of two to three hours, the tower fell. On April 19, Elizabeth's forces marched to the fortresses of Lords Ferniehurst and Hunthill. Ferniehurst Castle resisted efforts to blow it up, but fell to the determined efforts of English laborers who effectively leveled it piece by piece. The English continued on their way, burning a swath of some three to four miles on either side of their route.

Sir John Forster had set out with his forces from the Middle March on April 18, leaving a similar trail of devastation in his wake. The two groups met and descended upon Hawick, as the bailiff of the town had promised them food and shelter. Again, the locals had tried to prepare for their arrival, but again, with little success. They had unthatched their houses and set the materials alight at the entrance to the town. Hunsdon noted that "there was such a smoke as we were scant able to enter." But enter they did, and as soon as they quenched the one fire, they set the roofless houses to the flame in retaliation. After a cold and hungry night, Sussex, Hunsdon, and Forster left their footmen near the smoldering remains of Hawick and dispersed in different directions with their horse. Descending on Branxholm, Buccleuch's principal residence, Sussex and Hunsdon found that the Scot had tried to deprive them of their sport by torching it himself. But Sussex, in Hunsdon's words, "thinking that not sufficient, found one little vault in it wherein there was no fire. He caused powder to be set and so blew up the one half from the other. It was a very strong house and well set and very pleasant gardens and orchards above it and well kept, but all destroyed."

On Friday, the forces with Sussex, Hunsdon, and Forster split along three paths, burning all they encountered save for the property of those who submitted. The Lord of Cessford appeared to plead for East Teviotdale. As he could not offer proper compensation for the earlier raids into England, the English left his own property untouched but still burnt the countryside. After a brief gathering at Kelso, the three leaders again split up, with plans to reconvene at Hume Castle the following day. Lord Hume had arrived to offer compensation for the earlier raids into England, but Sussex refused him as he would not turn over the rebels. Hume found himself with a brief reprieve, however, due to a farcical misunderstanding with the ordnance master: the horses needed to draw the ordnance to Hume had been returned to Berwick, and so the English followed suit. They reached Berwick on Saturday. In little less than a week, as Hunsdon reported, "her Majesty had as honorable avenging of the receivers of her rebels and of all such as have been spoilers of her people and burners of her county as ever any of her predecessors had."[63] Few who had supported the rebels went untouched.

Sussex had explained his failure to take Hume Castle as a gracious reprieve. He notified the Scot that he had forborne, owing to his desire to see Hume reformed rather than punished. No one believed this, of course, and within a week Sussex returned to complete his task. The men under Hunsdon and Sussex placed their great ordnance along the north side of the castle, greeting anyone who peeked from the fortress with gunfire. When the defenders finally surrendered, the English spoiled the castle, "very rich in goods and food," and left two captains with two hundred shot to guard their prize. A contingent under William Drury's command seized and garrisoned Fast Castle for good measure, then rejoined the others for a brief rest in Berwick.

An impressively devastating set of forays without doubt, it nevertheless did little more than wreak revenge and enrich a few English soldiers. The raids netted only two associates of the rebels, one a servant of Northumberland's and the other an unnamed "vagrant man." Sussex had both executed promptly upon the return to Berwick, but this could not have seemed a satisfactory number of captives for all the effort.[64] The borderers had assured Sussex of their newfound desire to aid the English Queen when standing in front of the smoking wreckage of their villages, but they resumed their open support of the English rebels almost immediately upon his departure. Lord Scrope had spared the lands of Lords Maxwell and Herries on his foray into Scotland, upon their own and Morton's assurances that their loyalties lay on the right side. Nevertheless, Maxwell and Herries also openly began to shelter English fugitives. The Scots still refused to hand over the rebels; the Queen's party still refused to come to terms with the King's faction.[65] If anything, the English attacks had merely given new determination to the Marians. Kirkaldy of Grange, a much-respected soldier and supporter of the King's faction, now defected and the same was feared of Morton. Lord Herries openly proclaimed himself warden in Dumfries in Mary's name and all border lords of substance soon joined him. Sussex warned that the "son's party daily decayeth, the mother's party daily increaseth, and if the matter be left to themselves, the whole will be shortly on that side, and then no party but one."[66]

This, of course, would not do. Elizabeth had opened negotiations with Mary, and needed the Scots divided in order to ensure acquiescence to her remarkably ambitious demands. According to a note in Cecil's hand, the negotiators asked Mary not just to hand over the rebels, but in exchange for restoring her to her throne, to send young James to the English for "safe-keeping," to deliver Hume and Dumbarton castles into English hands, to retain the members of the King's party in their various estates and offices, and to give as hostages such men as lords Argyll and Flemming, all in addition to a binding league of peace promising no shelter for French or Spanish "strangers," no aid to the Irish, and the maintenance of the Protestant faith.[67]

As these negotiations continued, so too did the punitive raids into Scotland. On May 6, Lord Scrope entered the northern kingdom and burned many villages, primarily in the lands of Herries and Johnston. While intended ostensibly to punish them for maintaining the English rebels, it was also, explicitly, a strategy to keep these border lords from joining the Marian convention at Linlithgow.[68] On May 12 the English set out once again for a more ambitious excursion deeper into Scotland, this time under the direction of the newly knighted Sir William Drury and openly in the company of the King's faction. They traveled through Dunbar, Edinburgh, Linlithgow, Stirling, Glasgow, and Dumbarton. Lord Flemming, the captain of Dumbarton, had hidden two harquebusiers in an attempt to dispatch the English commander, but the harquebus had deficiencies as a sniper weapon. After Dumbarton, the English turned on the duke of Chatelhérault. Using ordnance provided by the lords of the King's party, they put three of his castles to the torch before returning to Edinburgh. On their first visit to the capital, a number of the English soldiers had been beaten and robbed by townsmen; on this visit, the King's lords had the city better in hand and produced the miscreants for execution, which the English "graciously" refused. By June 2, the English soldiers had returned to Berwick. They had done good work for their Queen. In all, between April 17 and June 2, they had burnt or leveled ninety castles and fortified houses and some three hundred villages and towns. All of these ostensibly belonged to Marian supporters suspected of harboring the English rebels. Subject to the three and sometimes four pronged attack from the English, and abandoned by the King's faction, the southern Scots had been unable to mount effective resistance. The English lost a few men, but Hunsdon felt fully justified in proclaiming this the most successful assault "that ever was made into Scotland with so few men with so safe a return."[69]

On their latter foray, the English had not just focused on punishing those who aided the rebels, but had also escorted to Edinburgh the earl of Lennox, Elizabeth's handpicked choice to assume young James's regency. As the King's grandfather, Lennox seemed a plausible choice, but having spent some twenty years of his life at the English court, he engendered enough suspicion that he could not be the leader required to unite the Scottish factions; as such, he perfectly fit Elizabeth's needs. Drury had also acted on a commission to negotiate a "surcease of arms" between the two parties and had extracted ambiguous, and in the event unheeded, promises to hand over English rebels. Discussions with Mary continued fitfully, taking on the appearance of urgency and sincerity only when the French threatened to provide their own assistance to their dowager Queen. In other words, nothing was yet settled.

Members of both factions found reasons to doubt English motives. James Melville, the Marians' envoy to Sussex, reported that the earl publicly maintained English neutrality, insisting that he had orders only to capture rebels and not to aid one faction over another. In private, however, Sussex intimated that he preferred those who had befriended the duke of Norfolk and accounted Mary and her son the rightful heirs of the English throne. Melville concluded that Sussex had come to play the two sides off each other, by appearing to support the King's faction while privately encouraging the Queen's party to hold strong.[70] Richard Bannatyne, secretary to John Knox, lauded English intervention on behalf of the King, but feared that members of Sussex's entourage were "over familiar" with Lethington. Hearing of Sussex's encouraging letters to the Marians, Bannatyne noted darkly that "the godly have always suspected the dealing of that man." Nor was the problem limited to the inclinations of a few doubtful individuals. Bannatyne solemnly recorded his concerns that "England we fear to be to us as Egypt was to Israel, a broken reed in time of greatest need; but that will turn to their own destruction."[71]

On July 10, Sussex wrote to Cecil of the renewed or continued support offered to the English rebels by Herries and others. He urged the Queen to use these provocations as a pretext for another raid. Whatever she might decide about the relative rights of Mary and James, another punitive foray into Scotland would benefit the future security of the borders. Sussex, at least, saw this pragmatically as an opportunity to settle the marches more to English advantage. An attack might also prevent the parliament intended by the Marians for Linlithgow in August.[72] Elizabeth liked the plan, and her response demonstrated the same cold calculation of appearances and future benefits evident in the earl's proposal. She noted that Sussex should first demand Dacre and the others from Herries, and as the Scot would likely refuse, Sussex "shall [thereby] have in the sight of the world sufficient appearance to allow your actions."[73] She did not, however, immediately dispatch sufficient funds. Sickness and heavy rain also hindered their plans. Many suffered from a new, feverish ague and the rains made it too difficult to transport heavy ordnance.[74] As desultory negotiations continued, the Marians conveyed the English rebels to their assemblies as a "spectacle" and fostered rumors of their Queen's imminent return, rumors that became "as common as meal in the market."[75] Sussex issued his demands that the border lords deliver the rebels in their keeping (naming among them his brother Egremont Radcliffe).[76] He obtained the replies he expected. Finally, on August 22, Sussex entered Scotland once more. He proceeded to burn the castles of Herries, Maxwell, and several lesser lairds. Returning to Carlisle on the August 28, he reported that this time he had burned little corn and few homes, offering two reasons. He had "some scruple of conscience to destroy the simple and poor for the offences of the greater." He also hoped to maintain the appearance that the raid was genuinely intended to punish the abettors of the English rebels. Sussex wanted to "make revenge appear to be for honor only" and yet reassured his Queen that he had "not left a stone house to an ill neighbor within twenty miles of this town that is guardable in any normal raid."[77]

Flight

For Elizabeth, the August raid served as a successful culmination to the events of the spring and summer. Ferniehurst, Buccleuch, Herries, and others submitted to the King's men. Both sides agreed to a truce. On September 3, Chatelhérault, Huntley, and Argyll signed an accord with Sussex, promising to abstain from hostilities, to refrain from any innovation in government for the space of two months, and finally, to abandon the English rebels.[78] The Marians were by no means yet defeated, but no longer had the upper hand they had enjoyed early in the year. Elizabeth now held the stronger position in determining the outcome. A little too optimistic, but not much, Sussex had declared that "For anything that may be done in Scotland, her Majesty may hold the helm and guide the ship where she lists."[79] The two sides remained roughly evenly matched until April of the following year, when against the odds, a surprise attack by the King's faction took Dumbarton castle. This had been the most important of the Marian strongholds as it presented the ideal landing place for French or Spanish troops; its capture lessened the English fears of quick and easy foreign intervention north of the border. Elizabeth soon had even less reason to prolong the Scottish conflict. The "discovery" of Mary's involvement in the Ridolfi plot in 1571 drove Elizabeth to abandon all thought of restoring the Scottish Queen. The French, miffed by Mary's dealings with the Spanish in this plot, also concluded the Treaty of Blois with the English in 1572 and embarked on rounds of marriage negotiations with Elizabeth. By 1573, then, the international situation allowed Elizabeth to send her troops openly to support the King by driving the remaining

Marians out of their last refuge in Edinburgh Castle.[80] While the Scottish civil war dragged on for years after Sussex's troops left in the fall of 1570, in the crucial early phase of the conflict, the English rebels had acted as a volatile precipitant. Their arrival renewed the hopes and efforts of the Marians, but in giving Elizabeth a pretext for armed intervention, also contributed to the defeat of Mary's men.

In the wake of the September agreement, reports of rebels fleeing to the continent multiplied. The countess of Northumberland, accompanied by Lord Seton, had already left for Flanders on August 23 to secure foreign aid. The earl of Westmorland had followed a few days later. Others now joined the migration.[81] There they added to communities of Catholics in place since Elizabeth's accession. English spies reported the pensions that the more prominent rebels received from the Spanish, the attendance of some at the new seminaries founded for English Catholics, and the continued plotting of many.[82]

One of the stranger conjunctures of spying and plotting surrounded a man named John Prestall. In the immediate aftermath of the 1569 rebellion, Elizabeth's northern agents had shown great determination in tracking Prestall, who consorted with the English rebels first in Scotland and then on the continent. The councilors' correspondence never clarified quite why they were so interested in him, yet looking back, we find Prestall to have been a key player in a 1561 Catholic plot to make Mary Stewart Queen of England. The conspirators had drawn encouragement from prophecies, and proceeded only after Prestall had invoked spirits to ask of them the best way to effect their intended treasons.[83] What precisely Prestall contributed to the northern rebels' aims or motivations in 1569–70 is unclear, but one of Cecil's continental spies felt sure that he was the "chief captain of those who are busy in practices."[84] An anonymous pamphlet writer affirmed that Prestall had joined himself with the rebels and "attempted sundry treasons against her Majesty," perhaps related to his boast that he "had an art to poison any body a far off, being not present with them, and that none could do it but he."[85] Yet, in the interval between the 1561 plot and the 1569 rebellion, it seems that Prestall had himself become an operative in Cecil's extensive spy network, so any offer of aid to the rebels was presumably disingenuous. He, and others like him, helped the crown watch over and interfere in the fugitives' activities.

Some of the best information about the exiles came not from the spies but from the interrogations of one Henry Simpson, captured as he tried to relay messages and tokens to the rebels' families and friends left behind in the north. Simpson was no rebel himself; he had first gone to the continent years before as a soldier in the English expedition against Newhaven. Having contracted the plague, he remained behind when the English departed. He then traveled throughout western Europe, marrying a French woman and working variously as a painter, stationer, and hatmaker. It was in the latter capacity that he first came in contact with the rebels, when the earl of Westmorland purchased from him some twelve or more hats for his servants. Soon, Simpson fell in with his fellow countrymen. Some that he met, such as Ralph Stansall of York, were there merely to avoid creditors. Others had come at the accession of Elizabeth to practice their faith without hindrance, and others yet came after the failed rebellion. More arrived all the time. Indeed, when coming toward England, Simpson had met a wagon with fourteen men, women, and children from Oxfordshire, with additional servants walking on foot. Simpson talked of English communities at Mechlin, Bruges, Tournai, and elsewhere, but knew Louvain best. In Louvain, the earlier Catholic exiles and the rebels did not always get along, but on Thursdays, all the English attended mass together to pray for their country. Simpson decided to return briefly to England to visit his friends and family; having heard of the many executions in the aftermath of the rising, and of a recent bout of the plague, he wanted to learn which of them still lived. As he prepared for his journey, many of his fellow Englishmen asked him to relay messages to their own loved ones. Mrs. Lassells, a gentlewoman in the service of the countess of Northumberland, asked him to pass her commendations to her elderly parents. Thomas Taylor gave Simpson locks of his hair and a note to assure his wife in Tadcaster that he and the other rebels would return in victory the following spring.[86] Sadly, none of these particular tokens and messages reached their intended recipients.

Nor did the fugitives' many plans ever come to fruition. It is easy to dismiss the exiles as cranks, until we remember the success enjoyed by their earlier Protestant counterparts in flight from Mary Tudor's Catholic regime, or indeed the many French and Dutch Protestants then busily plotting away in England.[87] Yet, while they sought assistance from the Spanish, the French, and the papacy by turns, they never again enjoyed the same degree of hope and support as they had had in Scotland. English raids into Scotland had failed to retrieve many rebels to join their fellows on the gallows. Nevertheless, they had successfully averted the very real threat of renewed rebellion in England, destroyed the dangerous bond between the English rebels and Marian loyalists, and strengthened the Anglo-Scots Protestant alliance that would prove so important in the future.

A "British" identity?

The links between the English rebels and Scottish loyalists were significant in their own right. Equally remarkable is that the English invasions, designed to entrench English hegemony, had the support of a good number of Scots and generally received little or no comment in the subsequent Scottish historiography. This was made possible by the emergence of a newer "British" identity, an identity premised on a shared Protestantism in the face of a pan-European Catholic foe, that began to compete with older national identities and hatreds. While Elizabeth justified her armed intervention with talk of law and justice, others turned to a more potent rhetoric of Protestantism under siege.

Certainly, many expressions of the traditional Anglo-Scots animosities were heard on both sides. Sussex and others of Elizabeth's agents frequently complained of the perfidy and guile of the Scots. Hunsdon on several occasions questioned the wisdom of sending money to train their old enemies to produce new and better soldiers.[88] Sussex noted of the Scots that he was "naturally born to distrust them," as his grandfather, "who was a long counselor and of great experience and service, charged me upon his blessing never to trust Scot or Frenchman further than I had the surety in my own hands."[89] On the other side, one writer left a "Memorial of the hard fortunes of such as ... have privily or publicly dealt with the estate of England." He narrated the grisly fates of Scotsmen foolish enough to think favorably of the English, whose touch apparently had much the same effect as a mummy's curse.[90] Both Moray and Lennox faced charges that they had "sworn English," a practice remembered with contempt from the "rough wooing" of mid-century.[91] One member of the King's party acknowledged that "as to our practices with England, the world says it has been most treasonable. I know they thunder out against us that we are traitors to our country, who would sell us to be slaves to our old enemies of England, [and] put our King and strengths in their hands." He countered this by pointing out that the Marians secretly confederated with foreigners from across Europe, all of them papists, and asked rather weakly how much worse a slavery it would be to live under "our Queen, Enemy to Christ's Evangel."[92]

This response is instructive. Among some, a new sense had emerged that despite their various flaws, their neighbors were at least Protestant, ranged beside them in a dire struggle against the papacy. The King's faction and their English allies had found a new way to challenge old prejudices and defend their actions. As Jane Dawson, Stephen Alford, and others have shown, since the Scottish reformation of 1560, a new discourse of "British" amity based on a shared religious identity and a shared enemy had emerged.[93] William Cecil himself had a profound sense of the need for such links. And it is in this light that the Marians' miscalculation in supporting the English rebels becomes most evident. Cecil and others of his countrymen had already interpreted the English rising as part of a conspiracy by the Pope and the Catholic powers.[94] The stain spread. In 1570, the King's faction sought to strengthen this association by consistently referring to the Marians as papists. English observers frequently discussed the conflict as one between "the godly Scots" and "the papists." Scottish prelate John Spottiswoode acknowledged that the two sides did not consist simply of Catholics and Protestants in neat polarity, but still saw the conflict as essentially religious: "Albeit that all the papists within the realm of Scotland had joined with [Mary], the danger had not been great...But alas!...to see the hands of such as were esteemed the principal within the flock to arm themselves against God."[95] In August 1570, Bishop Jewel explained to a continental counterpart that in Scotland, "there are at this time two parties: one of which cherishes the pure religion and the gospel, and depend upon us; the other are enemies to godliness, and friendly to popery, and are inclined toward the French."[96] George Buchanan's *Admonition*, written in the spring of 1570, elaborated on such characterizations. None of the Marians had pure motives, he insisted. Their actions betrayed the falsity of their avowals of friendship with England. Surely, if they wanted such an alliance, they would do their best to please Elizabeth, and not favor her rebels or join them in harrying her realm. Some openly called themselves papists, and the rest were but "feigned Protestants," secret "scorners of all religion" who desired the return of the old faith in hopes of promoting their "idle bellies to benefices."[97]

No matter how diverse their motives, no matter the Protestant, pro-English credentials of some of their number, the Marians were indelibly stained by association with popery and all its dangers. The Protestant William Maitland could try to excuse his association with Catholic rebels by insisting that their real motivation had been to secure Mary the succession,[98] but few others were willing or able to make such a distinction. Wrapped in a rhetoric of "British" Protestantism under papal siege, English military intervention ultimately dashed the hopes of the Marians and their own cross-border confederates.

The Earl of Northumberland

Meanwhile, the earl of Northumberland and a handful of other prominent rebels continued in Scottish captivity. About some, Elizabeth
seemed remarkably unconcerned, considering their capture had served
as the rationale for her invasions. Lord Lindsay had had several in
captivity since early 1570, including John Swinburne, Brian Palmes, and
William Smith the younger. Tired of his troublesome prisoners, Lindsay
sent repeated queries to the English asking what they wanted him to
do. He asked that his prisoners' lives be spared and to be reimbursed for
his pains. Getting no response whatsoever, he finally accepted bribes
from the rebels and sent them on their way.[99] The earl of Northumberland was another matter, however, and in him both his Queen and
his wife showed much interest. The countess of Northumberland had
tirelessly worked to secure her husband's freedom. In January of 1572
she finally obtained money for his ransom, with both the Pope and the
King of Spain contributing to a purse of some 10,000 crowns.[100] It was,
however, to no avail. She wrote a letter, ostensibly to her husband but
for Morton's eyes, in which she dismissed rumors that he was about
to be conveyed to England, assuring him that a lord as honorable as
Morton would never allow such a thing. Indeed, no one "of honor or
credit would agree" to a betrayal of this magnitude, "especially in that
nation that have so often tasted of the love of their neighbors in cases
like to yours and that hath so often needed thereto."[101]

With renewed rumors of plans afoot in Flanders and reports of rebels
returning throughout the north, Elizabeth stepped up her demands.
Throughout the early months of 1572, offers and counter-offers traveled
between Scotland and England. The keeper of Lochleven demanded
a minimum of 2000 pounds to give up his prisoner. Morton, not so
crass as to demand cash in exchange for his support, hinted that he
deserved redress for damages suffered during the English invasions that
had propped up his faction.[102] In May, Elizabeth sent a formal demand
for Northumberland, now able to cite not just treaties but also the recent
act of parliament that had attainted him as a traitor.[103] Finally, the
regent dropped his condition that Northumberland be spared execution.
Then, the problem was merely one of effecting safe passage. Finally, the
transfer was made: 2000 pounds in return for the rebel earl, conveyed to
Berwick by sea to avoid the dangers of travel by land.[104] The anonymous
Scottish author of the *Diurnal* inaccurately inflated the sum accepted
for the earl, suggesting that he was sold to the English for ten thousand
pounds; whatever the sum involved and despite his own political and

religious inclinations, the author had no doubt that the transaction worked "to the great shame of this realm." He noted how both Morton and the late earl of Moray had found refuge in an earlier day with Northumberland. Darkly he ended: "Judge ye therefore his reward."[105]

Like that of so many of his earlier followers, Northumberland's reward was betrayal and execution. Throughout the Scottish chapter of the rebellion, he had been a cipher, at best a pretext for action by others. His attempt at a cross-border confederacy had drawn on the traditional ties of the borderers, on shared concerns for the succession to the British thrones, and to a lesser extent on ties of common faith. His attempt had failed, and in so doing had strengthened the Protestant "confederacy for God's cause" so long sought by John Knox and others of his ilk.

The ironies did not stop there. Whereas the English Catholics had had difficulties justifying their rebellion, in order to defeat them Elizabeth sided with the King's faction in Scotland, men who had had no such problems sanctioning their own rebellion against an anointed Queen. With only Nicholas Sander as an exception, English Catholic writers for many years denied the right of political resistance, and favorably compared their hierarchical doctrines of obedience to the dangerously unruly Protestant theories first developed in opposition to Mary Tudor. Even those who came to endorse a limited right to resistance insisted that their rebellions followed more respectable, orderly paths than those of Protestants, in first appealing to the higher authority of the Pope.[106] The Scottish opponents of Mary Stewart, by contrast, had honed early Protestant justifications of disobedience to a fine point. The Scottish rebels had drawn on and developed a concept of a limited monarchy, rooted in the consent of the community, and subject to rightful resistance. As John Milton later noted in his defense of regicide, the Scots' action against Mary "bore witness that regal power was nothing else but a mutual covenant or stipulation between King and people."[107] The English harvest from such seeds would take many years to grow. In the meantime, Elizabeth turned to the scaffold as a pulpit for the doctrine of absolute obedience.

4
The Aftermath

John James attended the Hereford bonfire lit to celebrate the defeat of the rebellion. A servant previously in trouble for hearing mass, James was in no mood for festivities and muttered bitterly, "now you have the day you looked for."[1] Others, pleased with the outcome, expressed their own bitterness that the rebellion had ever happened. Only rigorous justice would ensure such danger never appeared again. Protestant polemicists argued that Catholics had long benefited from tenderness and clemency. But instead of learning the lessons of mercy, they had grown bolder, sufficiently bold, in fact, to launch a rebellion that threatened the entire realm. The purpose of pardons was to make offenders better subjects but, according to these Protestant writers, by the very nature of their faith, papists could never become loyal. They did not offer deference and repentance in exchange for mercy, seeing it as a vindication rather than a gracious reprieve, and believing that God stood by the righteous and protected them in their time of need.[2] One author argued that those who moved the Queen to pardon the rebels brought suspicion upon themselves. He went so far as to suggest that the Queen had no right to pardon these rebels and threatened that "overmuch cherishing of papists" might make the better sort less likely to defend their Queen in the future.[3] In a sermon preached before the royal court, Thomas Drant argued that "mildness to some is oft times unmildness and cruelty to many others." He insisted that because the northerners had rebelled not just against the Queen but also against God, they must suffer severe punishment. Just as David smote the Amalekites, so must Elizabeth destroy the Lord's Catholic enemies. He assured the Queen, "let them in God's name feel the punishment of a club, an hatchet, or an halter and in so doing, I dare say God shall be highly pleased."[4]

Halters appeared in abundance. In the weeks following the collapse of the rebellion in England, Elizabeth's agents exacted harsh retribution, far more deadly than that after the Pilgrimage of Grace or most other past English rebellions. Technically, none died for their part in the Pilgrimage, as all received pardons, but some 144–153 people had died for their involvement in the smaller revolts that followed.[5] The precise number of Wyatt's rebels who suffered execution in 1554 is unknown but was probably less than 100.[6] The revolts of 1549 witnessed horrendous carnage, but then most of the deaths happened in unmatched battles of peasants against foreign mercenaries, rather than through executions after the fact. The judicial death toll after the events of 1569 came nearer to that of contemporaneous Irish revolts; in early 1570, roughly 600 rebels swung on marshals' gallows. Memories of the 1549 tumults may well have played a part in the crown's responses to the Northern Rebellion, as many of Elizabeth's councilors had served under Edward and may well have drawn a lesson from the way lenience had allowed early protests to grow nearly out of control. Certainly, lenience was lacking in the early weeks of 1570. Unlike previous rebels, the 1569 rebels had surrendered in the field without negotiations for mercy. The only pardon in effect was that given on November 19, which had offered a few days grace to those who would abandon their protest and return to their homes. Anyone who had persisted in rebellion past November 22 faced the full danger of the laws and the crown's determination to provide plentiful examples of the dangers of dissent. This, combined with the heightened religious tensions and a firmer sense that obedience must be unqualified, ensured a violent attempt to repress the "rebellious instinct" both physically and ideologically.

Furthermore, the disobedient were to pay for their sins not just with their lives but also with their goods. By ancient custom and law, individuals guilty of treason forfeited their property to their prince.[7] Elizabeth would use this practice to unparalleled effect. Even before the rebels laid down their arms, Lord Hunsdon opined that "if this rebellion be well used, it will be very beneficial to her Majesty."[8] Sussex wrote much the same to Cecil, noting that the whole matter had been a blessing in disguise. With some care, he considered, "great commodity" might thereby come to the Queen, both in revenue and in the chance to settle northern affairs permanently to her liking.[9] In the aftermath of the revolt, the dictates of finance and patronage became intertwined with those of justice and mercy as Elizabeth sought profit from protest: she would gain from the disobedient the resources needed to cement the loyalty of others, while teaching a clear lesson on the rewards due to rebels. The Queen seized rebels' assets to secure the goodwill of others in the governing elite, and left the families of prominent rebels with little land but much incentive to conform. Her response to this rebellion drew on precedents and was shaped in part by the particularities of the rebellion itself, but differed in degree and determination from the resolution of previous risings. The suppression of the revolt did not just give expression to royal power, nor did it merely further the ascendancy of the Protestant faith over the Catholic. It also increased the capital at the disposal of the crown in concrete, practical ways.

The profits of protest

In the days immediately following the earls' flight, Sussex and Cecil planned their strategy. Sussex intended to execute some from each order of society, to exact especially harsh retribution from constables and officers who had abused their positions to deceive the people, and to hang some in every town that had sent men or aid to the rebels.[10] Always fond of lists, Cecil devised detailed plans not just to punish participants but also to teach others of the perils of protest. He penned a reminder that "Durham is a principal place of all other to make a memorial of by example." Drawing from existing repertoires of repression that blended practical and admonitory measures, he ordered that some bodies be left long on their gallows, to "continue hanging for terror." In any church where bells had rung to raise the countryside, all but one bell should be removed as a perpetual reminder of the infamy of rebellion.[11] At the same time, Sussex and the Queen's other agents in the north immediately set out to seize and catalogue rebel goods and to survey rebel lands. Much like the executions, the property seizures served ends both admonitory and practical. Elizabeth had spent a prodigious sum on suppressing the rebellion, and would spend even more chasing those who fled into Scotland. Despite rigorous attempts to limit costs, the crown spent roughly £42,300 to suppress the 1569 rebellion itself, and a further £52,608 on the army that it sent to deal with the troubles north of the border, for a total of nearly £95,000. It spent a further £71,288 on the concurrent Irish rebellions.[12] Forfeitures would help chip away at these costs, provide valuable rewards for loyalists, and warn other potential rebels that their actions risked not only their own lives but also the security of their families.

Yet Sussex and the others soon found that Elizabeth was not the only one who expected a return on her efforts. Members of the bloated southern army began looting and spoiling the region, taking everything from pigs to church lead for their own use. Sussex maintained that the southern soldiers, with the encouragement of their two lords lieutenant, "made such open and common spoil, as the like, I think, was never heard of, putting no difference between the good and the bad." They looted the property of those covered by the Queen's first pardon, "to her dishonor and my shame." Although the earl of Warwick did hang two men for plundering, Sussex thought he and the Lord Admiral did too little to restrain their soldiers and too much to impinge upon his own commission; he complained of them "crowing upon my dunghill."[13] As early as January 1, Sussex warned that the Queen had lost some £10,000 worth of rebel property, thanks to the depredations of southern soldiers. Angered by the slight to his authority, Sussex may have offered a peevish overestimate of the losses, but other observers concurred in their complaints of goods gone astray. Sheriff Thomas Gargrave and Attorney General Gerard made similar reports, the latter noting that the fines imposed on offenders would have to be lessened, for the locals had suffered such spoil that "there is almost nothing left for the Queen to take."[14]

A second and potentially graver problem appeared. The bulk of the goods and lands were located in Durham and thus might well forfeit to the bishop rather than to the Queen. In their anomalous capacity as secular lords of an ancient liberty, the bishops of Durham had long enjoyed rights in their diocese that rivaled those of a sovereign ruler. Statutes passed earlier in the century had extended royal jurisdiction in the palatinate, but had not deprived the bishop of all his privileges. Sussex advised that Elizabeth move quickly either to compound with the bishop for the proceeds, or to move him elsewhere so that she might collect the revenues of the vacant see.[15] Not about to let this golden goose get away without a fight, Bishop Pilkington refused to retreat and pressed his claims over the region. Thus, while the Queen's agents continued to gather and survey rebel possessions, they postponed the trials of the wealthier rebels to await the resolution of this issue. In February, Attorney General Gerard demanded to see proof of the bishop's rights. In his opinion, the Treason Act of 1352 cancelled all claims of lesser lords to the forfeitures of traitors. Consequently, the bishop might have the forfeitures of felons, but not of rebels who sinned against their sovereign. The bishop's counsel, in response, quickly brought forward a number of precedents that documented his master's rights, including some as recent as the Pilgrimage of Grace. In a test case in March, all but one of the justices rejected Gerard's reading of the 1352 statute and determined that the bishop had rights at least to lands held in fee simple, if not those in fee tail.[16] By April, Gerard still delayed the indictments of a number of Durham rebels, planning to bring them into King's Bench in the hope that some way might be found to protect Elizabeth's claims.[17]

Martial law and the "meaner sort"

These disputes over illicit plundering and the bishop's rights, and a concern that impartial jurors might prove impossible to find, delayed the punishment of the wealthier offenders but not that of the rank and file. Sussex and Cecil concurred that while care had to be taken with the rebels of substance, those without lands and goods of great worth might hastily be dispatched at martial law. Sussex assured Cecil and the Queen that even "before the receipt of the Queen's Majesty's letters," he had resolved "not to execute the martial law against any person that had inheritance or great wealth, for that I know the law in that case."[18] The Queen's agents had to send a clear message about the dangers of disobedience, but why imperil possible forfeitures to do so? Cecil urged that "in every special place where the rebels did gather any people, and in every market town or great parish, there be execution by martial law, of some of the rebels that had no freehold, nor copyhold, nor any substance of lands."[19] Together with the need to offer memorable examples of the perils of protest, blunt considerations of rebel wealth shaped the resolution of this rising.

People executed at martial law lost a third of their moveable possessions, but did not forfeit all their property. As such, martial law had little appeal for the crown in dealing with wealthy offenders. Aside from this drawback, it had much to recommend it to the authorities, most notably the speed of summary convictions without the need for potentially sympathetic jurors or rigorous standards of proof. Traditionally, martial law was to be used only in times of war, when the King's banner was unfurled and disorder such that the usual courts could not function. Over the sixteenth century, these traditional limits were ignored more and more often. Previously, the use of martial law had vested in the Court of the High Steward and Constable, but beginning in the reign of Henry VIII, it came to be operated by commissioners as need arose. "Need" seemed to arise more frequently. The use of martial law broadened to include preventative aims, and beyond all previous boundaries to cover vagrants, pirates, and notoriously, the owners of seditious books.[20] While all agreed on its use for soldiers – what we might think of as military rather than martial law – not all were so sanguine about its use on others. In 1565, Sir Thomas Smith noted his reservations about using martial law outside of time of war:

> In times of war and in the field, the Prince hath also absolute power, so that his word is a law. He may put to death, or to other bodily punishment, whom he shall think so to deserve, without process of law or form of judgment. This hath been sometime used within the realm before any open war, in sudden insurrections and rebellions, but that not allowed of wise and grave men, who in that their judgment had consideration of the consequent example, as much as of the present necessity, especially when by any means the punishment might have been done by order of law.[21]

But this was well before the members of the Stewart parliament of 1628 would denounce martial law and enshrine their objections in the Petition of Right; despite qualms such as Smith's, its use became ever more common. Royal agents had imposed martial law in the aftermath of the Pilgrimage of Grace and the 1549 rebellions. After those two rebellions, as in 1570, the regular courts could still have operated and sheriffs' writs been heeded, but expedience held sway. In the twenty years that followed Elizabeth's accession, her officials issued 259 commissions of martial law. As David Edwards notes, a great many of these commissions were for Ireland, "the perfect breeding ground for royal draconianism."[22] Significantly, perhaps, they first appeared in Ireland when the earl of Sussex had served as its Lord Lieutenant. In Ireland, Sussex valued martial law both for its speed and for its ability to keep costs low, as commissioners received no pay other than the proceeds of their grisly labor extracted from their victims' goods. "Enchanted" by its use in his previous command, Sussex now supervised its frighteningly efficient operation in the north of England.[23]

Sussex had to learn who precisely had participated, and who among the nobility might have considered doing so. In its efforts to gather information, the crown flirted with another measure of expedience and dubious legality. In his 1565 tract, Sir Thomas Smith had also praised English law for allowing no place for torture. But Smith himself would supervise the racking of prisoners before his career in royal service came to an end, as the crown came to use torture, like martial law, more often over the late sixteenth century.[24] Cecil ordered that captured rebels be closely interrogated; he wanted some from all parts committed to straight prison, deprived of food, and at least put in fear of torment to ease their examinations.[25] As the Privy Council issued commissions for torture, the loss of the council registers for this period means we can never know how much it was used in these months. That it *was* used is clear from random references in other records. Notations in the state papers suggest that in late November, a priest was put to the rack to extract whatever knowledge of the rebellion he might have. In coming months, two servants of the duke of Norfolk and one of the Pope faced similar treatment.[26] One other case ensuing from the rebellion earned a mention in Sir Edward's Coke's writings on the law, having established that a pre-trial confession might secure a treason conviction, but only if given willingly and without torture.[27] Of course, means other than torture often sufficed. People wanting pardon for themselves or for loved ones offered information in exchange, and some relieved northern loyalists willingly shared such knowledge as they had.

With their information in hand, Sussex and his men drew up lists of those involved in the rebellion and "appointed" a number to die from each area. The quotas ranged from 16 to 39 percent of the known rebels in any given district: "the number of such as joined themselves in Gillingeast, 225; whereof appointed to be executed, 37"; "the number of such as joined themselves from Gillingwest, 141; whereof appointed to be executed, 30." Of some 794 men identified from Durham, 308 were selected. From Richmondshire, 1241 had joined; of that total, 231 seemed a good number to die.[28] Although Sussex and his agents took care to avoid killing the innocent, their decisions on the fate of the guilty had all the appearance of a lottery. In one particularly egregious example, a list of Ryedale men slated for execution included a note that "these four are stayed to see if they can get two of a worse sort to be executed in their place."[29] Such was the calculus of death in 1570.

Many decisions remained at the discretion of Sir George Bowes, fresh from his humiliation at Barnard Castle to his appointment as provost marshal. Sussex told him to execute more or fewer in each town as he saw fit, basing his decisions on the degree of the individuals' offences and the need for example in each community. On his own initiative, Bowes added two days to the expiration of the November pardon: those who had persisted past November 24 bore the brunt of his commission, with special attention also given to those who had deserted him at Barnard Castle and those who were "stirrers of the rest of their neighbors."[30] Unsurprisingly, he found that many had fled, further decreasing his totals; hunting them in the heavily snowed paths and byways proved difficult. He began first in Durham, which on January 4 and 5 hosted the memorable display desired by Cecil. Accounts vary, but confirm the execution of at least one alderman and sixty-six constables and serving men. Thomas Plumtree, a priest who had preached for the rebel army and was reportedly arrested at the cathedral altar, also died in Durham's marketplace. According to one later report, Plumtree was "an old Queen Mary's priest, and... as some writers affirm, had mercy offered him, in case he would go to church, which he refused to do."[31] Next Bowes and his guard of sixty horse and many foot went to Darlington, where seven constables were among those executed on January 6. Bowes then moved on to Richmond, Allerton, Ripon, and Tadcaster. Executions in Thirsk continued from January 18 to 24. Bowes listed twenty-three sites of execution in his records, but also noted of other rebels simply that he had dispatched them in the villages from whence they came.[32] Obtaining word from Sussex to speed up his proceedings to appease the Queen's growing impatience, he delegated duties: Sir Thomas Middleton, Henry Wandisford, and others received warrants to execute named men "with all convenient speed."[33] In Hanlith, he discharged rebel William Lawson in exchange for his service as a hangman for his fellows (Map 4.1).[34]

While traveling through the towns and villages that had sent men to the earls, Bowes appropriated and assessed the goods of these "meaner" rebels. His servants carried warrants "to take, carry away, seize, or otherwise dispose and sell to the Queen's Majesty's use the goods, cattle, and chattels of all such as be executed by judgment of the martial law," and also to gather the fees of those committed to gaol for his own use.[35] His assistants submitted the money they received for selling "dead men's goods," keeping a bit for themselves. The possessions of executed rebel Robert Peverelt of Ingleton, for example, sold for £3 9s 6d, of which £3 went to Bowes.[36] In return, Bowes offered mercy of a dubious sort: he urged deputies charged with hanging rebels and cataloguing their goods to promise "the wives and children that I will be good with them." He met with widows to discuss composition; from women with many children, he noted his special clemency in taking nothing at all.[37]

Bowes did not execute as many persons as his initial orders had stipulated and he professed to kill only those who had marched willingly and in the final stages of the revolt. Practical impediments and the local ties of the men ordered to do the killing meant that the Queen would not get quite so many deaths as she had hoped. None the less, in late January, Bowes noted in a letter to a family member that some "600 and odd" of the meaner sort had died at his hands.[38] If contemporaries' rough estimates of about 6000 rebels in arms are accurate, Bowes quite

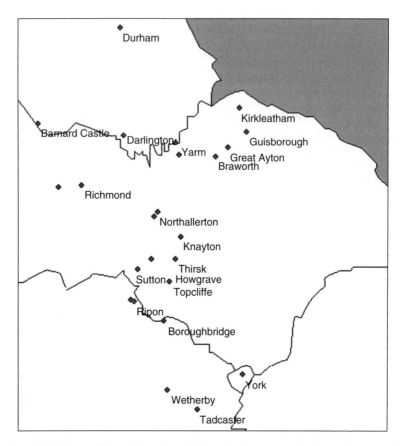

Map 4.1 Known Sites of Execution (Other rebels were noted as being "executed in the towns where they dwell.")

literally decimated the earls' followers. An impressively bloody tally, in its own way it confirmed the degree of willing popular participation in the rising, as well as the limits placed upon such participation in sixteenth-century political culture.

Pardons

But still the Queen gave no sign of mercy. Bowes asked Sussex to move Elizabeth to offer pardon. These "miserable people," he wrote, must be allowed to "redeem themselves into the case of subjects, with the uttermost of their substance."[39] Sheriff Gargrave dispatched a similar message to Cecil on February 1. Because many of the poorer offenders dared not return home, he noted, some towns had few men left and were thus undefended against any further trouble. "Commissions might be made to some discreet persons to call them all home by proclamation, except certain persons to be named and excepted," he wrote. Those with the ability to do so should pay fines, and then all save the named exceptions should receive pardon, for until "those that standeth as rebels be made by pardon lawful subjects, it is dangerous dealing with them."[40] With the ongoing rebel activities in Scotland, settling people's status quickly assumed special importance. A few days later, in response to the Queen's plan for a commission of oyer and terminer to attaint all offenders with property, Gargrave again warned of leaving the place bare of inhabitants. He urged that after a few salutary executions of papists, the rest be pardoned, "for, in mine opinion, the poor husbandman and mean subject (if he be not a great papist) will become good subjects. And there is by martial law already executed above 500 of the poor sort."[41]

Finally, reports of Leonard Dacre's plotting acted as the catalyst for a carefully penned pardon. Fearing his intentions, and the desperation of the former rebels, the Queen decided to proclaim her pardon to the humbler sort on February 18.[42] News of her belated clemency failed to reach the north before Dacre rose in open rebellion, but luckily for Elizabeth, his prompt defeat meant that he had no time to seek support from those who had nothing to lose. Realizing more quickly than their mistress the danger posed by desperate men, Hunsdon and Scrope endeavored to "comfort" as many of Dacre's men as possible. They announced that while they had no authority to grant pardon, they would intercede for all who submitted themselves to the Queen's mercy.[43] Accordingly, some 500 presented themselves to beg for clemency and on March 4, the Queen proclaimed her pardon to all who fully repented of their confederacy with Dacre.[44]

The resolution of the first, more serious rebellion continued. Throughout the north, heralds proclaimed the pardon issued just before the Dacre rising. It covered those who:

> will acknowledge themselves bound to her majesty as her true and natural subjects, and as persons that have received their lives and beings from her highness as the minister of Almighty God, for the which they be bound by double bond to serve her majesty faithfully and truly during the continuance of their lives to come, and to spend in her service that which from her clemency they have received.[45]

The pardon explicitly applied only to rebels without estates of value, those "who neither hath at this present nor heretofore hath any lands, tenements, or hereditaments of any estate of inheritance."[46] Finally, on March 22 the remainder of the rebels, excepting those still reserved for trial, received word to submit before the Queen's agents.[47] Many came forward who had not directly participated in the rising itself, but who had offered financial or other support; Bowes later reported that some eleven to twelve thousand presented themselves.[48] All had to attend a sermon that recounted the heinousness of their sins and to swear an oath of loyalty to the Queen before receiving her mercy.[49] During the revolt, these people had assumed the role of the religious crusader. Now the time had come to play the parts of the humble penitent and deferential subject. Significantly, Catholics were not to receive pardon until they repented not only of their actions in the rebellion but also of their faith. The oath bound them to "declare in [their] consciences" that the Queen was the supreme governor in matters spiritual as well as temporal, and that the Pope had no authority within the realm. They admitted their wrongdoing and acknowledged themselves the humbled, grateful recipients of the Queen's saving grace.[50]

The submissions served as pieces of political theatre redolent with explicitly stark messages about political power, helping both to communicate and construct royal authority; but they offered more immediate and tangible returns as well.[51] The Queen instructed the commissioners to compound with the offenders for their pardons, and to base their assessments upon a list of considerations that included the length of time the individual had remained in rebellion, whether he had stirred up others, whether he had participated in previous risings, and the size of his family. Persons with lands worth £5 per annum or less might redeem them "at a reasonable rate." If the commissioners did not know the value of an individual's property, they were to have the individual make his own declaration, but to caution him that he might only have restitution of that to which he confessed.[52] Despite the warnings of Elizabeth's agents that post-revolt plundering had left the rebels little to forfeit, the total sum collected was still impressive: one damaged and incomplete list of fines paid to the commissioners at Durham survives with the names of 4311 men who together paid roughly £3260.[53] Gargrave later reported revenue of £4800 from fines.[54] Some of this he disbursed immediately to pay the costs of soldiers remaining in the north and of those sent into Scotland to pursue the last of the rebels. The offenders did not just "pay for their rebellion": they also helped to finance its suppression.[55] Nor did the fines represent the only source of income from this procedure. The pardons themselves required a payment if the recipients wanted them formally enrolled, and such fees collectively added up to substantial amounts. Again, Elizabeth had to make allowances for the extreme poverty in the north, and noted that up to ten individuals might be listed in any one charter. In April, Chancery issued pardons for some 3840 individuals, which brought perhaps a further £600 into the royal coffers.[56] As Sussex had noted of the fines, "by many littles a great sum will raise."[57]

Forfeitures

The common law trials of the wealthier rebels finally commenced at York on March 20. The commissioners indicted sixty-four men, many *in absentia*. Others were later indicted at Durham and Carlisle. Of the eleven men condemned at York, four died on March 24: Simon Digby of Bedale, John Fulthrope of Islebeck, Robert Pennyman, and Thomas Bishop. Sussex and the commissioners held the rest back and asked for pardons. One man had apparently only stayed with the rebels under duress. The notes made concerning the others confirmed the heavy influence of the dictates of finance, rather than clemency, in the wake of this rebellion. Sussex wrote that the commissioners had attainted one young man simply to bring the title of his brother's lands into the Queen's hands, "and it was not meant he should die, for that he hath no land, and is within the compass of the commission for composition."[58] Lord Hunsdon intervened for a second man, Asculphe Cleasby, who he explained was "no notorious offender" and "hath not one foot of land." More important, perhaps, Hunsdon hoped to arrange a marriage between his son and one of the Conyers daughters, now financially attractive prospects on the attainder of their father. He believed that Cleasby's close friendship with the young women would help further his plans; thinking that the marriage "will the better be brought to pass by him, being in great credit with all the sisters," Hunsdon hoped to obtain his pardon as a bargaining chip.[59]

The other five were all reputed to be good, honest men and fully repentant; two had large families to support and one rather simple man had apparently been led astray by his wife. In case these reasons did not suffice to prompt pardon, Sussex pointed out that their lands were either entailed or the property of their wives, and hence would revert to their families, rather than the Queen, upon their deaths. An entail settled property on a specific succession of heirs, usually male; a tenant in tail was in effect a life tenant only, unable to alienate the land beyond his lifetime. Entails are best known to historians – and to readers of Jane Austen – as devices that allowed for the accumulation of large estates, free of the risk of an affectionate father splitting the property among all his children, as well as for the disservice they did to the claims of female heiresses.[60] In 1570, they also provided an incentive to keep some traitors alive. If the men received pardons for life only, their entailed property forfeited to the Queen during their lifetimes. Any other property they held in their own right remained safe in the Queen's hands. Pardons had the effect of resurrecting their recipients from the "legal death" imposed by their convictions, thus enabling such persons to start afresh, but conveniently for the Queen did not restore their rights in lost lands or goods. As Sussex bluntly observed of the rebel Leonard Metcalf: "the Queen shall win by his life, and lose by his death."[61] Elizabeth granted pardon to three of the men. As for the others, she professed to be unmoved by the prospect of profit, and thought they should be executed, as some observers might deem the execution of only four men of property unfair after so many deaths among the poor.[62] Wealth might privilege its beneficiaries in matters of life and death, but must not appear to do so too blatantly. Before long, however, she relented. Their entailed land saved their lives: the men received their pardons and the Queen leased their estates to others as rewards for service.[63] Still others received their lives in return for straightforward cash payments: for example, Sussex successfully argued for the pardon of one young man whose father had offered £500 in exchange for his life, noting expressly that if the culprit was executed, the Queen would receive nothing from him.[64]

Sussex and Gargrave originally believed that those who had levied war against the crown automatically forfeited their lands without need for trial. To ensure the legality of the forfeitures, however, the Queen required that all the captured rebels of wealth be brought before one court or another.[65] The justices of King's Bench dispelled any concerns about the propriety of seizing the land of rebels outlawed *in absentia*, but again, to be sure, the Queen had an act of attainder passed in the parliament of 1571 to confirm her right to rebel property.[66] The act was cast as a petition from the Queen's "loving and obedient subjects" who hoped that the fifty-seven named individuals "shall be by authority of this present act convicted and attainted of high treason" and all their property "deemed, vested, and judged to be in the actual and real possession of your Majesty without any office or inquisition thereof hereafter to be taken." The act also resolved another of Elizabeth's legal difficulties: with a case to determine the bishop of Durham's rights to rebel property stalled in King's Bench, Elizabeth managed to preempt the justices' decision through statute. The act of attainder noted that as the bishop and his bishopric had been preserved only by the Queen's great expenditures, all relevant forfeitures belonged to the crown. If the justices should again happen to rule in the bishop's favor, then the Queen might bestow upon him such proceeds as she thought "meet and convenient."[67]

After the resolution of these legal problems, the Queen received land worth a minimum of £5300 a year from the attainted rebels.[68] A good deal of this belonged to the earl of Northumberland, of which the bulk was entailed to his brother.[69] Nevertheless, the Queen managed to hold on to his land for a period of five to eight years, collecting its proceeds and plundering its assets. She kept intact the core estates of the earl of Westmorland, thereby leaving open the possibility that the family might be restored, but in the end, she left it to her successor to devise the estates and title anew. After the seizure of the bishops' temporalities at her accession, these forfeitures represented the largest single accrual of estates in Elizabeth's reign.[70] Some of the lands she retained in her own hands. As D.S. Reid notes, after 1570, crown-administered property in Durham exceeded in area and value the land of any lay magnate.[71] Some she sold for ready money: surviving documents reveal, for instance, that her commissioners sold lands that were worth £418 in annual rent for £10,447.[72] Much of the rest she distributed through grants and leases to favored courtiers and petitioners. In all, the patent rolls record that within five years of the rising, the crown made 126 leases of rebel land, with entry fines of roughly £5000 and annual rents of some £3300.[73]

Politics and patronage

Sussex and Hunsdon had been correct. With some care, "great commodity" had come to the Queen from the rebellion and, as Sussex had noted, the value of the forfeitures was not just financial but political as well. Joel Hurstfield once argued that the real importance to the crown of such feudal relics as the Court of Wards was indirect rather than direct. The proceeds entered in treasurers' accounts reflected only a small part of their worth, for ministers and civil servants regularly collected and doled out from the Court's business the unofficial perquisites that greased the gears of Elizabethan governance.[74] Much the same can be said of the proceeds from the Northern Rebellion. While the forfeited property gave the crown additional annual revenues and land that could be sold for ready money, it also offered new resources for patronage and reward. Patronage was of paramount importance in creating and maintaining the bonds of obligation on which order relied.[75] Contemporaries expected "liberality and bountifulness" from their sovereigns; and, as a councilor to Henry VII had long before opined, a King's "true profit dependeth on the grace of God, which is won by mercy and liberality."[76] Such bounty represented a quintessential duty of Kings and Queens. It reinforced the hierarchical social structure of early modern England, deeply imbued as it was with cultural codes of "good lordship" and reciprocal responsibilities. Patronage allowed the crown to cement the loyalty of the nobles, gentry, and servants whose help it needed in order to rule effectively. In the aftermath of the rebellion of 1569, Elizabeth used the bounty provided by the rebellious to tie the faithful more firmly to her.

Nor were the men who provided such loyal service slow in seeking their rewards. Even as the leading rebels made their way over the border into Scotland, the men who had armed against them began their suits for favor. Thomas Cecil wrote to his father at court on December 21, noting that "there are diverse gentlemen that mean at the end of this journey to crave in recompense of their chargeable journey at the Queen's majesty's hands some preferment of such of those goods and livings as are by reason of this rebellion forfeit." He protested that he "would be loath to account myself as one that hath deserved any recompense" and added that "since the victory is gotten without any strokes I would think my labor and charges well bestowed" if rewarded with command of one of the garrisons to be left in the north.[77] Others showed less modesty, sending business-like lists of choice morsels of rebel property with which they should like to be recompensed.[78] Some hinted quite broadly that their service came at such cost. Sir Henry Gate, a member of the Council in the North, detailed three different parcels of property that seemed appropriate compensation for his efforts. He asked that the Queen grant him one of these or "such other consideration as shall best please her majesty, without the which the said Sir Henry Gate shall not be able to continue his tarrying in the north parts."[79] As Thomas Cecil had ended his own suit, with such a grant "I should think myself not a little bound and encouraged to employ myself to the uttermost of my power and to the spending of my life to serve her majesty."

Many individuals who had written to sue for favor in the final days of the rising had their requests met. Lord Hunsdon, for example, asked for and received the stewardship of the crown's Richmond estates, a position formerly held by the earl of Northumberland. Sussex and Bowes, other key figures in the suppression of the revolt, eventually received their rewards as well. The grants that gave the earldoms of Essex and Lincoln to Walter, Viscount Hereford and Edward Fynes, Lord Clinton, respectively, noted their service in the revolt as a reason for their elevation.[80] Sir John Forster profited from both official rewards and his own initiatives of dubious legality. Lord Hunsdon later reckoned that Forster had gained from the rebellion property worth £500 a year and spoils valued at some three to four thousand pounds. It was, Hunsdon wryly noted, "a happy rebellion for him."[81] Many of the grants of rebel land made explicit mention of the Queen's desire to reward the recipient's faithful service. Twenty-six of these specified service during the rebellion itself as the reason for favor. Attainder acted as both carrot and stick for the Tudors: when its threat did not suffice to ensure the loyalty of some, its promise meant that others lined up to offer their services in hopes of reward.

The failure of the rebellion also allowed the crown and bishops somewhat more control over the character of the northern clergy. A few vacancies immediately opened up. Only one priest was executed for his part in the rising, but a few others fled or lost their positions. Of the Durham cathedral staff, fourteen known to have participated in the Catholic services performed during the rebellion retained their positions after confessing their guilt and performing penance. However, four lost their livings and were replaced with more amenable men.[82] Efforts to reform the clergy frequently ran into difficulties as both livings and advowsons, the rights to present candidates to vacant positions, were considered property and hence protected by law. Advowsons in the hands of conservative laymen had pernicious effects, as demonstrated by John Swinburne's nomination of a candidate to the vicarage of Bywell St. Andrew in 1564. With suspicions but no overt evidence that the candidate shared Swinburne's Catholicism, the bishop had been forced to respect Swinburne's property rights and allow the appointment to happen.[83] Only in 1571 did legislation allow bishops to deprive an incumbent who refused to take the oath of supremacy.[84] After the rebellion, a number of these advowsons in lay hands now passed to the crown. In her study of the distribution and use of ecclesiastical patronage in the diocese of Durham, Jane Freeman found that the post-rebellion forfeitures considerably increased the crown's resources; two of particular importance were the wealthy livings of Morpeth and Brancepeth, the latter a prebendal parish.[85] These rights of presentation had value as sources of both influence and profit. Their acquisition allowed the crown to select candidates with suitable religious inclinations, and added yet another item to the range of patronage resources at its disposal. Together with the appointment of Edmund Grindal as the new and ardently reforming archbishop of York in May of 1570 and the nomination of the "Protestant earl" Henry Hastings, earl of Huntington as the new president of the Council in the North two years later, such changes helped further the religious reformation of the region.[86]

With these grants, the Queen recognized past service and also created a vested interest in the success of her regime. She continued a process begun by her father in the 1530s, raising to positions of influence in the northern counties new men who owed much of their wealth and status directly to the crown. Of course, she had to take some care with the grants of rebel property; gifts that rewarded and established potentially more loyal men simultaneously risked the further alienation of others. As Steven Ellis has demonstrated, when the Tudors adopted a more interventionist approach to the assimilation of the borderlands after 1534, their attempts to extend royal authority resulted in new and destabilizing tensions.[87] The crown's selective use of patronage over the previous forty years had sparked intense northern feuding and had, in fact, contributed to the rising itself.[88] Sir Henry Percy, brother of the earl of Northumberland, stayed scrupulously loyal during the revolt in hopes of preserving his rights to the estates and title; the delays in receiving these from the Queen apparently drove him into the arms of conspirators a few years later.[89] Furthermore, Bishop Pilkington warned Cecil that "if the forfeited lands be bestowed on such as be strangers and will not dwell in the country, the people shall be without heads, the country desert, and no number of free holders to do justice by juries."[90] Elizabeth also had to consider defense of the border. Accordingly, most of the crown's grants included a standard stipulation that the grantee or a suitable deputy occupy the premises and provide border service when required. With due care, the forfeited properties offered a valuable resource for the consolidation of state power in the north. They allowed the Queen an opportunity to shape the character and personnel of her northern gentry. Sussex may well have been correct when he enthused that "the like commodity was never raised to any prince in any rebellion" as in this.[91]

As Sussex's comment implies, there was nothing particularly novel about the crown making a financial and political profit from protest. Henry VII took few lives after the revolts of 1497, but ensured that his mercy came at a heavy price. His commissioners compounded with the rebels and those who had given them aid, taking fines in exchange for their pardons. The surviving fine rolls for Somerset, Dorset,

Wiltshire, and Hampshire alone recorded payments of slightly more than £13,439. Known tallies for Cornwall and Devon came to £623 and £527 respectively.[92] In like fashion, Henry VIII seized the lands of those attainted for their involvement in the post-Pilgrimage revolts of 1537. The involvement of various monks also gave a delighted Henry yet one more means of obtaining monastic property.[93] Acquiring the estates of disobedient lords had long been a favored way to tame the nobility and fill royal coffers.[94] Indeed, the rebels of 1569 appear to have recognized and planned for this. Several of the Queen's northern agents noted that while sons joined the rebels, the fathers fought on the Queen's side or remained neutral, presumably in an effort to preserve the family estates from forfeiture.[95] With the same goal, others hurriedly transferred assets to family or friends in trust, ensuring the courts much business over the coming years in sorting out the legality of such conveyances.[96]

Thus, Elizabeth's efforts had a certain continuity with those made after earlier risings. Nonetheless, the scale and near single-mindedness of the pursuit of rebel goods appear greater in 1570, and the extent to which this pursuit affected who lived and died also seems magnified. The crown's heightened ability to profit from the rebels' disobedience may well have been partly fortuitous, a consequence of the specific course of this rising, as much as it was the result of altered policy or a reflection of Elizabeth's infamous parsimony. But precedents and the particular contours of this rebellion alone do not suffice as explanations, since Elizabeth treated these rebels differently than previous monarchs had theirs, from beginning to end. Unlike most earlier rebellions, this one did not end with a pardon of rebels on the field. Henry VIII and Mary may well have wanted to pluck the plumage of a few more wealthy rebels after the Pilgrimage of Grace and Wyatt's revolt, for instance, but both brought these risings to an end by offering their mercy to the bulk of the rebel hosts. Unlike her predecessors, Elizabeth made little use of mercy to convince the rebels to disband. In the early stage of the rising, she resisted advice to grant pardons to all, and made only one offer of mercy in the first days of the revolt to the "meaner" rebels who agreed to return to their homes. When the rebellion collapsed on its own, she was able to arrange the confiscations and trials before granting her pardons, and then to precisely those she wanted to pardon, and for life only. In his account of Henry VII's resolution of the 1497 revolts, Sir Francis Bacon noted that "the commissioners proceeded with such strictness and severity as did much obscure the king's mercy in sparing of blood, with the bleeding of so much treasure."[97] Henry opted for money over executions. The precipitous end to the rebellion of 1569 allowed Elizabeth to exact both. And the context encouraged such resolve. Intense anti-papist sentiment in the south demanded harsh, exemplary punishment; Elizabeth and her agents chose the victims needed to placate this sentiment in such a way as to maximize returns.

Local effects and the rebels' families

What did all this mean for the families and tenants of the dispossessed? Certainly, the rebellion itself took a heavy toll. Surveys made by the border wardens some ten years later testified to the long-term devastation that some individuals suffered. In 1580, many people professed themselves unable to provide the materials required for effective border service because of the spoils inflicted by the rebels who had fled to Scotland during retaliatory cross-border raids, and by the Queen's own soldiers. The men of Abell, for instance, declared that "in the rebellion they were so sore spoiled by the Queen's majesty's garrisons serving in these north parts they were never able to get or provide themselves of horse or armor again." The tenants of Lowick encountered a different problem, one that may not have been terribly unusual amidst the plethora of forfeitures and grants that marked the aftermath of the revolt. Their village had once been in the possession of Leonard Dacre. After his attainder, they had paid their rents to the Queen's receiver, but now faced an injunction to pay the same again to Lady Brandon, who claimed the land as her own. These tenants maintained themselves to be too poor to serve, "being uncertain whose tenants they are."[98] The number of commissions charged over the next few decades to sort out who owned what suggests that such uncertainty was not limited to the people of Lowick.[99] Landlord–tenant bonds presumably weakened for many, heightening the dislocation already caused by the previous twenty-year forfeiture of the Percy estates earlier in the century.[100] With new landlords, individuals who held their land by tenant right – one of the more common forms of peasant tenure in the area – had to pay new entry fines, a potentially ruinous burden on those already spoiled by the Queen's soldiers and commissioners.[101] Some new landlords took the opportunity to increase rents or fines, but a few of the grants forbade the recipient to expel current tenants or to increase the charges.[102] On the other hand, those who now found themselves tenants of the crown may well have seen their situation improve – the crown notoriously lagged behind other landlords in increasing the rents and fines owed by its tenants. Furthermore, as M.E. James has noted, many of the northerners who had struggled to assert their claims to the more secure customary tenure rather than tenancies at will found their case strengthened after 1569: the royal surveyors asserted that the Percy lands were copyholds of inheritance.[103] Most tenants of the dispossessed rebels had probably suffered spoiling or heavy fines of one degree or another, but further generalizations must be made with caution.

For the families of the rebels themselves, the crown's policy of exploiting the rebellion for all its economic and political value had dire results that left them more firmly at the Queen's mercy. Children obviously lost their paternal inheritances, and in theory at least, the children of those formally attainted lost any maternal inheritance they may have expected: attainder corrupted the blood, not just of the guilty individual, but also of any offspring born before the event.[104] While women were tried in the church courts for their activities during the rebellion, no women were called to account for participating in the rebellion itself, save for Anne, countess of Northumberland; she had ridden daily with the rebels and had the dubious honor of being specifically named as an individual in the parliamentary act of attainder.[105] Nevertheless, the realities of coverture and forfeiture meant that many suffered anyway, whether guilty of involvement or not. For a woman, marriage had consequences not unlike conviction for a crime, that is, civil death. According to the legal doctrine of coverture, husband and wife were to be treated as one person at law. As such, any moveable property a woman brought to the marriage became her husband's for good, and land became his for his lifetime. When a wife's coverture was compounded by her husband's conviction, the results might be disastrous. The effects of a man's attainder on his wife had long been confused by competing interests, as were most questions about property. Baronial opposition to the policy of complete forfeiture of a traitor's possessions had resulted in a 1285 statute that included amongst its provisions protection for the wife's own inheritance. The statute provided similar security for a woman's jointure, the lands or their proceeds settled on a bride just prior to marriage, which some couples adopted as a provision for widowhood in lieu of dower, the traditional and more common right to a portion of the husband's lands at his death.[106] Because a wife's rights to an inheritance or jointure antedated her husband's misdeeds, they were judged safe from permanent forfeiture, although they were confiscated for the remainder of her husband's life. In contrast, right to dower, the main source of support for widows and usually accounted as one-third of the husband's property, began only at the moment of the husband's death and was thus canceled by his attainder. Later statutes did little to change the situation. An act of 1547 explicitly protected the dower rights of a traitor's wife, but another passed just four years later included a last-minute proviso that just as carefully prohibited dower claims. This state of affairs remained in effect for the remainder of the Tudor years. Three Elizabethan statutes that created new treasons did exclude dower from forfeiture, but only in regard to the specific offence in question.[107] Thus, the wives and widows of the attainted northern rebels found themselves largely dispossessed.

The wives of rebels who had obtained pardons faced particular difficulties, because such land as they might otherwise have been able to claim, their jointure or inheritance, remained in the crown's hands until the husbands died. For instance, at the time of their attainders, both William Smith and Thomas Norton shared possession of a parcel of land, both in right of their wives. Norton was executed for his treasons, and so his portion reverted to his wife Elizabeth. William Smith, in contrast, received a pardon, and thus the land in question was destined to remain in the Queen's hands for the time being.[108] Similarly, Isabel Saltmarshe had brought two thirds of the capital tenement of Redness to her marriage; her husband John received a pardon for his part in the rising, but for life only. As such, Isabel's property passed to the crown for the remainder of her life, to be granted in turn to Thomas Yonge in return for a healthy rent and entry fine paid to the Queen.[109] It is perhaps no coincidence that at least a few men whose wives had brought substantial amounts of property to the marriage were pardoned; while they lived, the Queen had use of the estates.[110]

The wives of rebels who had fled lost their own land in what became a legal labyrinth. The estates they had brought to their spouses as marriage portions were also considered forfeit for the duration of their husbands' lives, leaving them in much the same predicament as women whose husbands received pardons. When the husband had not been formally attainted, however, questions arose about the propriety of such seizures. The Queen and her council were unwilling to forgo these valuable resources, and certainly did not want their proceeds to fall to the rebels in exile. The parliament of 1571, therefore, passed the "Act against Fugitives over the Sea," which dealt with those who, "contrary to the duty of good and lawful subjects, as though they were Sovereign Rulers themselves and not under rule and commandment," left the realm without license and plotted against the Queen. It spoke specifically of the recent flight of "rebels, fugitives, and traitors." The statute decreed that anyone who had left the realm without permission since the first year of the Queen's reign and who did not return within six months would lose all goods and chattels and forfeit for their lifetimes all proceeds from their lands. This clause explicitly included lands held in right of their wives. Apprehensive members of the House of Lords added a proviso whereby peers of the realm incurred this penalty only eight months after they had received personal notice from the Queen. Another amendment made allowance for the families of those men who left by reason of "blind zeal and conscience only," and who did not in any way attack the Queen's authority. In such cases, the "desolate wife and children" might petition for up to a third part of the value of the lands.[111] The wives and children of the 1569 fugitives, however, now found their own land wholly forfeited for the men's lifetimes. Margaret Danby, for example, had had one-third of the manor of Beeston assigned to her as dower and by the will of her first husband. When her current spouse, Christopher Danby, rebelled and then fled to the continent, her interest in Beeston was forfeit until either she or Christopher died, and in the event Elizabeth granted it to one of her favorites, Sir Christopher Hatton. Margaret's husband wrote letters from Louvain praising God, who "punishes where he loveth" and had lifted from them the vanities of the world; whether Margaret also saw the forfeiture of her property as a blessing is unclear.[112] The massive forfeitures after the rebellion, compounded by the complexities of coverture, thus ensured that the families of the guilty paid a heavy price.

Not everyone submitted quietly. Bridget Norton persistently harassed George Bowes for debts he had owed her husband Sampson, despite Bowes's insistence that Sampson's attainder canceled his obligations.[113] When Anne Bishop learned from Nicholas Naddall, a family servant, that her brother Thomas had been apprehended at the close of the rising, she and Naddall immediately gathered from Thomas's home various items to keep for the use of his wife and children. She secured pewter dishes, a table, brass pots, wall hangings, a chest of linens, and other necessary household implements.[114] They were not alone in attempting such concealments. Thomas Gorge, a Groom of the Privy Chamber, received a commission to hunt for concealed rebel property and share the proceeds with the Queen; Gorge found it a healthy source of income.[115] Some people, such as Elizabeth Troloppe, offered overt resistance. Her husband had occupied a parcel of lands leased to him by Robert Tempest, a kinsman and also a prominent rebel. Tempest's possessions forfeited to the crown, and Elizabeth's husband died without a pardon. Widow Troloppe, however, simply refused to quit the land, even when offered compensation. The owner found himself unable to find a new tenant, complaining that "no one will deal with the purchase thereof because they stand in such fear of her and her children's great speeches."[116]

Others, however, decided that deference offered the best solution to their personal crises. The Queen was not completely insensitive to the plight of rebel kin, and proved happy to depict herself as the protector of the innocent and downtrodden. Accordingly, she made several grants to the wives and children of the attainted. Margaret Norton, for instance, the daughter-in-law of rebel Richard Norton, lost an inheritance by his attainder, but received from the crown an annuity of £10.[117] A handful of the subsequent land grants included provisions to support widows and wives of the rebels. In December of 1572, William Inglebye received a twenty-one year lease of lands once held by his son-in-law Thomas Markenfeld; Inglebye paid a reduced rent for the duration of Isabel Markenfeld's life, owing to her a yearly payment of some £20 for her "better relief and support."[118] Notoriously, the countess of Westmorland received a substantial grant of lands once in her husband's possession. (From her importunate pleas for aid with all their effusions of humble deference, one would hardly suspect that she had played an active role in encouraging the rebellion.) The provision of such grants, of course, remained discretionary and informal, conditional on the individual's compliant demeanor, connections, and good luck. Some might even hope to exchange tractability for more than annuities and small leases: the same parliament that attainted the rebels of 1569 restored to their blood the heirs of an earlier rebel, Sir Thomas Wyatt.[119] The widows and children of rebels, and the surviving rebels themselves, found themselves with much incentive to behave appropriately.[120]

Thus, Elizabeth approached the resolution of the rising in a mercenary manner, determined not just to use fines and forfeitures as a form of punishment, but willing also to manipulate the principles of justice and mercy to extract a profit from protest. This is not to suggest that mercy was routinely and crassly sold to the highest bidders in a manner that would have been deemed corrupt: the benefit the crown sought was political as much as financial, and made in accordance with the cultural codes of patronage and lordship upon which early modern order relied. Exchanges of value shaped the resolution of the rising: outward shows of deference for reprieves from the gallows; money for pardons; loyalty for land.

It might be argued that resort to such measures undermined the crown: alienating land as a form of patronage and relying on such fortuitous revenues as forfeitures weakened the crown by failing to increase its reserves of land and postponing a much needed reform of taxation.[121]

In the long-term and with the benefit of hindsight, such an argument has some merit. Yet it goes too far from the evidence of 1569. In the short term, such policies had much to recommend them. The proceeds of protest generated the capital needed to pay for the support of persons friendlier to Tudor rule. The repression of some fostered the participation of others, and vice versa. Normally a careful (or parsimonious) steward of her patronage resources, Elizabeth acquired from the rebels a bounty that allowed her to reward the faithful without diminishing her own reserves. A number of the leading rebels had found their motivation partly in the challenges to their local authority posed by the arrival and promotion of Protestant protégés of the crown. Ironically, their rebellion speeded the transition of power against which they fought. Ultimately, the suppression of the rebellion offered more than just a tangible expression of royal power: it increased the capital of the early modern state, and hence its ability to police and suppress disorder in the future.

While the pursuit of profit sometimes overshadowed the dictates of punishment and mercy, Elizabeth was no stranger to the value of public, gruesome executions in teaching lessons in loyalty. The many bodies that crowded the gallows and trees of Durham and Yorkshire presented those lessons most vividly to the surviving rebels themselves, their neighbors, and to the men brought from all parts of England to serve in the north. Rumblings and rumors of trouble elsewhere also ensured a few displays of royal power and vengeance in London itself.

Executions and examples

On April 6, 1570, eight of the rebels were arraigned at Westminster. Three pleaded not guilty and thus forced trials, but five, including four of the Norton family, confessed and threw themselves on the Queen's mercy. Some of these men, such as Northumberland's servant Thomas Bates, languished in prison for years; others compounded for their pardons. Three were selected for death: Thomas and Christopher Norton, the brother and son of old Richard Norton respectively, and Oswald Wilkinson. The Nortons suffered first. On May 27, they were drawn on hurdles from the Tower to Tyburn. On the scaffold, Thomas Norton refused to repent, and insisted on saying his prayers in Latin. Reciting the Ave Maria and requesting help from the saints, he suffered all the special penalties reserved for traitors. Christopher Norton, having watched his uncle's execution, proved more pliable. Following the scripted performance of so many earlier traitors, he repented his actions, urged all to take heed from his example, and sought forgiveness. "Being hanged a little while, and then cut down, the butcher opened him, and, as he took out his bowels, he cried and said, 'Oh Lord, Lord, have mercy upon me!,' and so yielded up the ghost." Their severed heads were placed on London Bridge, their quartered bodies distributed for display about the city.[122] Oswald Wilkinson remained in prison a while longer. He had been the York gaoler and, according to one man, "the most pernicious, railing, and obstinate papist in all this country."[123] He was also a tenant of Northumberland's and had served as the latter's messenger to the Spanish ambassador in the final days before the revolt. When arraigned in April, he pleaded not guilty and professed to be "no more privy to this rebellion than the child of two years old."[124] Found guilty nevertheless, he too was eventually drawn and quartered at Tyburn. London audiences were thus not deprived of the scaffold's stark teachings on the dangers of dissent.

Perhaps the most widely noted and discussed execution, the one that marked the final end to the rebellion and its aftermath, was that of the man behind it, Thomas Percy. He remained on the border in the garrison town of Berwick for some time after his purchase from the Scots in the early summer of 1572. In August, finally, he was conveyed from Berwick to York. Lord Hunsdon had done his best to avoid the task when asked. Sir John Forster, the man subsequently chosen for the job and an old enemy of the earl's, took to it with alacrity. The parliamentary act of attainder offered sufficient declaration of Northumberland's guilt that no trial was needed. Instead, he was taken directly to the Pavement at the center of the city at three o'clock on August 22. In his confession, Northumberland had expressed the tragically naïve belief he had held before his rebellion, that the truth of the Catholic faith was so evident that even Cecil and Leicester would come to "discern cheese from chalk." "To be short," he said, "the unity which ever hath been, throughout Christendom, among those called papists; the disagreement and great dissension continually growing, and that ever hath been among the Protestants; methink was, and is sufficient, to allure all godly and humble minds."[125] This conviction remained firm even at his end. Gargrave reported to Cecil that Northumberland neither prayed for the Queen, "nor even wished her well, nor yet would confess that he had offended her majesty." To the end, "he continued obstinate in religion, and declared he would die a Catholic of the Pope's church . . . he affirmed this realm was in a schism, and that all were schismatics. He said here there was neither pity nor mercy."[126] Once he finished his speeches, the executioner had him lay his head upon the block and severed it with a carpenter's axe. The earl's head was hoisted atop one of the where it remained until it was stolen several years later. H buried without memorial in Crux Church, now the site of tea shop.

No formal memorial, but well remembered nonetheless. Almost immediately some of his coreligionists thought of him as a martyr. One man took clippings from the earl's beard while the head waited to be lifted to its grisly perch, and wrapped them with a note that read: "This is the hair of the good earl of Northumberland Lord Percy."[127]

Yet, we might better end not with Northumberland but with some of the other men, largely nameless and forgotten, but whose involvement made the revolt possible and made them the special targets of the Queen's ire. Here we might return to Sedgefield, one of the communities that had so exuberantly restored Catholic services and sent so many to join the rebel army. The altar they had twice reerected – once in 1567 and again during the rebellion – was torn down by the Queen's soldiers from the south as they marched through the area. The parishioners paid to replace the Protestant books they had burnt, and some paid fines for their part in the rebellion. A few found that their pardon failed to cover their acts of destruction and had to answer before the ecclesiastical court in Durham. Some may well have been among the people who found that their pardons similarly failed to protect them from the subsequent suits launched by Protestant gentlemen who had been spoiled during the revolt. Others yet received no pardons at all. Sir George Bowes had the names of eighteen men from the village on his list, and a note that five had been executed. We do not know precisely which men suffered; eight of the men known to have participated did not appear on the lists of the pardoned. Presumably the five who died were among their number. The other three may just not have paid the additional fee required to have their pardon formally enrolled. Roland Hixson, the churchwarden who stoked the fire at the town gate with service books, obtained mercy. Brian Hedlam, who had earlier been in trouble for his "lewd speeches" to the vicar, did not. Hedlam was quite probably among the Sedgefield men chosen for death, and chosen to act as an example to their neighbors of the perils of protest.

5
Meanings and Memories

Once the rebellion had ended, Bishop Pilkington wrote to a continental colleague, Heinrich Bullinger, with news of his tribulations cast in epic terms. The rebels, he said, had "persecuted us with the greatest harshness. They offered all manner of violence to religion and its ministers. But the Lord has delivered us all from the mouths of the lions...our good Lord disappointed all of them of their hope." In 1571, Bishop Horn similarly characterized the rebels as "the brood and offspring of popery, that pernicious and accursed fury of the whole world." Yet, he noted happily, "everything turned out so unexpectedly as it were from above, that it seemed as though the Lord of Hosts and of might had undertaken from his heaven the cause of his gospel, and had fought, as it were, with his own hands."[1] In such ways did good Protestants of the day interpret the rebellion: directed by a foreign, anti-religious Pope, and suppressed by a God intent on preserving his true church. But this, of course, was not the only way the rebellion could be understood. Much more recently, George Thornton drew a different moral from the story, urging modern readers to see the rebels as role models of a sort: "For Catholics today it is salutary to reflect on the high price Blessed Thomas Percy, his fellow martyrs and commoners placed on the Faith we so often take for granted in our freedom to worship."[2]

It should not surprise us that the rebellion acquired different meanings for different people through time. Its significance was invented, imagined, and contested in ways both spontaneous and deliberate, then and later. Such varied depictions reflected but also enhanced pre-existing differences, often justifying subsequent belief and action, each in their own fashion. The battle to determine the history of these events began even before the earls raised their standards, and continued long after their flight. The rebels' own attempts to shape the meanings of their actions via proclamations, banners, and targeted actions have already been discussed in a previous chapter. The first sections of this chapter examine the reception of and responses to those efforts. The crown sought to contain this rebellion and to prevent future challenges, not just through executions and forfeitures, but also by carefully constructing messages about the meanings of such protest. Much as Elizabeth was able to use the material repression of the revolt to her political advantage, so too would the cultural significance assigned to the rebellion promote a heightened loyalty. The politicized, instrumental ways in which contemporaries discussed the rebellion demonstrate again the significance of its popular and religious elements; they also shaped subsequent histories of the revolt. Accordingly, this chapter ends with an examination of the afterlife of these various interpretations in memory and history.

Rumors and popular news networks

Listening as best we can to the public conversations about the events of 1569 helps to resituate the rebellion in our own narratives of Elizabethan history, in part because the form and content of those conversations demonstrate that contemporaries recognized the active participation of people outside the halls of power. Rumors – the stuff and substance of politics in a pre-literate society – had to be countered and controlled. And rumors raced throughout the north in the fall of 1569. Whispers spread not only of an intended rising but of a rising accomplished. Some individuals reported hearing that the people of Durham had risen and sacked the bishop's palace; that a castle had been seized; that prominent Protestants had been marked for death, and more. Sir George Bowes noted that "the assembly and conference of people at fairs" constituted a seedbed of seditious talk and wanton rumormongering.[3] Accounts of high political intrigue thus found a receptive audience and special resonance in a population already resentful of recent assaults on their churches.

Disturbed by the rumors, the Queen issued her fateful summons to the earls of Northumberland and Westmorland. She also dispatched letters to justices throughout the realm, requiring them to gather the leading men of each county and have them swear to abide by the Act of Uniformity and the new Protestant services. She also repeated earlier orders that local justices keep a close eye on fairs and markets and interrogate any who spread seditious tales. She demanded that they seize vagrants, who both contributed to the general sense of disorder and were thought especially prone to spreading dangerous reports far and wide.[4] In response to these repeated injunctions the Councilors of the North gathered inn holders and taverners before them and asked whether they had "heard talk in their houses by any manner of person of any news, tales, reports, or rumors between the Queen's Majesty and her nobles or commons or between the nobles and commons or between any of them."[5] Similar enquiries occurred throughout the realm.

Once the rising began, individuals throughout the country spread the story and often added their own glosses. One unnamed northerner who arrived at the Blackborough fair in Norfolk reported to William Shuckforth, a local husbandman, that "they were up in the north, a hundred thousand men, and more than there be men and bullocks in this fair." Shuckforth in turn relayed the story to others. He spoke approvingly of the stir, linking it with the duke of Norfolk's arrest, the stranglehold the earl of Leicester held on the country's affairs, and the laxity newly allowed by priests. When he repeated his news yet again on November 29, he asserted: "By God's blood it is true that I told the last day. They are up in the North, for every body talks of it now, gentlemen and others. And [for] all this business we may thank the knave priests, for they have preached so largely and set such liberty that men may eat all things and keep no time for on Fridays they are not well without a piece of beef."[6]

Tales about the Northern Rebellion and rumors of other sympathetic uprisings continued to spread. In one London conversation, when vintner Harry Shadwell was asked, "What news?," he responded with claims that some 15 000 Scots had joined "the noble men of the north, whom he would not deem as rebels." He, too, thought the earl of Leicester somehow responsible for making revolt necessary. Shadwell added that the duke of Alba had promised aid and asserted that by Candlemas next, the Queen would be attending mass at St Paul's. He had heard this news, he said, from a "wench," two unnamed gentlemen, and the waterman who rowed him across the Thames earlier that day. When interrogated, the waterman admitted that he had talked of the rebellion, but insisted he had told his passengers that the Scots fought on the Queen's side, with some 5000 now lying dead in the field. He opined that if the earl of Leicester and his brother had been among the fatalities, the rebels "would soon be quiet, for as he thought the whole grudge was more against them ... than against the Queen's Majesty."[7] Leicester had clearly become to Elizabeth what Cromwell had been to her father – an object of displaced antagonism – and despite the threat of official reprisal, individuals offered independent interpretations of the news they received.

Sometimes such rumors threatened to spark sympathetic risings, or at least provoked such a fear from worried officials. John Welles of Norfolk recounted news of the rising and urged his hearers to take this as encouragement to rise for their duke: "There are two earls amongst others in the north who [have] been in great business and trouble, and except they be helped they be but undone, but if all men would do as I would, they should have help." He remonstrated with one neighbor: "It is a pity you live and that one hundredth of you were not hanged one against another, for that you have not stirred all this while, for those that dwelled three hundred miles off have done more for his Grace than you, but if you will do as I will, we should rise for the deliverance of the duke out of the Tower." He then proclaimed that he knew where to find the key for the church door and would ring the bells to raise the countryside. If the key could not be found, he would go in a window or burn down the door. Welles referred to his own military experience and said he could captain at least a few hundred men. John Barnard, a local linen weaver, added that he had a drum with which to marshal men, one used in a previous excursion into Scotland. They believed the duke's councilors would allow them the weapons from Kenninghall. Together, they would march to Cambridge, find the duke's brother to lead them, and go north to aid the rebels.[8] Welles managed to gather a handful of followers, but the conspirators quickly found themselves in the Norwich gaol.[9]

In Hereford, several men of suspect religious habits confidently reported that King Philip of Spain had arrived and marched along with the men of Lancashire to aid those of the north.[10] A drover living near Bedford relayed reports of a rebellion in Cornwall and Devon, the site of the 1549 rebellion against religious innovation.[11] Lancashire, too, remained a concern. In addition to the memories of an intended revolt there the previous year, the earl of Derby's loyalty was in some doubt. Sir Francis Leek tinged his report on Lancashire with cautious optimism, "yet, considering the late factions which have, within these two years, grown in that country, as well for foolish opinions of religion as other common actions between the earl of Derby and others, it resteth doubtful that all the keys of Lancashire do not presently hang at the earl of Derby's old girdle."[12] The bishop of Worcester warned the Privy Council that this "storm makes many to shrink. Hard is it to find one faithful." He added that "Wales with the borderers thereof is vehemently to be suspected."[13] Rumors thus reached the Council of various plots, each supposedly inspired by the actions taken in the north.

The stories that spread through taverns, fairs, and other informal news networks thus helped spark the 1569 rebellion, shaped understandings of its intent, and threatened to lead to other risings. There has been a recent spate of historical interest in this popular news culture as both an aspect of mass politicization and a potentially subversive force. As Adam Fox has noted, many conversations began with the enquiry, "What news?" and progressed to discussions of national and even international concerns. Fox and others have shown that the political culture of early modern England had a broader social base than one might expect in an age predating mass literacy and the proliferation of works from the popular presses.[14] Recapturing such popular political speech is difficult, however. It appears in the archives only when others reported the speaker to the authorities, and accusations sometimes derived as much from private malice as public loyalty.[15] Nevertheless, even if the claims were false they had to be believable, and the records leave no doubt that many busily shared news and views of the rising. Clearly, many people in 1569 had an interest in great affairs of state and felt themselves fully competent to form and communicate their own opinions and, indeed, to act upon them, whether in support of or in opposition to the rising. They did not constitute a passively accepting audience but a public capable of independent judgment. All those with interests at stake recognized the need to appeal to this broader audience, to explain the rationale for their actions, and to impose meaning. They knew they had to arm for a battle that occurred not just on the field but also in the more nebulous domain of public interpretation.

The Crown's response

While some historians have doubted the importance of popular involvement in this rising in particular and in sixteenth-century politics in general, the governors of Elizabethan England did not. Elizabeth and her councilors recognized the dangers rumormongers and talebearers posed. After the rising began, the Queen continued to order justices throughout the realm to watch the activity at fairs and markets and to arrest any who spread stories that threatened to promote disorder.[16] Councilors again asked inn holders and alehouse keepers to report anyone who shared news of the events in the north.[17] Those rumor spreaders we know by name are known because of arrests. Elizabeth and her councilors recognized, however, that repressive measures on their own did not suffice. The crown enjoyed an advantage, but had no guarantee of winning the contest for public sentiment. Much as her predecessors had done when faced with armed protest, Elizabeth now mobilized print, pulpits, and proclamations to dissuade the rebels and their potential supporters. To contain the rising, the Queen and her agents had to depict it in ways sure to weaken rebel resolve and to strengthen the loyal or uncommitted.

The first step, as usual, was to proclaim the leaders of the revolt traitors and thus reject outright their claims to loyalty. Elizabeth sought to disabuse those who saw no contradiction between their aims and faithfulness to their sovereign.[18] Attentive to the various modes of communication, the Queen resorted to public ceremony as well as proclamations to have the two earls ritually proclaimed as traitors. Heralds gathered at Windsor on November 26 and to the sound of trumpets declared the earls' treachery to all in attendance. Elizabeth also had the earl of Northumberland publicly divested of his membership in the prestigious Order of the Garter. Election to the Garter denoted perhaps the highest honor available to an Englishman, "an elevation beyond ordinary nobility to a privileged role of trust and intimacy" with the monarch.[19] Degradation from the historic order thus constituted a devastating public shaming and repudiation of noble status, especially significant for a lord who appealed to the sanctity of nobility to help justify his revolt. On November 27, Elizabeth gathered a group of her lords in the Garter Chapel at Windsor to witness the heralds "hurl down with violence the earl's banner of arms to the ground and then his sword and after his crest and lastly his helm and mantel." The heralds then "spurned" these objects from the chapel and finally from the castle gates in a manner that deliberately recalled the official ceremony of dishonor under the law of arms.[20] As Sir John Hayward noted of Elizabeth in another context, she knew "right well that in pompous ceremonies a secret of government doth much consist, for that the people are naturally both taken and held with exterior shows."[21] While this specific ritual was aimed primarily at Elizabeth's most powerful subjects, an admonition for lords who might be torn between obedience and honor much like the northern nobles, the Queen also ensured that the population at large learned of the falsity of the earls' claims to loyalty.

Countering the rebels' claims to loyalty represented the first step, but how then to respond to the religious element of the revolt? Here, the official response is revealing of the progress of religious reform and conversion after a decade of Elizabethan Protestantism. The Queen and her agents knew, or at least believed, that they had too many favorers of the old faith on their hands to make religious truth the focus of their arguments against the rising. Instead, they personalized the conflict. They attacked not the integrity of the old religious establishment but the integrity of the rebel earls. They questioned not the rebels' faith, but their faith in their leaders. The real choice people had to make was not between the Catholic church and the Protestant, as the earls proclaimed, but between two dim-witted, dissolute, and dishonest leaders and a Queen known for her kindness, care, and love of peace. The Queen's first proclamation provided a remarkable, lengthy narrative of the events preceding the rising. It declared the earls rebels, but also detailed the Queen's patient responses to their refusals to attend upon her at court, their persistent perfidy, and even their inability to manage their own estates. It noted that "as for reformation of any great matter, it is evident they be as evil chosen two persons (if their qualities be well considered) to have credit as can be in the whole Realm." It dismissed the earls' claim to loyalty as "a pretence always first published by all traitors." Despite its length, however, the proclamation had one glaring omission: it made no reference to the earls' reasons for rebellion other than their personal desperation and poverty. It thus assiduously and skillfully ignored the religious question.[22]

Even when Cecil decided to mobilize the resources of the church to oppose the rebels, he knew to proceed carefully. He wrote to Sussex in the north and noted that just as the rebels drew strength and identity from attending masses, so too ought the Queen's forces attend to their own "spiritual arming." He suggested that Sussex impose mandatory public prayers on the loyal forces, but cautioned him to find "discrete" preachers who would talk only of "matter proper for the common people . . . and not to entreat of hard matters in question, being not so mete for the multitude nor for the time." Instead, the preachers must speak only of the Queen's care for her people and the sinfulness of rebellion.[23]

In the north, however, the earl of Sussex could not completely ignore the religious question. In a missive to Sussex, the Queen noted that "these rebels do make religion to be the show of their enterprise," and urged him to use any means he could devise to convince the northerners of the falsity of this pretence and that the earls secretly intended to bring the country under the yoke of a foreign prince.[24] Sussex accordingly issued a proclamation that set out the "falsehoods and vain delusions" offered by the earls. It went through the rebel proclamations point-by-point, criticizing and refuting each. Sussex talked of the goodness of the Queen and the unnaturalness of rebellion. He insisted that the earls used religion only as a cloak for baser motives: they were "pretending for conscience sake to seek to reform religion, where in deed it is manifestly known many of them never had care of conscience not ever respected any religion, but continued a dissolute life until at this present day they were driven to pretend a popish holiness to put some false color upon their manifest treasons."[25] This talk of religious concerns as a "cloak" or "false color" became the standard line in official pronouncements on the revolt. Thus, during the rising itself, the official attempts to shape interpretation focused on power struggles within the elite and either ignored or discounted the religious motivation of the bulk of the rebel force.

Only with the rebellion suppressed did this focus begin to change, as seen in two later official efforts to impose meaning and elicit obedience. In the immediate aftermath of the revolt, Elizabeth and Cecil drafted an elaborate defense of the Queen's proceedings since her reign commenced. The document began with a reference to the recent "unnatural commotion of certain of our subjects" that a small few seditious persons had instigated for their private benefit. In order that all might "beware hereafter of such blind inveiglings, crafty abusings, and perilous enticements... we will that it shall be briefly understood both what our former intentions have been in our government... and what course we intend in God's grace to hold."[26] The document spoke not of the specifics of religious doctrine and practice, but instead offered proof that the Queen had a legitimate, God-given right to see that all live in obedience to the Lord. It sought to convince its audience that the Queen had long provided "mild, merciful, and reasonable government." It warned, however, that since lenience had led some to disobedience, the Queen now felt compelled to wield the Sword of Justice as well. Recognizing the need for oral as well as written distribution, it ended with a note that as the bulk of her good subjects were unable to read, the text was to be read aloud in all parish churches. The document is striking in its open attempt to explain, defend, and convince. Yet, for reasons unknown, the Queen may not have issued it. No printed copies of it survive, and while churchwardens' accounts throughout the country record payments for official prayers and ballads against the rebels, no such records have been found for this defense.[27]

The *Homily Against Disobedience and Wilful Rebellion*, however, most certainly reached a wide audience from the pulpits. Two collections of official homilies already circulated in England, one devised in 1547 and the other in 1563. These set, compulsory sermons served both to aid weak preachers and to regulate the pulpit in the interests of conformity. In early 1570, a new homily joined these pre-packaged sermons, to be delivered at regular times throughout the year. The *Homily Against... Rebellion*, nearly four times the length of the other homilies, had as its primary message the insistence that disobedience to one's prince equaled disobedience to God, full stop.[28] It endeavored to show that "obedience is the principal virtue of all virtues" and warned that subjects must not resist even an evil leader, as "a rebel is worse than the worst prince."[29] Just as David refrained from smiting Saul, so too must subjects leave the correction of misguided lords to God. Examples drawn from both sacred and secular history demonstrated that God never bestowed his blessing on the rebellious. Disobedience left fields untilled and wives unprotected. Revolt entailed all seven of the deadly sins. It led to famine and plague not just for the rebels themselves but also for their fellow countrymen. The homily even described how the congregation of large groups inevitably caused the "corruption of the air and place when they do lie with ordure and much filth in hot weather." Above all, it showed the futility of those who rebelled with the aim of bettering the commonwealth and asked, "Surely, that which they falsely call reformation is in deed not only a defacing or a deformation, but also an utter destruction of all common wealth?" History demonstrated that rebels were unfailingly "rewarded with shameful deaths, their heads and carcasses set upon poles, or hanged in chains, eaten with kites and crows, judged unworthy the honor of burial."[30]

The bulk of the homily relied on Scripture and history to make its case for the evils of rebellion in general. Now that the Northern Rebellion had safely reached its end, however, the time had come to acknowledge the rebels' motives and actions and to condemn them appropriately. The text noted that some "make rebellion for the maintenance of their images and idols...and in despite of God, cut and tear in sunder his Holy Word, and tread it under their feet, as of late ye know was done." It explained both the sinfulness and futility of such revolt, and now used the rebellion itself as proof that the old religion came of the Devil rather than the Lord. It exclaimed: "what a religion it is that such men and by such means would restore may easily be judged: even as good a religion, surely, as rebels be good men and obedient subjects." Only a "frantic religion" needed such assistance.[31] The Devil generally used both ambition and ignorance to stoke troubles, and had done so throughout history with the assistance of the Bishop of Rome. In recent years, the text asserted, the Pope had provoked the Pilgrimage of Grace and the 1549 Prayer Book rebellion. So, too, had he clearly instigated the rebellion of the previous year. The homily addressed those legitimizing symbols advanced by rebels and warned, "Let no good and discreet subjects, therefore, follow the flag or banner displayed to rebellion and born by rebels, though it have the image of the plough painted therein." Beware, too, those who "bear the picture of the five wounds of Christ against those who put their only hope of salvation in the wounds of Christ, not those wounds which are painted in a cloth by some lewd painter, but in those wounds which Christ himself bare in his precious body." Those who "bear the image of the cross painted in a rag against those that have the cross of Christ painted in their hearts" would find only ruin and destruction.[32] With the rebels safely disarmed, the crown could now denounce papistry itself and abandon the attempt to convince them and their coreligionists that the earls simply used religion as a mask for private motives.

The contrast between the messages crafted during and after the rising is instructive, but so too are their forms. Elizabeth and her agents recognized the need to address an audience broader than just the nobility and gentry from whom the conspiracies had first sprung. Rumors had helped spark the rebellion and might easily allow it to spread unless countered. The Queen addressed audiences both elite and plebeian, literate and illiterate, and drew liberally on print, pulpit, and public performance. The political culture of Elizabethan England involved both high and low elements, and order relied on both policing and persuasion.

Protestant pamphleteers and anti-papistry

While royal agents either ignored the religious motivation of the rebels or dismissed it merely as a "false cloak" during the course of the rising, there were others who felt less compunction about offering a frontal assault on the religious rhetoric coming out of the north. An impressive stream of vituperative polemic poured off the presses. Dismayed southern Protestants printed ballads, sermon texts, pamphlets, and lengthier tracts in condemnation of the rising. Some of these may have had quiet sponsorship from the crown, or at least from Cecil: two of the authors would later have overt ties to Cecilian propaganda initiatives. They must have had tacit official approval in order to make their way past the censors, but neither they nor their words received open official endorsement.[33]

One of these pamphleteers, Thomas Norton, wrote disparagingly of the papists who thronged St Paul's Cathedral seeking and reporting news, and according to him, making it up to suit their needs. He accused papist rumormongers of writing letters to themselves and brandishing them about, ink not yet dried, as proof of the news they imparted. He warned of the danger of such unbridled rumormongering and observed that tales of rebel strength were "no more but to discourage the Queen's true subjects and soldiers, and to rail up in doubtful men inclined to papistry a daring to join themselves to such a supposed strong side."[34] Similarly, John Phillips penned his *Friendly Larum . . . to the True Hearted Subjects of England* to comfort those disquieted by the "papists which mutter there and here, as opportunity serveth their turns, strange lies and news far distant from the truth." He warned these papist talebearers that:

> Your golden day may chance to cause
> Your necks to stand a crook.
> And therefore leave your whispering you,
> That daily gape for news:
> Take heed all ye that do Paul's Church,
> In order much abuse.[35]

As Norton and Phillips explained, loyal subjects needed to counter such false tales and to set the true meaning straight. The sinful needed to be confounded, and the wavering to be strengthened. These polemicists, at least, had no doubt that even those formally excluded from politics might sometimes play a role. News and rumor spread well beyond the literate elite and had to be directed and controlled.

The three works that appeared during the rising acknowledged the religious motives of the rebels and linked them firmly with the Pope, that stalking-horse of the antichrist if not the antichrist himself. All three demonstrated a very real perception of the danger the revolt posed to the security of the state and its religious settlement. For them, ignorant dupes may have filled the rebel ranks, but they were dupes of the Roman bishop rather than feudal instinct. William Seres's *An Answer to the Proclamation of the Rebels in the North* offered a versified, point-by-point refutation of the rebels' claims, while John Awdely penned a short *Godly Ditty or Prayer to be sung unto God for the Preservation of his Church, our Queen and Realm, against all Traitors, Rebels, and Papistical Enemies*. The longest and most elaborate response published during the rebellion was Thomas Norton's missive *To the Queen's Majesty's Poor Deceived Subjects of the North Country, Drawn into Rebellion by the Earls of Northumberland and Westmorland*.

Norton acknowledged the sincerity of the religious sentiments of the bulk of the rebel host, but sought to convince these good, if misguided, people that their leaders did not share these views. He insisted that, no matter how noble the men might think their goals to be, the earls planned to waste their lives merely to further their own evil ends.

Even if the rebel rank and file only wanted a return to the old faith, they were participating in a plot designed to overthrow the Queen, bring in foreign enemies, and enrich the earls. Echoing the official line, Norton talked repeatedly of deception, seduction, "erroneous shows," "false colors," and "false persuasions." He claimed to write in order to counter such falsehoods: "I impute one great part of your most heinous fault to other men's wicked persuasions, so I do not wholly despair of your amendment by better advices." He accused the earls of "an apish counterfeiting of feigned popish devotion." If these be good Catholic men, he suggested, make them demonstrate the good works upon which they so insist. Norton went even further in his warnings of deceit: he argued that the wives who spurred the men to rise for the old faith only wanted the return of unmarried, lascivious priests to satisfy their own carnal lusts. "Few women storm against the marriage of priests, calling it unlawful, and incensing men against it, but such as have been priests' harlots, or fain would be. Content your wives yourselves, and let priests have their own." He added: "This is a quarrel wholly like the old rebels' complaint of enclosing of commons. Many of your disordered and evil-disposed wives are much aggrieved that Priests which were wont to be common be now made several... there is the grief indeed."[36] He hoped to convince both the rebel ranks and their favorers elsewhere that they had, quite simply, been had. They must open their eyes, return to their homes, and trust in the clemency of their Queen.[37]

These and some of the later works about the rebellion mobilized all the traditional arguments used to deter and condemn revolt. Several reminded the men of their paternal duties and warned of the perils to which they exposed their families. Some sought to disabuse them of the notion that loyalty and protest were compatible; they might claim to oppose only "evil councilors," yet everything they objected to had been approved by the Queen and the nobles, bishops, and commons gathered in parliament. And while the rebels appealed to the symbols and messages of history, so too did these polemicists. Many reminded their readers or hearers to resort to the chronicles to see that rebels never prevailed. Edmund Elvidian sought to persuade by descriptions of "perils past... of the discommodities of rebellion."[38] William Seres admonished that "You never heard nor ever read that rebels did prevail."[39] William Elderton and others cautioned of the punishments rebels faced for their acts, deliberately contrasting the images used by the rebel host with those of Tyburn and the rituals of death. Just as the rebels' priests had hung up crosses, so too would they be hanged; they would soon lose their elaborate robes for a "Tyburn tippet, a cope, or a halter."[40] Others resorted to mockery, such as Thomas Preston's ballad account of the Pope's lamentation upon hearing of the rebels' defeat, told from the perspective of a fly in the pontiff's nose.[41]

Some of the works, however, especially those that celebrated the end of the rising, took a new tone. They confronted the question of identity, but went further than just calling the men of the north unlawful rebels and poor, deceived fools: rather, they were also enemies of God. The authors of these works recognized the conscious, willing participation of the individuals who "so well liked the earls' cause of religion" and attacked that cause directly. In doing so, they appealed not just to the standard historical examples of the futility of revolt, but also to a newly emerging view of history that saw the true and false churches engaged in an enduring apocalyptic struggle. Some authors referred explicitly to John Foxe's recently published *Book of Martyrs* to offer context for recent events.[42] The rebels' religion did not represent a cloak or false cover; it constituted the fundamental issue. These polemicists sharpened a rhetoric that had its tentative beginnings in the denunciations of the earlier Pilgrims of Grace and Prayer Book rebels of 1549. They used the terms "papist" and "traitor" as synonyms, and deployed an anti-Catholic vocabulary that came to mould the events of subsequent decades.

Thomas Norton soon threw off the moderation and restraint of his first publication on the rising. In his *Warning Against the Dangerous Practices of the Papists and Specially the Partners of the Late Rebellion*, he set out to prove "that every papist, that is to say everyone that believeth all the pope's doctrine to be true, is an enemy and a traitor." According to Norton, "no clemency, gentleness, ... or loving dealing can win a papist while he continueth a papist, to love her Majesty."[43] The rebellion itself had offered proof of the equation between papistry and treason, whether the rebels had been deceived or not. If the banners, actions, and proclamations of the rebels truly reflected their aims, then no more needed to be said. Yet, even if these were "false and vain colors, abused by these rebels to deceive and draw more subjects to take their parts, then see what followeth, then must it needs consequently be evident that they themselves yet supposed and knew papistry to be the very likely and apt color and mean to allure men to rebellion and treason against the queen."[44] He did briefly acknowledge some distinctions among favorers of the old faith: "Many men, otherwise good and honest subjects, are not yet purged of all errors wherewith Rome hath infected them and must have their time to be better instructed." Not all could be considered "perfect papists" and hence "perfect traitors" worthy of death. Yet, as the late rebellion had shown, even these "imperfect papists" posed a danger: "late experience hath taught how very many that pretend themselves to be but unsatisfied in some Popish opinions, and yet do renounce the Pope's usurped jurisdiction, have a certain aptness to receive also his traitorous articles and supremacy, when opportunity serveth."[45] They must therefore be rooted out of the commonwealth and destroyed.

Norton and his fellow polemicists urged unmitigated severity for these rebels, and harsher penalties for all such papists, for the rising had proven the treason that lay within every adherent of Rome. They argued for stern justice rather than the usual displays of mercy that followed a rising. Normally, rulers used mercy to prompt contrition and amendment in essentially good but misguided subjects. These rebels, being papists, were different; with them, mercy had no chance. They might repent of their rebellion, but would not give up their inherently traitorous faith. In a sermon preached at court and later published, Thomas Drant counseled that "as it is true that two and two make four, that when the sun is in the midst of heaven it is noontime,...so it is infallibly true that no perfect papist can be to any Christian prince a good subject."[46] The author of the ballad *A Cold Pie for the Papists* similarly adduced the rising as proof that all favorers of Rome were traitors, and that all such papists deserved retribution. He insisted that nothing differentiated those who had taken up arms from their fellows in faith. He prayed, "Unto our Queen, Lord grant thy grace/That she the sword from sheath may draw/To vanquish such as hate thy law/Then shall we be from danger free...God grant our Queen may look about/From hence to weed such Papists stout/Then shall we be from danger free."[47]

This depiction of the rising, which saw it as one of a series of confrontations between the true and false churches, won the field and became the standard perspective in most of the later domestic narratives of the rebellion. The stain applied primarily to the Romanists, but also bled onto all Catholics and favorers of the old ways more generally. In assigning religious significance to the rising, these Protestant writers noted the participation and aims of the rank and file and turned them into something extremely sinister. It was precisely the broad, popular attachment to the old ways demonstrated by the rebels that allowed Protestants to look back and depict the rising as yet one more link in the "chain of treasons" tied to Rome, and its resolution as yet one more sign of God's blessings for their own efforts. In so doing, they helped forge a virulent anti-Catholic Protestant identity that was to endure and shape responses to future events.[48]

Foreign foes

This view seemed to be endorsed by the Pope's excommunication and deposition of the Queen in February of 1570. Long pressured by a group of English exiles to clarify Elizabeth's status, Pius V had sent Nicholas Morton to England the previous year to sound out the likely responses of sympathetic noblemen to such a move. Morton returned full of encouragement, and news of the rebellion along with the earls' belated request for help provided further impetus to act. Pius opened proceedings on February 5, hearing testimony from twelve English exiles. The questions put to them focused on whether the Queen had deprived ordained bishops and put in their place laymen, heretics, and schismatics (the clearest evidence of which was the appointment of married men); whether she had the power to prohibit the spread of heresy if she so wished, as her sister Mary had done; and, on a related note, whether she had the freedom to act against the wishes of her council and parliament if she so desired. Receiving answers in the affirmative, the Pope issued his sentence on February 25. He declared "Elizabeth, pretended queen and daughter of iniquity," a heretic and excommunicate. As such, her one-time subjects were now absolved of their duties to her.[49] Copies of the sentence were sent to Alba in March, to be posted in the seaports and smuggled into England. On the morning of May 25, 1570, one John Felton nailed a copy of the papal bull to the doors of the bishop of London's palace near St. Paul's Church. With this publication, the bull (arguably) gained canonical effect. Felton's efforts were too late to help the rebels of 1569, although his timing helps to explain that of English attempts to quell trouble in Scotland before the rebels could make use of the bull to recruit more participants. The authorities promptly arrested, tortured, and tried Felton, executing him in St. Paul's churchyard on August 8.

The bull provoked a good deal of fear among Protestants, now anticipating further troubles, but also provided them further proof of the ties between Catholicism and treason. Now, both rebel actions and papal words proved the treason inherent in the Roman faith. Yet, not content with this link, they argued that the bull had in fact preceded and caused the rebellion. If moved back in time, the bull conveniently proved the Pope to be the author of the recent troubles. In his *Addition Declaratory to the Bulls*, Thomas Norton described the existence of two bulls: one of absolution, given to Harding and used to gather rebels since 1567; and the second, the bull of excommunication, which he claimed had been prepared, but not publicized, as early as February of 1569. Norton believed "that the original of the bull was among the rebels, brought by Markenfeld or some such other ... [and] kept close to be publicized so soon as they should have been able to get into their company such a head as they desired to set up."[50] Such arguments became especially credible after being endorsed by a Catholic writer. In 1571, Nicholas Sander published his vehemently pro-papal *De visibili monarchia ecclesiae*, in which he maintained that the papal sentence preceded the rising. According to Sander, on his 1569 mission, Morton actually told the northern lords that the Queen had already been excommunicated, rather than that this was simply an imminent possibility. For Sander, of course, such a claim legitimated the rebellion. For the Protestants who delightedly latched onto his words, however, it further delegitimated what the rebels had done. The rebellion thus became the first fruit, or first calf, of the papal bull, an accusation that quickly became a standard assumption in writings on the rebellion.[51]

While the Protestant polemicists immediately and insistently accused the Pope of causing the rebellion, they initially showed surprising restraint in respect to Mary Stewart. Much like the crown and even the rebels themselves, they remained largely silent regarding the role of the Scottish Queen. Only the most oblique references appeared in their earliest works. Thomas Norton again proved most daring, dancing around the topic of Mary's complicity in his missive *To the Queen's Majesty's Poor Deceived Subjects of the North Country*. He noted darkly that when the rebels shouted, "God save the Queen ... they have plainly showed it is not our Queen, Queen Elizabeth, that they mean." Later in the same work, after referring to Elizabeth as both "most loving mother and nurse of all her good subjects" and "husband of the commonweal," he accused the rebels of breaking the bonds of this "sacred wedlock" by yielding their bodies to a "notorious adulterer."[52] Norton became only slightly more explicit in the tract he wrote immediately after the rebellion. Next to a marginal reference to the "Lady of the North" he referred his readers to the common knowledge that groups of criminals become even more dangerous "where there is a woman in the company." This could, possibly, refer to the countess of Northumberland, but Norton had shown no compunction in naming others of the domestic rebels. Later in the work he discussed the Guise family and alluded to "that foreign title which was made the title and foundation of this last rebellion." Even these few subtle accusations may have earned him a rebuke, for on the title page of his collected works he included a disclaimer that he "meaneth not herein to hurt the fame of any singular person unnamed."[53]

This public silence on the role of Mary, as either direct agent or merely as inspiration, persisted through the first post-rebellion parliament, which convened in April 1571. The anti-papist characterization of the rebels' identity and place in history was, however, on full display and guided the deliberations of men now determined to eliminate the Catholic threat.[54] The rebellion remained fresh in memory, and shaped much of the business. In his speech on the supply, Lord Keeper Sir Nicholas Bacon explained the Queen's need for money in reference to the recent revolt and her ongoing duty to protect the nation from such popish plots.[55] Accordingly, the preamble of the subsidy act noted the nation's humble desire to give the Queen this "little and small present" to repay her for saving them from an "evil, unnatural, Popish and rebellious attempt." Perhaps responding to the sense that the rebellion had been a punishment, or "fatherly correction," for wicked living and temporizing, a few members thought the best response to be a wiping away of ambiguities.[56] Some of the more thoroughly Calvinist members pushed for a purer, more complete reformation. Measures were introduced to make the Eucharist, rather than mere church attendance, the test of conformity and to reform offending ceremonies and clerical vestments.

These attempts ran afoul of the Queen's determination to keep her church unchanged, but in other respects the Elizabethan religious settlement did tighten. In addition to the act of attainder against the leading rebels and the act to deprive fugitives of their estates, this parliament passed a statute against bringing in or executing papal bulls and another that required all clerics to subscribe to the 1563 articles of religion or suffer deprivation. It also passed a harsh new treason law. To the treason bill, Thomas Norton attempted to make an addition dealing with the succession, which would have barred from the throne anyone who had laid claim to it during Elizabeth's lifetime, as well as the children of such a claimant. This suggested amendment was quite obviously, although not explicitly, an attack on Mary. In the end, the statute abandoned Norton's attempt to impose the bar retroactively and on the children of such claimants, but did disable any who thenceforth laid claim to the throne. Furthermore, anyone who helped such a claimant in any way became guilty of treason and anyone who advocated the rights of someone not recognized by parliament as the lawful successor risked imprisonment. More broadly, the act made certain criticisms of Elizabeth, whether printed or simply spoken, treasonous offences. Any written or verbal statement that Elizabeth was a heretic or schismatic, or not the legitimate Queen, thenceforth merited death.[57]

During this session of parliament, a series of events began to unfold that would undermine the public reticence about Mary Stewart's supposed role in the events of 1569. The revelation of the Ridolfi plot would finally allow all the elements of the Protestant memory of the revolt to come together. A Florentine merchant and banker, Roberto di Ridolfi had resided in London since 1562. He had quickly established contacts with men of every conceivable party, acting as a financier for William Cecil and other prominent English councilors, receiving pensions from both the Spanish and French ambassadors, and serving as an agent of the Pope from 1566. In 1568 he had offered his assistance in arbitrating between Elizabeth and Alba in their trade dispute.

His actions in 1569 are unclear, but he did enough to provoke the suspicions of the Elizabethan government. Arrested in October of that year on suspicion of complicity in the Norfolk marriage plan, he was kept under house arrest in the care of Francis Walsingham. Walsingham later became Elizabeth's principal secretary and an invaluable spymaster, but had not yet entered official government service. Nevertheless, it seems that he, with Cecil's help, "turned" Ridolfi in the few weeks the Florentine remained in his custody. It was for this service, perhaps, that Walsingham soon received his first official appointment. At any rate, Ridolfi was released on November 11 on the stipulation that he not "deal directly or indirectly in any matters concerning her Majesty or the state of this realm except by her consent."[58] He immediately resumed his earlier plotting, but now relaying at least some information to Walsingham. He presented to Norfolk and Mary's agent, the bishop of Ross, a plan for a new Catholic uprising to free Mary and put her and Norfolk on the throne, this time with guaranteed financial aid from the Pope and military support from the Spanish, the latter to come primarily from Alba and include the refugees from the previous rebellion. Whether the outlines of the plot were suggested to him by Walsingham and Cecil, or whether he acted on his own initiative remains unknowable.[59]

Norfolk and Mary took the bait. Norfolk disregarded his promise to Elizabeth to deal no more with talk of the marriage; even while still in confinement he resumed correspondence with Mary. In August 1570 he was released from the Tower and allowed a form of house arrest in London. Within days, Ridolfi visited the duke and explained his plan. Initially Norfolk refused, but after receiving encouragement from Mary in January of 1571, he seemed to accept it at least in principle, although he refused to put his name to any related document. The Pope, in contrast, enthusiastically endorsed Ridolfi's plan. King Philip initially offered his support, but proved indecisive. With the duke of

Feria and others of his advisors pushing him forward, Philip did in July of 1571 order Alba to invade. Soon after, however, he left the matter to Alba's discretion. In doing so, he must have known that in effect he had abandoned the plan, for Alba had made his opposition clear from the beginning. At one point, the duke had dismissed Ridolfi as a great talker with no substance, nothing more than "un hombre muy vacio."[60] In a letter sent in August, he bluntly criticized the plotters for thinking "that one can conjure up armies out of thin air or pull them out of one's sleeve." Reciting their overly ambitious aims, Alba concluded sarcastically that "even if Your Majesty and the Queen of England agreed to cooperate to make it happen, even that would not suffice to make it happen at the time they propose."[61]

By this point, the investigation of the plot had begun in England. The "fortuitous" seizure of a servant carrying letters from Ridolfi, then in Flanders, to the bishop of Ross in April 1571 led to Ross's detention in May. Two of Norfolk's servants were also arrested and tortured into admitting their master's complicity. Accordingly, Norfolk found himself in the Tower once more. Whereas the duke's earlier plans to wed the Scottish Queen had not sufficed for a charge of treason, Cecil now had what he needed. In January of 1572, Norfolk went on trial for a series of charges that included his continued dealings with Mary even after his submission, which seemed proof of his nefarious intent, and his aid to the rebels and their abettors after their flight to Scotland. The third focus was his involvement in Ridolfi's scheme: plotting with foreign leaders to bring in foreign powers. He was found guilty but languished in prison for months, as Elizabeth signed and then cancelled one death warrant after another.[62] The Spanish ambassador was finally expelled. The bishop of Ross, who had sung like a canary under interrogation, was eventually released to spend his last years on the continent. Ridolfi remained in Europe, where he later told a thrilling, self-serving version of the story to Girolamo Catena, the biographer of the then deceased Pius V, which became yet more fodder for Protestants intent on proving the perils of the papacy.[63]

With the unveiling of the Ridolfi Plot, the linkage between the rebellion and the papacy became complete, and so too did Mary come to be publicly associated with the events of 1569. *Salutem in Christo*, the first printed work to accuse Mary of complicity in the revolt, appeared in these months. While she was to remain physically secure for years yet, her credit with Elizabeth and hence her protection from public calumny diminished. The next parliament met in May of 1572. The mood was rabid and the muzzles removed. Members established a select committee to consider the problem of Mary Stewart. Within two days it returned with a lengthy report of her procurement of the Northern Rebellion, her support for the English rebels in Scotland and on the continent, and her complicity in the recent plot.[64] In stark contrast to the earlier reticence about Mary, members of parliament now denounced her as "a Scot, an enemy to England, an adulterous woman, a homicide, a traitor to the queen, a subverter of the state, an underminer of titles"; or, more simply, "as vile and as naughty a creature as ever the earth bare." They demanded her execution, citing precedents from both sacred and secular history, and ominously intimated that if the Queen failed to kill her, God would require blood of her instead. In their petition, the bishops noted that:

> The late Queen of Scots hath not only sought and wrought by all means she can to seduce the people of God in this realm from true religion, but is the only hope of all the adversaries of God throughout all Europe and the instrument whereby they trust to overthrow the gospel of Christ in all countries, and therefore if she have not that punishment which God in this place aforementioned appointeth, it is of all Christian hearts to be feared that God's just plague will light both upon the magistrates and subjects for that by our slackness and remiss justice we give occasion of the overthrow of God's glory and truth in his Church mercifully restored to us in these latter days.[65]

When Elizabeth told them to set aside the question of Mary's guilt and execution, the members consoled themselves by passing a bill that explicitly barred Mary from the succession. Even this the Queen put off, but asked that the usual formula for a veto – "La roigne se avisera" – be taken literally. In the interim, the members turned more fiercely on Norfolk. One petition for his death had concluded, with some asperity, that the Queen must see justice done, "lest her Majesty be recorded for the only prince of this land with whom the subjects thereof could never prevail in any one suit."[66] It was perhaps to appease and divert her critical MPs that Elizabeth finally ordered his execution. On June 2, 1572, Norfolk died on Tower Hill, attended by his former tutor, the martyrologist John Foxe, and protesting to the end his innocence of any treasonous intent or support for Catholicism.

With Norfolk dead and Northumberland soon to join him, the crisis that began with Mary's arrival was near its end. Together with the conspiracy that brought down Norfolk, there had been a series of smaller, sometimes harebrained schemes to free Mary and a set of near-rebellions in Norfolk, in at least one of which the participants envisioned calling on Alba to provide support. Taken together, these events confirmed an apocalyptic, providential view of the past and expecta-tions for the future. Whatever the variety of motives that had guided the many members of the rebel army of 1569, or later their supporters in Scotland, they became even more strongly tied to a militant, interna-tional Catholic conspiracy led by the Pope with the King of Spain and Queen of Scots as his instruments.

People must be able to make sense of their experiences, to give meaning to the things happening about them, before they can respond. The crown and worried, outraged Protestants and loyalists sought to shape those meanings, even if not always to precisely the same ends. During the rising, the crown attempted to dissuade rebels and their potential supporters by focusing on the deceit practiced by self-serving men who had the title but not the substance of nobility. The crown tried to diminish future dangers by teaching a doctrine of unquestioning obedience as the highest good expected of a subject to God and Queen. After the rebels' defeat, the crown and its allies added a potent condem-nation of the rising as not just religious but anti-religious, and tied to the needs of a foreign Pope and an equally foreign Queen. Some such works had a critical, even subversive edge in implying that Elizabeth's hold on God's favor, and hence on her crown, required more vigilant opposition to God's enemies. Yet, for the time being at least, the dangers of international Catholic conspiracy worked to reinforce the need for absolute obedience.[67] Recognition that despite her flaws, their Queen offered the only security against the Pope restrained Protestant oppon-ents; the firmer linking of foreign foes and Catholicism did the same for many religious traditionalists. Nor could people be allowed to forget such lessons. The task of assigning meaning continued in coming years, as the rebellion became part of rival understandings of history that shaped subsequent beliefs and actions.

Protestant memorials

The process of making the rebellion meaningful by putting it into a specific sequence of events and strand of history began almost imme-diately. The bonfires that celebrated the nation's deliverance at the end of the rebellion helped spark a tradition of Protestant, nation-alist commemoration. The anniversary of Elizabeth's accession day, November 17, became the first state holiday to supplement the dimin-ished roster of religious holidays.[68] While a few parishes had offered some festivities on this date even earlier, from 1570 the practice became increasingly common. According to Elizabethan chronicler William

Camden, it did so as a response to the rebellion and the papal bull, twinned threats to Elizabeth and to her people: "the twelfth year of the reign of Queen Elizabeth being now happily expired, wherein some credulous papists expected, according to the prediction of certain wizards, their golden days, as they termed it, all good men through England joyfully triumphed and with thanksgiving, sermons in churches, multiplied prayers, joyful ringing of bells, running at tilt, and festival mirth, began to celebrate the seventeenth day of November, being the anniversary day of the beginning of her reign."[69]

Parishes and towns marked the holiday in various ways: with plays, bonfires, bell ringing, free food and drink, or special prayers, sermons, and ballads. In 1576, Archbishop Grindal issued *A form of prayer with thanksgiving, to be used every year, the 17th November, being the day of the Queen's Majesty's entry to her reign.*[70] From the 1580s, Accession Day tilts and jousts entertained those at court. What began spontaneously with local initiatives acquired official sanction as a reminder of providential deliverance. It served as an injunction, to both the Queen and her subjects, to remain vigilant against the threat of popery. Edwin Sandys explained the purpose of the celebration in one Accession Day sermon: "When your children shall ask you what this our assembly meaneth, you shall answer, that it is to give God thanks for that great benefit which we received at his hands this day, when in his mercy he gave us our gracious elect Elizabeth, whom he hath used as his mighty arm, to work our deliverance, to bring us out of Egypt, the house of Romish servitude." In another of his November 17 sermons, Sandys preached on the biblical reference to foxes that threatened the vineyard and spoke of "the late rebellion in this realm, raised for no other cause but by force to subvert religion, by no other man than the father of these foxes, [which] is fresh in memory."[71] An important addition to the "protestant calendar" and cult of Elizabeth, Accession Day both took on new significance after the 1569 rebellion and, like the post-rebellion Homily and official prayers, also helped shape and preserve memories of the rebellion in turn. Just as the rebels of 1569 had had the examples of history cited to them, so too would they become examples to others.

Memorials of the events of 1569 continued to be crafted and constructed as the years progressed. The rebellion never achieved quite the same prominence in the litany of providential deliverances as did the Armada of 1588 or Gunpowder Plot of 1605, yet it received frequent mention alongside these two favorite object lessons of history. Almanacs listed the rebellion with the Armada and Gunpowder Plot as three of the most important historical events since the creation of the world, or at least since the biblical flood. (Of course, Jonathan Dove's "Brief computation of some memorable accidents" listed among its thirty-four items not just the rebellion but also the first appearance of tobacco in England).[72] The rebellion appeared in a number of the many sermons preached on the anniversary of the 1605 plot as yet another example of the perfidy of papists and yet another reason for godly diligence. In his November 5, 1641 sermon before the House of Commons, for instance, Cornelius Burgess cited the rebellion "as the first poisoned fruit of the Pope's Bull" before moving on to more recent challenges.[73] Similarly, the rising made its appearance in the "deliverance" literature that poured off the presses in the early seventeenth century. In his tract on *God's Manifold Mercies in these Miraculous Deliverances*, John Taylor repeated the standard description of the rebellion as sparked by the papal bull and funded by the papacy. He concluded, "Thus we (by proof) must thankfully confess, that where the Pope doth curse, there God doth bless."[74] Miracles proper might no longer have a place among Protestants, but "miraculous deliverances" were theirs alone. Yet, such comforting messages always carried an implicit threat. God had saved the English from their oppressors many times, a fact that signified God's favor for their church, but one that bore the implication that He might not always do so should the English regress.

Bishop George Carleton of Chichester accorded the rebellion somewhat lengthier treatment than most others in his compendious *Thankfull Remembrance of God's Mercy*, first published in 1624. Carleton wrote his work so that "by examples of things past, we may better judge of things to come." The rebellion was the first fruit of the papal bull, devised by the Pope and Spanish King; to prove this, he offered a lengthy quotation from Catena, the Catholic hagiographer of Pope Pius V. They had planned two risings, one led by the northern earls and one by Norfolk, to be joined by an army from Ireland and one from Alba. Yet, before long, it all collapsed and left its noble leaders ruined. This outcome should serve as a warning to others similarly inclined: "it may teach others to beware of those that bring such poisoned and intoxicating cups from Rome." Surely, any "religion that bringeth always a curse is to be suspected." Carleton labored to dissuade any who might be tempted by talk of returning to the faith of their fathers both with a description of the failed attempt in 1569 and with an explanation that the Council of Trent had completely altered the Catholic faith. "And therefore men may observe a great difference between these men that are now called Papists, and their forefathers." God had blessed their fathers, who served Him sincerely and according to such knowledge as they had. "But after that God hath revealed a greater measure of knowledge by the spreading of the favor of his Gospel, they who then forsake the truth offered are followed with great curses." In this way, he carefully separated the histories of the pre- and post-reformation Catholic churches, allowing opprobrium to be cast more securely on the latter. While the narrative of the revolt served to warn those with similarly rebellious inclinations, it also proved the veracity of the Protestants' faith. That "the Pope's curse is turned by the favor of God into an extraordinary blessing" was proof enough that the Pope was not Christ's Vicar. And a victory against the formidable combined forces of the Papacy, the Spanish, and other foreigners surely signaled God's intervention: "For what power could be able to keep his church from being swallowed up by such cruel adversaries, but only the hand and holy protection of our God?"[75]

Carleton's effort is perhaps most distinctive for its images. The title page gave clear pride of place to the Armada and Gunpowder Plot, God's deliverances from water and from fire. Its second and subsequent editions, however, included iconic depictions of the popish onslaughts

Illustration 5.1 The Rebellion of the Earls of Northumberland and Westmorland.
Source: George Carleton, *Thankfull Remembrance of Gods Mercie*. 4th edn. (London, 1630). Huntington Library Rare Books 16378. This item is reproduced by permission of *The Huntington Library, San Marino, California*.

narrated in the book, each accompanied by an image of the divine retribution that ensued. One edition included a separate foldout sheet of the pictures, which served "for strengthening of our hearts when we shall be called to the like trials; for in these days of peace it is good to prepare against a storm." This foldout also sold separately from the volume itself.[76] Meant as aids to memory, these separate images might be hung in homes or pasted up in pubs and helped disperse the central admonitions of the text to a larger and non-literate audience. In the tradition of John Foxe's notorious, gruesome depictions of Protestant sufferings at the hands of papists throughout history, they acted as constant reminders of God's grace to true believers (Illustrations 5.1–5.3).

In word and sometimes in pictures, then, the rebellion survived as an example to dissuade future would-be rebels, to brand Catholics as foes of good order, and to hearten and admonish the faithful. If never the most prominent, it did inaugurate a list of divine deliverances that, as Alexandra Walsham notes, served as "tangible seals of the Lord's special covenant with the elect." Protestants used such tales of providential intervention as weapons to win converts, to strengthen the resolve of the faithful, and to weaken that of their opponents. Furthermore, for a time

Illustration 5.2 The Pope's Bull Against the Queen.
Source: George Carleton, *Thankfull Remembrance of Gods Mercie*. 4th edn. (London, 1630). Huntington Library Rare Books 16378. This item is reproduced by permission of *The Huntington Library, San Marino, California.*

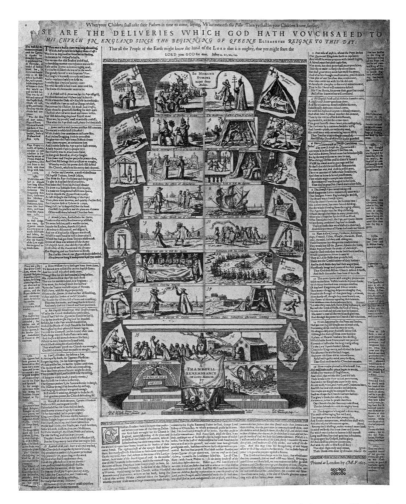

Illustration 5.3 The Deliverances which God Hath Vouchsafed to His Church.
Source: Sutherland Collection LIII. 101, Ashmolean Museum. This item is reproduced by permission of *The Ashmolean Museum, Oxford*.

at least, these celebrations served as a "kind of cultural cement, a ligature linking the learned culture of Protestant elites with the street culture of those they condemned as the 'carnal multitude.'" Yet, they became increasingly divisive and contentious during the reign of King Charles, with his French Catholic wife and foreign and ecclesiastical policies that sought conciliation with continental powers. Walsham notes that under Charles's Archbishop Laud, some anniversary sermons shifted their focus to the sinfulness of disobedience in general rather than the dangers of Catholicism in particular.[77]

In these disordered years immediately preceding the Civil Wars, a rebellion so often used to depict the evils of Catholic conspirators could be redeployed to attack the deceptive claims and self-depictions of even Protestant rebels. When Charles's Scottish Presbyterian subjects went to war with their King, all the while insisting upon their fidelity and attempting to enlist the support of their English neighbors, one anonymous author issued *Loyalty's Speech to England's Subjects* to strengthen support for the King. "Loyalty" listed previous examples of failed rebellions, and noted how most participants had tried to obscure their true nature by giving themselves names other than "rebel": "It were tedious and too long to repeat their names, who continually have slandered loyalty with base terms... Thus might I with tears remember the wrong that I suffered in the Northern Rebellion, where though the fact was so infamous as the memory is odious to this day, yet did they pretend a reforming of religion, a freedom of conscience, and a bettering of the commonwealth."[78] Attacking Presbyterian rebels, this author returned to the idea of religion as merely a false cloak for baser motives and simple disobedience, something he portrayed as more significant a failing than even Catholicism. John Walter has discerned a new frequency and intensity in admonitory tales of previous revolts in the years immediately preceding the Civil War. He suggests, quite plausibly, that this increase helped shape responses to events in the early 1640s.[79] As the English moved toward war with each other, they found different warnings embedded within the narratives of past protest.

Catholic renderings of the revolt

The past, and the place accorded to the 1569 rebellion within it, could be constructed differently according to the needs of different communities. Well before some English Protestants sought to use the rebellion to denounce the "false" claims of rebellious fellow Protestants, another group had offered a reading of the rebellion much at odds with the standard depiction of the dangers of popery.[80] Almost immediately upon the rebels' defeat, some Catholic writers began crafting their own interpretations, often no less providential than those of the victorious Protestants. Religious explanations can be wonderfully flexible: whereas Protestants had seen the occurrence of the revolt as a test or punishment from God, and their victory a sign of His favor, some Catholics saw its failure as a test and punishment for their lack of resolve. Yet, rather than focus solely on this rather depressing aspect of the rebellion's failure as a punishment, a number of writers decided to extol the participants as martyrs, men whose God-given ability to die strong in their faith signified the truth of their beliefs.

Nicholas Sander, whose earlier works had exerted such a profound influence on the earl of Northumberland, was in 1571 the first to print a characterization of those executed for their support of the rebellion or the papal bull as martyrs.[81] Another of his works, published in 1585 after his death while raising rebellion in Ireland, again referred to the men as martyrs. *De origine ac progressu schismatis anglicani* offered the first comprehensive Catholic history of the English reformation (or schism) and proved extremely popular. Six Latin editions as well as translations into English and six other languages appeared by 1628. Subsequent Catholic authors borrowed liberally from its account, ensuring it an even broader audience.[82] Others quickly followed Sander's lead in treating the rebels as martyrs. For instance, Richard Bristow's 1574 tract, *A brief treatise of diverse plain and sure ways to find out the truth*, included references to the 1569 martyrs in its attempt to provide reasons "to move a man to believe the Catholics and not the Heretics." Protestants who died for their faith, no matter how well intentioned, did not die within the faith of St. Stephen, the first Christian to die for his God, and hence were martyrs merely of the devil. He contrasted the earl of Northumberland, Thomas Plumtree, the Nortons, and "so many hundreds of the Northernmen" to "those stinking martyrs of the heretics." Bristow warned "that all men may easily see, that if they desire to be with those Martyrs, they must not be with the Protestants."[83]

Much like the Protestants' stories of providential deliverance, such Catholic martyrologies were intended to aid conversion and strengthen the committed. Accounts of martyrdoms validated one's faith by showing the strength God gave to his followers even at death. They tied recent events to a long, hallowed history that stretched back to the beginnings of Christianity. Protestants implicitly recognized the power of such accounts by trying to claim the genealogy of early church martyrs for themselves and by fashioning a modified rhetoric of suffering (stripped of its miraculous and interventionist aspects) for their own fallen coreligionists.[84] Borrowing in turn from the Protestants, Catholic polemicists also created iconic images of suffering that rivaled those of John Foxe's *Book of Martyrs*. Richard Verstegan, for instance, illustrated his *Theatrum crudelitatum haereticorum nostri temporis* (Antwerp, 1587) with gruesome woodcuts of Protestant atrocities.

A. Propter fedis Romanę et fidei catholicæ confeßionem, undecim Rᵐⁱ episcopi catholici ex diuturna carceris molestia contabescentes obierunt,

B. Plumtreus Wodhouin Nelsonus, Maijnus, Hansiusque facerdotes in partes disfecantur.

C. Storeus I.V. doctor. Feltonus etiam nobilis, et Shir Wodus idem supplicium subeunt, Regina Elizabetha Anglię imperante.

D. quidam uir illustris capite plexus est.

30

Illustration 5.4 The Sufferings of Catholics.

Source: Giovanni Battista Cavalieri, *Ecclesiae Anglicanae Trophaea* (Rome, 1584). Huntington Library Rare Books 14875. This item is reproduced by permission of *The Huntington Library, San Marino, California*.

Although some of these publications were successfully smuggled into England, they reached mainly a continental audience. Their influence in England was probably strongest, if indirect, through the many priests who received their training abroad, tutored in such tales, before returning to minister to the dwindling flock of fellow Catholics. Indeed, students at the English College in Rome had incorporated the martyrologies into their daily ritual. When Anthony Munday visited in 1579, he noted that at each dinner a student read from the Bible and then from the accounts of the English martyrs; he heard the stories of Felton and the two Nortons while in attendance.[85] In 1582, work began on a series of 34 frescoes at the College, of which 24 depicted early church martyrs and 10 showed martyrs from the time of the Reformation. One of the latter groups centered on those who died for their part in the Northern Rebellion. Giovanni Battista Cavalieri engraved versions of these frescoes for publication in *Ecclesiae Anglicae Trophaea* (Rome, 1584). As Anne Dillon notes, these were provocative images, intended to call men to action.[86] Thus, these Catholic authors and artists inserted the rebellion into an understanding of history that provided evidence of God's intervention on their side, challenging the Protestants' claim to the badge of persecution and suffering (Illustration 5.4).

Depicting the 1569 rebels as martyrs proved problematic for some Catholic writers, however. The martyrologists liked having elite and educated men to contrast with the low-status pseudo-martyrs of the Protestants, and in their efforts to secure aristocratic support for their cause, extolling men such as Northumberland had a certain appeal. But they also sought to portray victims who died for their faith alone and not for treason, the charge most commonly leveled against them by English Protestants. While Northumberland, Thomas Norton, and some of the others were men of status who had died firm in their faith for a rebellion intended to restore that faith, they had died for rebellion nonetheless. In fact, no one "Catholic interpretation" of the rising and its participants existed. Just as fissures appeared in Protestant depictions of the revolt, so too did differences exist among Catholics. While some Catholics readily embraced militant opposition to Elizabeth, many others insisted upon the wisdom and duty of obedience. Some authors argued repeatedly that Catholics, rather than Protestants, made the most loyal subjects. For them, the rebellion posed a challenge.[87]

Bishop Leslie published his own version of recent events soon after Protestant polemicists began attacking Queen Mary in print. The anonymous author of *Salutem in Christo* had denounced Mary as Elizabeth's "most dangerous enemy" and "the greatest cause of the

Rebellion lately in the north." Leslie responded with a vigorous defense and counterattack in his *Treatise of Treasons*. While he did not entirely repudiate armed resistance, he advanced the now common Catholic claim that Protestantism constituted the more dangerous and inherently rebellious "faith." For recent and evident proof, he said, one only had to look at the Protestants in the Netherlands, France, and Scotland. Leslie's work set out to reveal the less evident proof of "deep and hidden" Protestant treason within England itself. He urged Elizabeth and his readers to look to the past, and especially to the history of the Greek conquest of Troy through duplicity. Just as the Greeks had concealed their intentions to devastating effect with their infamous wooden horse, so too did ambitious men adopt this new, feigned religion to hide their treasonous aims. The recent supposed treasons of Catholics were merely the products of machinations by Elizabeth's Machiavellian, anti-aristocratic councilors. The northern earls had rebelled only when cunningly maneuvered into desperation by Cecil and other such wolves in sheep's clothing.[88]

While Leslie dealt with the rebellion by making it the product of Protestant conspiracy, some later Catholic writers emphatically denounced it and any violent resistance to their lawful Queen. English Catholics remained divided on how best to handle the crisis they faced: should they offer militant opposition or prudent accommodation and principled loyalty? Late in Elizabeth's reign, this basic difference crystallized into heated disputes between two factions: one, represented by the Jesuits and the other by the secular priests, the so-called Appellants. The latter hoped for some sort of toleration and tried to distance themselves from the militant Jesuit minority they blamed for counterproductively antagonizing the crown. William Watson and Thomas Bluet, leading members of the Appellant clergy, penned *Important Considerations* for their coreligionists; William Watson contributed the preface while Bluet wrote the body of the text. Bluet disparaged the 1569 rebellion as the first of the ill-advised provocations that had turned the crown against Catholics. Catholics had lived in tolerable conditions "till the said rebellion broke forth in the North." He criticized Sander's attempt to make martyrs out of men who had risen against their sovereign and died after being justly condemned under the ancient and approved law of treason. He condemned the rebels, their posthumous praise, and any other political opposition as being linked to the "Jesuitical Hispanized Faction of Falsehood." For Bluet, the Jesuits, like the Protestants, represented novelty. As one of "the ancienter sort of priests," Watson insisted that "the old approved paths of our forefathers...will always prove the best." Their forefathers had planted their faith through preaching and prayer, and had taught obedience rather than revolt. Priests ought "to fill men's hearts with joy and peace by the inward working of the holy Ghost, and not to feed them with hopes of invasions and treacheries."[89]

Yet, while Watson and Bluet wrote their tract to insist that Catholics could be loyal, obedient subjects, Protestants would use their words in much the same way as they did the works of Catena, Sander, and others. In that later time of anti-Catholic crisis, an anonymous work published in 1689 used Watson's preface, along with a copy of Pope Pius's encouraging letter to the rebels found in a 1640 collection of papal correspondence, to show that plots laid "to the charge of papists are...owned and acknowledged by Catholics themselves."[90] Fissures within the Catholic community, sometimes encouraged by the crown, ensured that no one interpretation of the 1569 rebellion dominated their accounts. And regardless of the differing political positions of the Catholic authors, and hence the different ways they framed the rebellion, their evidence provided fodder for Protestant polemicists in times of heightened crisis.

For all their differences, both Protestant and Catholic depictions concurred in some respects. Neither of the dominant traditions of written remembrance afforded much space for a complexity of motivation. In these accounts, the rebellion remained intrinsically an episode of religious conflict. Whereas the crown had sought to downplay the religious element during the revolt in an attempt to minimize its spread, in the ensuing months and years it endorsed a story of providential deliverance from the foreign forces of the antichrist. In the Protestant narrative of divine protection and popish conspiracy, those not fully committed to a Romanist Catholicism disappear. Much the same is true of the Catholic accounts; as Lucy Wooding notes more generally, the "hagiographies of the recusant tradition left little room for those who did not embrace the stark principles of the martyrs."[91]

Local and popular memories

But what of local understandings and memories of the revolt? Here, we encounter the problem of a primarily oral culture that left little trace in print. In his history of the afterlife of Owain Glyn Dŵr's revolt, R.R. Davies distinguished between written histories and "social memory," the latter being the "common collective memory of human groupings from the neighbourhood to the nation." The precise contours of social memory, he notes, are impossible to retrieve for periods before the last century. Fragments are the most to be hoped for.[92]

In the region that produced the rebellion one might expect fairly complicated memories. Certainly, there were reminders aplenty. The continual lawsuits over coming years to sort out who owned what in the wake of forfeitures and executions, or to satisfy men such as George Bowes who had been spoiled, would have kept memories fresh. Any church bells removed at Cecil's command or churches stripped by southern soldiers would have provided memorials of a sort, but with what specific connotations in unknown. A sense of remorse may have stayed with some, if not for their defiance at least for the damages they had inflicted on their neighbors: when William Hodgson died in 1598, he left money to John Longstaff "in consideration of his losses he sustained by me in the late rebellion in the north," and to two other men "in like manner."[93] In contrast, the man who tried suing for the losses he incurred when the Queen's soldiers captured him in his attempt to flee to Scotland presumably remembered his actions with little guilt.[94] One is only left to wonder what one "Gregson the north tale teller" thought of the rebellion; arrested in 1584, he had stolen the head of the executed earl of Northumberland from its grisly perch atop the York city walls for use in some sort of sorcery.[95] How northerners responded to the view of the rebellion presented in official homilies and prayers, or to that in tracts smuggled in from the continent, cannot be retrieved.

We can try to fall back upon the ballads that were later collected by antiquarians and folklorists. The ballads tend to focus on the romantic tragedy of the revolt, on great lords and their heraldic banners and badges, on futility and loss, and on treachery. The people of the north had looked to the lords and gentlemen for leadership and assistance, but had been abandoned. As one ends,

> But the dun bull is fled and gone,
> And the half moon vanished away:
> The Earls, though they were brave and bold,
> Against so many could not stay
>
> Thee Norton, with thine eight good sons,
> They doomed to die, alas! For ruth!
> Thy reverent locks thee could not save,
> Nor them their fair and blooming youth.

With them full many a gallant wight
They cruelly bereav'd of life:
And many a child made fatherless,
And widowed many a tender wife.

Unsurprisingly, a similar tone of loss pervaded many of the surviving ballads, with some even less sympathetic to the rebellion's leaders. Another version of the same ballad ends on an unflattering note:

But the dun bull is fled and gone,
And the half moon vanished away:
And Francis [sic] Norton and his eight sons,
Are fled away most cowardly.[96]

Treachery was thus a common theme – either the treachery of the leaders so disastrously abandoning their men on the field or, in other ballads, the treachery of the Scots in handing the earl back to the English. But with little firm knowledge of when, where, or by whom the ballads were composed, it would be unwise to attempt too close a reading of their significance for the contemporary social memory of the rebellion.

The dominant social memory of the revolt in the nation at large presumably fitted it into the larger narrative of papal danger, a narrative that became pervasively compelling.[97] There were, however, some early exceptions. In 1581, David Brown, a husbandman of East Tilbury in Essex, found himself in court after complaining "that it was a merry world when the service was used in the Latin tongue and now we are in an evil way and going to the devil and have all nations in our necks." He found hope, however, in the continued activities of the earl of Westmorland. The earl, he said, had received a wealthy dukedom from the King of Spain for his good services and was then in Ireland with a great army of soldiers, many of whom were men who had suffered under the Queen's unusually harsh laws. The earl planned to return in force to regain his estates, and Brown for one would help him to the best of his abilities.[98] Four years later, another Essex man was arrested after making similar claims. William Medcalfe, a laborer of Coggeshall, insisted that "this world will be in better case shortly" as "the king of Spain with the noble earl of Westmorland with Norton and six of his sons of noble birth are come into England with others, and with fifteen or else twenty thousand English men." These English men had suffered under Elizabeth's cruel vagrancy laws and fled, but now followed the earl who "did put his trust in God to be at the Tower of London shortly and there to apprehend all such as he thought good to be revenged of the death and blood of the late duke of Norfolk."[99] The second case had enough similarities with the first – particularly in maintaining that Westmorland gathered his army from the ranks of Englishmen burned or bored through the ears – to suggest that Brown and Medcalfe did not create these stories themselves but drew from a more common rumor.[100]

Like the people of the north, these men looked to great lords to help lead them out of their problems and into a better world. Brown and Medcalfe voiced the same preference for the old ways, the same sense of the links between the old religion and better days that had featured in the rebellion. They also manifested the same combination of a sturdy independence of mind and respect for lordly leadership as had so many in the north. Not living in an area that had been spoiled by soldiers or festooned with the corpses of defeated rebels, these Essex men, at least, remembered the rebellion not with the sense of treachery that pervaded the northern ballads but with a sense of hope. That was precisely what Elizabeth and her agents had tried to counter. In the effort to allocate meaning to action, the crown had immense advantages: a store of authority on which to draw and better access to the presses, pulpits, and gallows. Even with these advantages, however, it faced competing and incompletely eradicable narratives, be they from disappointed puritans, conspiring Catholics, or subjects not easily classifiable into categories. The rebellion of 1569 became part of a Protestant nation-building narrative, but also remained for years yet an event with some threatening potential, a resource to be used to different ends.

Conclusion

For many years after, historical understandings of the 1569 rebellion continued along the trajectories set by its contemporaries. The northern ballads might not allow us to speak with certainty of social memories of the revolt, but they did help shape the perception of those who lovingly retrieved, catalogued, and preserved them in later generations. Probably the best-known example of this lies in William Wordsworth's *White Doe of Rylstone; or The Fate of the Nortons* (1807). Wordsworth latched onto the rebellion as recorded in the ballads to elaborate on a northern legend of a white doe that had returned each Sunday to a parish church to lay beside a rocky mound. In Wordsworth's poem, the doe had been raised by Emily Norton, daughter of old Sir Richard and sister of his many sons, "doomed to be/ The last leaf on a blasted tree." A symbol of the comforts of memory and imagination to the desolate, the doe returned to console Emily after she lost all in the rebellion, becoming "Her only unextinguished light/ Her last companion in a dearth/ Of love, upon a hopeless earth." To set up Emily's crisis, the poem explored the romantic tragedy of chivalrous men dying in a doomed defense of an ancient faith. As men of all sorts flocked to the banner sewn by Emily, her father exclaimed:

> "...With festive din
> Lo! how the people are flocking in, –
> Like hungry fowl to the feeder's hand
> When snow lies heavy upon the land."
> He spake bare truth; for far and near
> From every side came noisy swarms
> Of Peasants in their homely gear;
> And, mixed with these, to Brancepeth came
> Grave Gentry of estate and name,

And Captains known for worth in arms

And prayed the Earls in self-defence
To rise, and prove their innocence.–
"Rise, noble Earls, put forth your might
For holy Church, and the People's right!" ...

He took the Banner, and unfurled
The precious folds – "behold," said he,
"The ransom of a sinful world;
Let this your preservation be;
The wounds of hands and feet and side,
And the sacred Cross on which Jesus died!"[1]

Wordsworth added to his tale of ancient families and doomed causes a measure of the broader, popular appeal of the religious element. He made clear his borrowings from local histories, legends, and ballads in an afterword. When Sir Walter Scott tried correcting some of the poem's factual inaccuracies, pointing out that most of the Nortons fled rather than died, for instance, Wordsworth responded: "I have followed (as I was in duty bound to do) the traditionary and common historic records...Therefore I shall say in this case, a plague upon your industrious Antiquarianism that has put my fine story to confusion."[2] Whether his poem reflects an earlier "social memory" of the revolt is unknowable. Yet, while obviously an overly romanticized account with few pretensions to historical accuracy, in some ways it strikes a truer note than much other early writing on the rebellion.

In the nineteenth century, the romantic engagement with the past was accompanied by two further developments that affected understandings of the rebellion's place in history. The first was the revival of Catholicism. Despite heated controversy, in 1829, the Emancipation Act lifted most civil and legal disabilities from Catholics and in 1850 the church hierarchy was restored. In the many anti-Catholic speeches and publications that greeted these changes, past instances of papal attempts to undermine the royal supremacy received a fresh airing. The anniversary of the Gunpowder Plot, for instance, had rather louder crowds than usual in 1850.[3] So, too, did Catholic characterizations of the rebels of 1569 as martyrs for their faith reappear. Attempts to have some of the rebels formally recognized as martyrs had continued intermittently over the years. Now, with new impetus and better resources – and less need to insist upon loyalty – the cause revived in 1855. After a lengthy investigation, Felton, Plumtree, and the earl of Northumberland were declared

Beati in 1888; that is, not canonized as saints but recognized as men of special status owed special honor in their localities. The Blessed Thomas Percy's festival was thenceforth to be celebrated every November 14 in the Catholic diocese of Hexham and Newcastle. Eight others of the rebels were listed among the *Praetermissi*, people who might possibly be worthy but requiring further investigation.[4]

The other nineteenth-century development was the rise of professional, academic historical writing. Despite its efforts to be scientific, dispassionate, and objective, initially this new mode of engagement with the past could barely help but be guided by the narratives earlier writers had offered. The religious aspect of the revolt was at first preserved, and came to signify either the weakness of the Protestant Reformation or its strength, depending on whether one focused on the rebellion's occurrence or its short duration. Soon, however, came a shift to a secular, political explanation that must have seemed to some a welcome change, but oddly enough one that recapitulated the essentials of the crown's depiction of the revolt at the time of the fighting. Perhaps due in part to increasing secularism or skepticism, the religious explanations fell from vogue and with them, any notice of the rank and file as willing actors. Surely, something more substantial, more material, must have lain behind the rebellion? Nor did the rise of social history in 1960s and 1970s challenge the premise of this recharacterization. This first generation of social historians reexamined many of the rebellions of the pre-modern period as part of their project to rescue the nameless from "the condescension of posterity." But the rebellion of 1569 must have seemed an unattractive prospect. It was, after all, a revolt led by two earls, paragons of the feudal class, and in which no expression of "independent social grievances" could be found. Since this was no longer a religious rising, feudal tenant loyalty came to serve as an explanation for why rebels joined. Such dismissals, shared by political and social historians alike, also drew support from a prevailing view of the north as a "dark, backwards corner" of the realm.

Yet, more recent historical research has undermined theories of northern exceptionalism, and in our own day, it is perhaps easier to accept that religious beliefs can move people of all sorts to action, for good or for ill. In his survey of late medieval and early modern revolts, Norman Housley has counseled against seeing the religious rhetoric, badges, and actions of rebels merely as ways to legitimize or justify protest for other ends, "for there are signs that religious belief was present, as a force shaping behaviour rather than just validating it."[5] Religious beliefs, in all their degrees and depths, were not somehow extraneous to or masks for "real" motives. That said, an insistence upon the formative role of religion in this and other revolts should not be seen as a critique of social history. Social historians long ago showed that riots and protests were not just unmediated, knee-jerk reactions to economic stimuli; by returning to the possibility of principled conflict and expanding our notion of the principles that might move common men and women to act, we may do more to revive a genuine social history that finds self-directed action with transformative potential, rather than just pragmatic calculated negotiation, even outside the manifestly "social" riots and revolts. Even in such ostensibly unattractive terrain for the social historian as a religious revolt directed by two earls, we see acts that cannot be dismissed as mere manipulation.

The evidence presented throughout this book does, I think, support the characterization of the rebels' involvement as conscious and willing, rather than instinctive responses to the call of their feudal lords, whether it be the earls' attempts to persuade people to join, the profile of the rebels' social and geographic origins, the worried statements of loyalists that too many joined willingly, the ferocity with which the rank and file were punished, or the determination with which the crown and allied polemicists sought to dissuade them. The context in which the rebellion occurred, the rhetoric chosen by rebel earls and loyal writers to persuade and cajole, and the actions and symbols seen in the revolt all argue for the importance of faith in moving men to participate, whether that faith consisted of a deep, doctrinal commitment to papal supremacy or a more straightforward preference for the old ways. The rebels acted on a range of motivations, not just religious but not just tenant loyalty either. Much the same can be said of those who chose not to rise; surely, we can leave aside suggestions that because not all traditionalists or Catholics joined, the rebellion cannot be characterized as having religious motivations. Loyalty to the old faith remained a strong force, but so too did a sense of loyalty to the crown, a habit of obedience, a preference for peace, and a fear of punishment.

Recognizing the active, willing participation of the rank and file, and the significance of faith for many of them, allows us to refine our own understanding of the rebellion's place in history. The rebellion of 1569 has sometimes been seen as the last of its kind; one of the appealing aspects of the neo-feudal explanation was that it seemed to explain the end of a particular style of revolt that drew lords and commoners together in a common effort by reference to the end of the feudal social formation that had sustained it. This is debateable in several respects. One might point to Monmouth's rebellion in 1685, in which some 3000 men of the lower orders volunteered to help the Protestant duke take the throne; its most recent historian describes it as the "last popular rebellion."[6] On the other hand, one might look to the lords who raised their tenantry to fight in the Civil Wars of the 1640s, or to the northern "aristocratic" insurrections that accompanied the Revolution of 1688.[7] But there was a significant pause, at least – a reduction in the frequency of major revolts and a long hiatus in any joint action of lords and commons after 1569. Collective action has a history of its own. As Charles Tilly and others have demonstrated, the "repertoires of contention" vary over time, in ways linked to the long, slow changes in economic and state forms and the culture that embodies those forms of power and constitutes social order. Arguably, the most significant transformation in the forms of collective action had to await the late eighteenth and nineteenth centuries, with the demonstrations and petitioning campaigns of mass politics or strikes and industrial action of a new economic age. What we see earlier are variations on old themes, uneven movements from one phase to another within a particular epoch rather than transitions from one historical epoch to the next.[8]

In some ways, the rebellion of 1569 resembled many of its predecessors quite closely. Like rebels before them, this group included a mix of lords and commoners that replicated the traditional social hierarchy, limited their violence and directed it primarily at property rather than persons, and made protestations of a fundamental loyalty and desire to correct and restore rather than overturn. The biggest differences lie in the responses of the crown. Drawing perhaps on experiences in Ireland and the earlier English revolts of 1536 and 1549, and from the contemporary climate of confessionalized antagonisms, the Elizabethan regime turned its back on earlier responses to revolt. Unlike previous rebellions, this one did not see repeated offers of mercy used as a means of negotiation and resolution. This one, instead, saw from the beginning the crown's determination "to invade, resist, repress, subdue, slay, kill, and put to execution of death by all ways and means."[9]

In their study of Tudor rebellions, Fletcher and MacCulloch note that the Elizabethan years saw little rebellion in comparison with the rest of the century. They observe that the Northern Rebellion of 1569 posed the only such serious threat and ask, "What was the recipe for neutralizing the rebellious instinct?...Why did the situation change after 1569?" Many of the ingredients, they argue, were contributed by Elizabeth herself. She refused to force a fundamental, much needed reform of taxation, a decision that left many problems for her successors but that avoided confrontation in the short term. They also emphasize that Elizabeth was simply better at the arts of governance than her predecessors had been: she more skillfully directed the public theatre of politics, constructed an imposing and yet sympathetic image of herself, played up the rhetoric of obedience, and generally showed herself more responsive to the demands of her subjects.[10] All of this is true. And as this study of the one serious revolt in Elizabethan England shows, she was also highly attentive to the potential that lay in the physical, material, and financial repression of "the rebellious instinct." The punishment of the rebels did much to limit the material ability of the former rebels to renew revolt, and provided encouragement for future obedience. Elizabeth was able to turn the rebellion to her financial and political advantage, extracting from it resources to cement or at least encourage the loyalty of others.

MacCulloch and Fletcher suggest two further explanations for the taming of the "rebellious instinct": part of the credit belonged to social changes that drew the yeomanry closer in material interest and intellectual inclination to their social superiors and away from the masses beneath them, and part belonged to accidents of international politics that promoted a greater sense of national loyalty. One wonders if this process of social distancing might have been speeded by members of the lower orders separating themselves from their superiors, too. Yes, one finds plenty of evidence for the continued strength of commoners' respect for their lords, for men's willingness to fight under their lords' command and to look to them to legitimize and enable protest: the Norfolk men who wanted to protect their duke, the Essex men who awaited the return of Westmorland to lead them against Elizabeth, the northern gentlemen who believed the leadership of at least one of their earls necessary before rising, and, of course, the bulk of the 1569 rebels themselves. Yet, there are hints, too, of a certain skepticism and suspicion, such as the rebels who feared early on that their lords would abandon them "in the briars" and the ballad singers who denounced the earls' treachery. Elizabeth and her agents certainly thought this skepticism worth encouragement; witness the many injunctions that the common man use his own judgment to detect "feigned nobility." As for the "accidents" of international politics that fostered a greater sense of national loyalty, the most potent of these emerged from the rebellion itself: the papal excommunication and the ways it solidified emerging new identities and loyalties. The "tolerant confusion" of the first years of Elizabeth's reign had eroded over the 1560s, an erosion that helped trigger the rebellion and would in turn be speeded by it. Spurred by the northern rebels, Pope Pius V finally issued his excommunication of the

Queen; spurred by the northern rebels, crown and parliament issued new definitions of treason, endorsed firmer doctrinal standards, and more firmly linked Protestant and English identities. Social hierarchies were slowly being supplemented or indeed supplanted by binary divisions. In the short term, however, a different binary division dominated: Protestant and Catholic came to denote inherently oppositional groups locked into an enduring and recurring struggle, representing all virtues and vices respectively, including obedience and disobedience, loyalty and disloyalty.

Together, all these elements suggest ways in which the 1569 rebellion remained, for many years, the last of its kind not because of factors extrinsic to it but because of the particular conjunction of actions, structures, and meanings that made it the event it was. As an "event," it was not just a symptom of broader changes and processes, but a formative moment in its own right, both a culmination and a beginning. This is not to say that the rebellion happened within a system capable of containing all subversion and drawing benefits from all instances of dissent; but this particular event was a rupture that closed off one set of circumstances while opening others, creating a new context for both obedience and dissent. One might point to the ways in which Elizabeth's efforts to defeat this rebellion and to benefit from it also contained the potential for future problems, such as the collaboration with men who had developed coherent justifications for overthrowing their own anointed Queen, the alienation of land to secure support and the reliance upon fortuitous revenues like forfeitures rather than effecting necessary fiscal reforms, or the creation of Protestant narratives of divine deliverance that could be turned against the crown. But all these problems would await a later day. In the short term, the Northern Rebellion closed off the possibilities for one type of protest and strengthened the Elizabethan regime. As such, it marked both a beginning and an end.

Notes

Preface

1. Strong, "Popular Celebration," p. 88.
2. Abrams, *Historical Sociology*, p. 192.

Introduction

1. Raine, *Depositions...From the Courts of Durham*, p. 160.
2. SP 15/15, no. 29(i).
3. Norton, "A Warning Against the Dangerous Practises of Papists," sig. A5v; Strype, *Annals*, I, ii, p. 323; SP 15/17, nos. 72 and 73.
4. DUL DDR/EJ.CCD/1/2, f. 195;DDCL Raine MS. 124, ff. 180–82d. Most of the relevant Durham material is included in Raine, *Depositions...From the Courts of Durham*.
5. *CPR Elizabeth I*, vol. VI, no. 1230.
6. Corporation of London Record Office, Repertories of the Court of Aldermen, vol. 16, fol. 520d.
7. Reid, "Rebellion of the Earls," pp. 171–203; MacCaffrey, *Elizabethan Regime*, p. 337; Wood, *Riot, Rebellion and Popular Politics*, pp. 72–3. Diarmaid MacCulloch and Anthony Fletcher differ somewhat in allowing that bastard feudal tenant loyalty had to be reinforced by "religious propaganda" to gather forces, but offer an explanation that remains focused on the lords and politics: The earls rebelled because denied the place in central affairs they thought rightfully theirs, and the significance of their failed efforts lie primarily in proving "that northern feudalism and particularism could no longer rival Tudor centralization": *Tudor Rebellions*, pp. 102–16.
8. James, "Concept of Order," p. 83. See also Meikle, "Godly Rogue," p. 139. Meikle notes that Lord Hunsdon's oft-quoted statement that the north "knew no prince but a Percy" should not be taken as accurate but rather as a "desperate plea for more military aid at the height of the rebellion."
9. Taylor, "Crown and the North of England." More accessible summaries of Taylor's findings can be found in Wall, *Power and Protest*, pp. 174–7, and Haigh, *English Reformations*, p. 260.
10. Elton, "Politics and the Pilgrimage," in *After the Reformation*, ed. B. Malament (London, 1979) and *Reform and Reformation*, pp. 260–70.
11. Davies "Popular Religion," pp. 90–1. See also Davies, "Pilgrimage of Grace Reconsidered," pp. 39–64.
12. Hoyle, *Pilgrimage of Grace*.
13. The literature on popular politics is now vast, but see for instance: Wood, *Riot, Rebellion and Popular Politics*; Braddick and Walter, *Negotiating Power*; and Shagan, *Popular Politics*.
14. Bernard, *King's Reformation*, pp. 293–404.

15. Davies, "Popular Religion," p. 59.
16. Loades, *Conspiracies*; Thorp, "Religion and the Wyatt Rebellion," pp. 363–80; Robison, "Wyatt's Rebellion in Surrey," pp. 769–90.
17. Pittock, *Jacobitism*, pp. 114–15.
18. Sharp, *Memorials*; reprinted with a new foreword by Robert Wood as *The Rising in the North: The 1569 Rebellion*. Sharp's book is an impressive feat of collection, including not just the papers of Sir George Bowes but also those found in other collections that pertained to the story. Although I have gone to the original documents in most cases, Sharp's book remains an invaluable aid.
19. Sharp, *Memorials*, pp. 61–3; BL Caligula B.IX, ii, f. 425.
20. SP 15/15, no. 30. See also SP 15/15, no. 41.
21. See, for example, Davies, "Popular Religion," pp. 58–91; Collinson, *Protestant England*, pp. 127–55; Walter, *Understanding Popular Violence*.
22. Fletcher and MacCulloch, *Tudor Rebellions*, pp. 6–7.

1   An Impending Crisis?

1. Cressy, *Agnes Bowker's Cat*, pp. 21–2.
2. Bullein, *A Dialogue ... Against the Fever Pestilence*, p. 107.
3. Anonymous, *Monstrous Child*.
4. Bodleian Library MS Eng Hist e. 198: William Woodwall, *The Acts of Queen Elizabeth Allegorized*, fols. 8–19d.
5. Woodwall, *Allegorized*, fol. 7.
6. Anonymous, *Meruaylous Straunge*. See also Brammall, "Monstrous Metamorphosis," pp. 3–21.
7. Strype, *Annals*, vol. 1, pt. 2, p. 346.
8. C 66/1073, m. 31 (*CPR Elizabeth I*, vol. V, no. 1818).
9. "Enclosure Riots at Chinley," pp. 61–8; Tawney, *Agrarian Problem*, pp. 327–9.
10. Thomas, *Religion and the Decline of Magic*, p. 404.
11. For the laws against the use of prophecy in protest, see 33 Henry VIII c. 14; 3 & 4 Edward VI c. 15; 5 Elizabeth I, cc. 15, 16; 23 Elizabeth I c. 2. See also Kesselring, "Deference and Dissent," pp. 1–16 and van Patten, "Magic, Prophecy, and the Law of Treason," pp. 1–32.
12. E 164/37, fol. 19d.
13. SP 15/14, no. 87; BL Cotton MS Titus F. III, fols. 112–14, 123.
14. SP 12/194, no. 75 (f. 159).
15. Slack, "Vagrants," p. 360. For the searches of 1569–72, see Beier, "Vagrancy," pp. 3–29.
16. Tawney and Power, *Tudor Economic Documents*, I, p. 325.
17. SP 15/14, no. 79; Corporation of London Record Office, Journal of the Court of Common Council, JORS 19, fols. 171d–174d.
18. SP 15/11/45; see also Wark, *Recusancy in Cheshire*, p. 2
19. Kemp, *John Fisher*, pp. 3–4, 113–15, quoted in Beier, "Vagrancy," p. 16.
20. BIHR HC.CP 1570/5.
21. See Shagan, *Popular Politics* and Whiting, *Blind Devotion*.
22. Pollard, *Tudor Treatises*, vol. 125, pp. 110, 125, 142.

23. Taylor, *Very Old Man*, sig. D3r.
24. Peters, *Patterns of Piety*; J. Maltby, *Prayer Book*; Walsham, *Providence*; for a particularly strong case for adaptation, although in a different context, see Todd, *Culture of Protestantism*.
25. Jones, *The English Reformation* and "Living the Reformation," pp. 273–88.
26. Jones, *Birth of the Elizabethan Age*, pp. 17–47.
27. See, for instance, Baskerville, "Religious Disturbance," pp. 340–48.
28. Fisher, "Coercion and Religious Conformity," pp. 305–24.
29. Foster, *Churchwardens' Accounts...Cambridge*, p. 164.
30. Drew, *Lambeth Churchwardens Accounts*, vol. 1, pp. 100–101.
31. Haugaard, *English Reformation*, p. 141; Aston, *England's Iconoclasts*, vol. 1, esp. p. 304; Litzenberger, *Reformation and the Laity*.
32. SP 12/18, no. 21.
33. SP 12/46, no. 33.
34. Haigh, *Reformation and Resistance*, pp. 210–23.
35. Green, "Mr. William Whittingham deane of Durham."
36. Marcombe, "Rude and Heady," pp. 117–51; Marcombe, "Dean and Chapter," p. 182.
37. SP 12/20, no. 25
38. Fowler, *The Rites of Durham*, pp. 23, 95; Marcombe, "Rude and Heady," p. 134.
39. DDCL Raine MS. 124, f. 52b.
40. *Works of Pilkington*, p. 129; quoted in Marcombe, "Rude and Heady," p. 134.
41. Bateson, "Original Letters," p. 64; SP 15/12, no. 108.
42. Bateson, "Original Letters," p. 67.
43. Marcombe, "Dean and Chapter," pp. 187–9.
44. BIHR HC.A.B. 3 fols. 169–75d, pp. 104–5.
45. Cheshire and Chester Record Office, EDA 12/2, fols. 122–122d.
46. BIHR HC.A.B. 3, fols. 189–90; HC.A.B. 4, fol. 24b; V. 1567–68 CB1, fols. 102d, 105–105d, 148d.
47. BIHR V. 1567–68, CB1, fols. 42–4, 203; CB2, fols. 36, 83.
48. See in particular Alford, *Succession* and also Thorp, "William Cecil," pp. 289–304 and Thorp, "Catholic Conspiracy," pp. 431–48. Alford and Thorp modify the older view of Cecil as a *politique*, most cogently presented in the works of Conyers Read.
49. Alford, *Succession*, pp. 27–8.
50. BL Cotton Caligula C.I, fol. 76.
51. Memo of 1568: BL Cotton Caligula C.1. fols. 76 ff; from summer of 1569: SP 12/51, fols. 9r-13v; Haynes, pp. 579–88. See also Alford's discussion of these memos and their significance; *Succession*, pp. 182–4.
52. Wormald, *Mary, Queen of Scots*; Wormald, "Politics and Government of Scotland," p. 153.
53. Guy, *Queen of Scots*; Warnicke, *Mary Queen of Scots*. There is dispute even about how to spell Mary's family name. She herself used "Stuart," in deference perhaps to the French, but Scottish historians tend to prefer the original "Stewart" spelling.
54. Guy, *Queen of Scots*, pp. 164, 184.
55. Guy, *Queen of Scots*, pp. 187–99.
56. Guy, *Queen of Scots*, pp. 266–8.

57. KB 8/40; Jones, "Defining Superstitions," pp. 187–203.
58. BL Cotton Caligula C.1, fols. 139–140.
59. BL Cotton Caligula C.1, fols. 76d, 98, and see Alford, *Succession*, pp. 166ff.
60. See Donaldson, *First Trial*, pp. 132–3.
61. Alford, *Succession*, p. 175; Guy, *Queen of Scots*, p. 418.
62. Quoted in Guy, *Queen of Scots*, p. 423.
63. *CSP Spanish*, II, no. 38 (p. 53).
64. Wernham, *Foreign Policy*, p. 34. Philip's "Iron Duke" often goes by "Alva" in English writing, but here I have followed the example of Geoffrey Parker and William Maltby in opting for the alternate spelling.
65. *CSP Spanish*, II, no. 20 (p. 29).
66. Maltby, *Alba*, p. 183.
67. Parker, *Grand Strategy*, pp. 155–9; Read, "Pay-Ships," pp. 443–64. But see also Ramsay, who argues that English intent in removing the money from the ships was still unclear and possibly benign before de Spes overreacted and took the crisis to the next level: *Queen's Merchants*, pp. 90–111.
68. Quoted in Alford, *Succession*, p. 187.
69. MacCaffrey, *Elizabethan Regime*, p. 282; Calder, *Revolutionary Empire*, pp. 69–70.
70. Quoted in MacCaffrey, *Elizabethan Regime*, p. 282.
71. Quoted in Parker, *Grand Strategy*, p. 157 from Don Francis de Alava y Beamonte, *Correspondencia inedita*, pp. 301–2, 317.
72. Parker, *Grand Strategy*, p. 159.
73. Parker, *Grand Strategy*, p. 158; *Relations politiques des Pays-Bas et d'Angleterre*, V, pp. 479, 508, 510, 539, 603; *CSP... Rome*, I, nos. 632, 638, 684. In February 1570, Philip did send a man ("Kempe") to assist the rebels and set aside money for their use, but by then of course, such aid was too late for the English rebellion. In August, he told the papal nuncio that it was too late to aid the rebels, but he would continue to await a good opportunity.
74. Meyer, *Catholic Church*, p. 56
75. Lemaitre, *Saint Pie V*, p. 296 and passim; Pastor, *Popes*, vol. 18, pp. 196–99; Laderchi, *Annales Ecclesiastici*, 1569, no. 270.
76. Alford, *Succession*; see also Anne McLaren, who discusses the broad "legitimist middle ground" of support for Mary's right to succeed Elizabeth that had to be actively campaigned against by Cecil, and the likely attractiveness of the Norfolk marriage plan to a range of Protestants: "Gender, Religion, and Early Modern Nationalism."
77. Haynes, *State Papers*, p. 509.
78. Haynes, *State Papers*, p. 572.
79. Haynes, *State Papers*, pp. 541–3.
80. Haynes, *State Papers*, p. 535.
81. See in particular Adams, "Eliza Enthroned?" pp. 55–77 and "Favourites and Factions," pp. 253–74, and more recently, Mears, *Queenship and Political Discourse*.
82. Alford, *Succession*, pp. 30, 185–6.
83. BL Salisbury MS vol. 4, fols. 134–134d; BL Cotton Titus B.II, fol. 338; BL Lansdowne 102, fol. 143d (no. 78); see MacCaffrey, *Elizabethan Regime*, pp. 316ff.
84. BL Salisbury MS vol. 156, nos. 95–6 (Haynes, *State Papers*, p. 549).

85. BL Salisbury MS vol. 5, nos. 7–8.
86. Sharp, *Memorials*, p. xvii; SP 59/16, f. 84.
87. Pembroke, at least, very quickly earned full forgiveness as he was appointed to command the Queen's personal guard during the rebellion. (*Sadler Papers*, II, p. 41.)
88. It was the report of a rising, not the investigation into the marriage plan, that prompted their call to court. See: BL Cotton Caligula C.I, fol. 472.
89. For Irish history in this period, see particularly: Ellis, *Age of the Tudors*; Brady, *Chief Governors*; Canny, *Conquest of Ireland*; and finally, although outdated in some respects, Bagwell, *Ireland Under the Tudors*, II, pp. 146–233.
90. BL Cotton Caligula B. IX, fol. 34, cited in Dawson, *Earl of Argyll*, p. 2. This paragraph and the one that follows draw heavily from Dawson.
91. BL Lansdowne 102 no. 71.
92. Dawson, *Earl of Argyll*, pp. 158, 167.
93. Dawson, *Earl of Argyll*, p. 164.
94. SP 63/26, no. 18.
95. BL Cotton Caligula C.I, fol. 100d.
96. SP 63/24, no. 16.
97. SP 63/23, no. 28.
98. In addition to the standard texts on sixteenth-century Irish history cited above, this paragraph and the one that follows draw heavily from David Edwards, "Butler Revolt," pp. 228–55 and Sasso, "Desmond."
99. Edwards, "Counter-Reformation," p. 322.
100. See Binchy, "Irish Ambassador," pp. 353–74, 573–84; quotes at pp. 364–5.
101. *CSP Spanish*, II, no. 158 (210).
102. Lyons, *Franco-Irish Relations*, p. 135.
103. SP 63/29, fol. 2.
104. SP 63/29, no. 8; Sasso, "Desmond," p. 127.
105. SP 63/29, fol. 50. Edmund Butler later claimed to have disagreed with Fitzmaurice's religious aims, but David Edwards finds reasons to doubt his protestations of innocence; "Butler Revolt," pp. 247–8.
106. See Churchyard, *General Rehersall of Warres*, sig. Q3v.
107. Sasso, "Desmond," pp. 160, 172.
108. Alford, *Succession*, p. 189.
109. BL Cotton Caligula C.I, fol. 465.

2   The Rebellion in the North

1. Anonymous, *False Rumours*.
2. SP 15/23, nos. 41, 41(i); SP 12/83, no. 28; BL Lansdowne 15, no. 95.
3. Haynes, *State Papers*, p. 538.
4. Phillips, *Frendly Larum*, title page and sig. A6v.
5. Norton, *All Such Treatises*, sig. H3v.
6. See Reid, "Rebellion of the Earls," pp. 178, 201–3; Reid, *Council in the North*, pp. 192, 199; E 134/12 Eliz/Trin 3. The copper mine dispute is sometimes erroneously dated to 1569, but as M.E. James noted, the case began in 1566, and judgment was given in the early months of 1568; "Concept of Order," 79 n. 135 and Plowden, *Commentaries* (London, 1761), p. 310. See also:

Meikle, "Godly Rogue," pp. 126–63; Hoyle, "Faction, Feud, and Reconciliation," pp. 590–613; and James, *Family, Lineage and Civil Society.*

7. Neale, *Elizabeth I and her Parliaments*, I, p. 117; Lock, "Percy, Thomas."
8. E 178/752.
9. Marcombe, "Rude and Heady," p. 128.
10. Marcombe, "Rude and Heady," passim.
11. Marcombe, "Rude and Heady," p. 125.
12. Reid, *Council in the North*, pp. 192, 200–1. See also Haynes, p. 445.
13. Ormsby, *Lord William Howard of Naworth*, pp. xi–xii, 365–409.
14. Bodleian Library, Tanner MS 50, no. 20. There is corroboration for enough parts of Bishop's tale to lend credence to the whole; see, for instance, Haynes, *State Papers*, p. 594; Murdin, *State Papers*, pp. 30–32; and SP 12/67, no. 59. On Bishop, an ardent Marian and perennial plotter, see Pollitt, "Old Practizer," pp. 59–84.
15. Sharp, *Memorials*, pp. 192–3 (Northumberland's confession).
16. SP 15/21, no. 56.1; reprinted in Sharp, *Memorials*, pp. 189–213. See also Norfolk's account of his dealings with the rebel earls: BL Cotton Caligula C.I, fols. 482–4.
17. *CSP Spanish*, II, pp. 96, 111, 136, 141, 145–7, 152, 164, 167, 171, 183, 186, 189.
18. National Library of Scotland Adv. MS 35.4.1, p. 25d (another copy is in BL Cotton Caligula C.4).
19. Murdin, *State Papers*, p. 42.
20. Sharp, *Memorials*, p. 196. (Northumberland's confession).
21. Sharp, *Memorials*, pp. 196–7 (Northumberland's confession).
22. Sharp, Memorials, p. 213 (Northumberland's confession). These were just some of the forty-one books written by Catholic exiles in the heated controversy between Harding and Bishop John Jewel. Nicholas Sander later claimed that some 20 000 copies of these works had been smuggled into England between 1564 and 1567. Pollen, *English Catholics*, p. 111.
23. SP 15/21, no. 29 (Sharp, *Memorials*, p. 281).
24. SP 15/14, nos. 90, 94, 98, 99; Bodleian Library Tanner MS 50 no. 20.
25. SP 15/15, no. 4 (i).
26. SP 15/15, nos. 18 and 18 (i).
27. Sharp, *Memorials*, p. 199 (Northumberland's confession).
28. Sharp, *Memorials*, p. 199. She, of course, later denied doing any such thing. It does seem somewhat incongruous, considering her ostensible Protestantism and that her brother, the duke of Norfolk, had asked them not to rise for fear of losing his head, something she should not have taken lightly as their father had previously been executed for treason. Others besides Northumberland, however, reported that she was at the least a "stiffener" of her husband's resolve.
29. Sharp, *Memorials*, pp. 199–200.
30. Bond, "An Exhortation to Obedience," p. 164.
31. For a discussion of the force of hierarchy and obedience in early modern England, see Marsh, "Order and Place," pp. 3–26.
32. Pastor, *Popes*, vol. 18, pp. 202–203, citing a letter from Nicholas Sander dated March 15, 1570 in the Graziani Archives, Citta del Castello, Instrutt., I., 26.
33. *Calendar of State Papers...Rome*, I, nos. 647, 649.

34. SP 15/15, no. 29 (i) and with minor variations elsewhere, that is, handwritten on the copy of the Queen's responding proclamation microfilmed as STC # 12 779.
35. BL Harleian MS 6990, fol. 44; printed in Sharp, *Memorials*, pp. 42–3.
36. Raine, *Dr. Matthew Hutton*, vol. 17, pp. 267–8.
37. Sharp, *Memorials*, p. 185; James, "Concept of Order," p. 70.
38. James, "Concept of Order," pp. 70–73.
39. On these men, see Sharp, *Memorials*, pp. 40, 59.
40. E 164/138, Homberston's survey of rebel property, compared with the list of rebels and their places of origin. The rebel list was compiled primarily from the list of men pardoned, included in the *CPR, Elizabeth*, vol. V, pp. 81–114; a list of rebels fined, in E 137/133/1; and various lists prepared for or by Sir George Bowes in his post-rebellion capacity as provost marshal, most significantly those in Strathmore Estates (Glamis Castle) Bowes MS vols. 13–15, but also BL Add MS 40746 fol. 23ff and DUL MS 534 Bowes Papers. The fines list is the most complete, but there are several hundred individuals who appear in only one or the other of the two other sets of names. Once duplications between the lists are eliminated, a total of 5561 names remain. (With all the opportunities for error in deciphering the handwritten names and entering them into the database, I was quite happy to find my total accord so nicely with Taylor's. She too found a total of 5561, but acknowledging that some might still be duplications allowed for a range between 5513–5561.) Of these, 4525 had places of origin that I felt could be identified and mapped with confidence. While the remainder could usually be located in either Yorkshire or Durham due to the organization of the original lists, if the precise location could not be identified the individual was not included on the map or list of known origins. As the references in the text to 6000+ rebels at any given point, with continual additions and defections, suggests, this is not a complete list of all rebels. Those from Tynedale and Redesdale, and those who joined late and briefly from Cumberland, are notably lacking. Yet, it is more than adequate for the sorts of general conclusions made here.
41. Taylor, "Crown and the North of England," pp. 216–19, 250–2. Taylor compared the lists of rebels with the muster lists produced the previous summer and the crown surveys of rebel lands in early 1570. Only 12–14% of rebels' names could be identified as tenants. Allowing that sons rather than the tenants themselves might have fulfilled tenurial obligations, Taylor included anyone of the same surname and township in her searches and concluded that of the Yorkshire and Durham rebels, 15.6 and 19.4%, respectively, could have had any tenurial connections with rebel leaders.
42. For the mustering of the Pilgrim hosts, see Bush, *Pilgrimage*.
43. SP 59/20, fol. 115.
44. SP 15/15, nos. 30, 31.
45. BL Cotton Caligula B.IX vol. 2, fols. 425–425d.
46. BL Cotton Caligula B.IX vol. 2, fols. 425–425d.
47. Unfortunately, I have not been able to locate a copy of the rebel oath; a clause in their oath of submission makes it clear, however, that such an oath was taken.
48. SP 15/15, nos. 71, 73.

49. SP 15/15, no. 44; Bush, *Pilgrimage*, p. 57.
50. For some unknown reason, Bowes's lists identify only the Yorkshire constables as such, although other records clarify that the Durham rebels often came accompanied by their village constables as well.
51. Kent, *Village Constable.*
52. Bowes Museum Bowes MS no. 45xx; BL Cotton Caligula B.IX vol. 2, fol. 425.
53. BL Cotton Caligula B.IX vol. 2, fols. 425–426; Sharp, *Memorials*, p. 63.
54. Sharp, *Memorials*, p. 62.
55. Pardon list, compared with leases in North Yorkshire Record Office DC/RMB 1/2, 4/2, 5/9.
56. Wenham, "The Chantries...of Richmond," pp. 97–111, 185–214, 310–22, esp. p. 99.
57. See, for example, Cheshire and Chester Record Office EDA 12/2 fols. 122–122d.
58. SP 15/17, no. 6. The sender's name is torn off, but the tone and language correspond with Wharton's other missives.
59. Foley, *Society of Jesus*, i., pp. 232–3; see Wenham, "The Chantries...of Richmond." Also: E 178/2552 m. 17.
60. SP 15/15/30. See also SP 15/15/41.
61. Norton, "A warning against the dangerous practices of papists," sig. A5v; Strype, *Annals*, I, ii, p. 323; SP 15/17, nos. 72, 73.
62. *Zurich Letters*, pp. 215, 218; SP 15/17, nos. 72, 73.
63. See Tyerman, *Crusades*, pp. 3, 343–67. Michael Bush and J.P.D. Cooper have explored the imagery and theatrics of earlier protests: Cooper, *Propaganda and the Tudor State*, pp. 118–19; Bush, "Pilgrim Tradition," pp. 178–98.
64. For the constitutive properties of dress in early modern England, see Jones and Stallybrass, *Renaissance Clothing.*
65. As Tyerman notes, the story of Constantine had remained readily available, at least until mid-century, in traditional and popular works such as James of Voragine's *Golden Legend*. (Ibid., p. 364.) The story and banner may also have had a newer resonance: several Protestant writers had depicted Elizabeth as the new Constantine and compared the conversion of the English to that of the great emperor. See Pucci, "Reforming Roman Emperors."
66. BIHR HC.CP 1570, 2.
67. Hussey, "Archbishop Parker's Visitation," p. 114.
68. Haigh, *Reformation and Resistance*, p. 221. For other instances of hostility to clerical wives, see Carlson, "Clerical Marriage," p. 7.
69. Haugaard, *English Reformation*, pp. 200–5. Brett Usher notes that Elizabeth's opposition to clerical marriage can too easily be exaggerated, and points out that however deep it may have been, it had little effect on clerical appointments: "Mrs Bishop," pp. 200–20.
70. Prior, "Crucified Marriages," p. 125.
71. Parish, *Clerical Marriage*, p. 183.
72. Kitching, *Royal Visitation of 1559*, p. xxv.
73. See, for example, Bannatyne, *Transactions in Scotland*, p. 2.
74. BIHR HC.AB 5; DUL DDR/EJ/CCD/1/2 fols. 170–200d; DDCL Raine MS. 124. Most of the Durham incidents are included in Raine, *Depositions...from the Courts of Durham.*
75. DDCL Raine MS. 124, f. 52b.

76. DDCL Raine MS. 124, f. 108.
77. On the varieties of "conservatism," see Shagan, "Rumours and Popular Politics."
78. DUL DDR/EJ.CCD/1/2, f. 195; DDCL Raine MS. 124, fols. 180–182d.
79. See, for example, DUL DDR/EJ/CCD/1/2, fols. 172d–173.
80. DUL DDR/EJ/CCD/1/2, fols. 170–171, 200d.
81. British Library Add Ms. 40746, f. 21; DUL DDR/EJ/CCD/1/2, fols. 179d–180d. On parish support for 1549 rebels, see Duffy, *Voices of Morebath*, pp. 134–40.
82. See, for instance, Fletcher and MacCulloch, *Tudor Rebellions*, p. 114.
83. Raine, *Depositions ... from the Courts of Durham*, pp. 138, 157, 158, 160, 177, 180, 200–201.
84. Whiting, "Abominable Idols," pp. 46–7.
85. DUL DDR/EJ/CCD/1/2 f. 195b.
86. DUL DDR/EJ/CCD/1/2 f. 193b.
87. Davis, "Rites of Violence," pp. 51–91; Crouzet, *Les Guerriers de Dieu*.
88. See Manning, "Patterns of Violence," pp. 120–33; Manning, "Violence and Social Conflict," pp. 18–40; James, *Society, Politics, and Culture*, pp. 333ff.
89. Sharp, *Memorials*, p. 209 (Northumberland's confession).
90. Bush, *Pilgrimage*, p. 56.
91. Sharp, *Memorials*, p. 183.
92. BL Cotton Caligula B.IX vol. 2, fol. 425; Harleian 6991, fol. 67.
93. SP 15/15, no. 76.
94. SP 15/15, no. 86.i.
95. BL Harleian, 6990 fol. 91.
96. SP 15/15, no. 73.
97. CSP Mary, II, no. 11.
98. CSP Mary, II, no. 17.
99. SP 15/15, nos. 23, 24.
100. SP 15/15, no. 25.
101. Haynes, *State Papers*, I, p. 557.
102. Raine, *York Civic Records*, VI, pp. 170–71; SP, 15/15, no. 30 (i).
103. *Sadler Papers*, II, pp. 54–6.
104. SP 15/15, no. 49. In several letters, Hundson displayed an evident respect for the countess, at one point memorably voicing the old adage for couples in which the wife was the stronger force: of the two, "the grey mare was the better horse."
105. SP 12/59, no. 65.
106. PRO 30/26/116, fol. 202.
107. SP 12/59, no. 68; E 351/228; *Sadler Papers*, II, p. 41. For the military preparations in 1569, see especially Fissel, *English Warfare*, pp. 123–34.
108. Raine, *York Civic Records*, VI, pp. 160–81.
109. *Sadler Papers*, II, p. 64; SP 15/14, no. 94; SP 15/15, nos. 14, 20, 33, 36, 46; BL Salisbury MS 70, no. 21. This 500li figure was, however, mentioned in the context of a much later suit by the townsmen in an effort to diminish later impositions and may well have been an exaggeration; my thanks to Dr. Helen Good for discussion on this point.
110. SP 15/15, nos. 46 and 49.

111. SP 15/15, no. 48.
112. Sharp, *Memorials*, pp. 47, 61–3; BL Caligula B.IX, ii, f. 425.
113. SP 15/15, no. 22.
114. *Sadler Papers*, II, pp. 54–6.
115. SP 15/15, no.49.
116. SP 15/15, no. 42.
117. SP 15/15, no. 46.
118. SP 15/15, no. 70.
119. SP 15/15, no. 39.
120. Sharp, *Memorials*, p. 54.
121. SP 15/15, no. 44, and also no. 42.
122. SP 15/15, no. 52.
123. SP 15/15, no. 54.
124. SP 15/15, nos. 39, 51 (i).
125. *CSP Foreign*, 1569–71, no. 507; SP 15/15, no. 55; Sharp, *Memorials*, pp. 15, 64. The man in question was Captain Reed, who joined the rebels for a time but later convinced the authorities that he had done so merely with the intent of spying upon them. Reed also had the grant of the fort on Holy Island, which helps explain the decision to send soldiers to protect it.
126. SP 15/15, no. 56.
127. Sharp, *Memorials*, pp. 64, 71.
128. SP 15/15, nos. 76 (i), (ii), and (iii). It perhaps did not help that Cumberland had been actively suspected of complicity with the rebels throughout. Scrope, too, had incurred some minor suspicion earlier for his friendly relations with Mary when she was in his custody, and as his wife was the sister of the duke of Norfolk and countess of Westmorland. Lord Wharton may also have been suspected of complicity: Thomas Bishop's later confession claimed that Wharton was "bruted" to be among the initial group of conspirators that surrounded the earls in September, only abandoning them when he learned of Norfolk's arrest. (Bodleian, Tanner MS 50, no. 20.)
129. SP 59/16, fol. 124 and Sharp, *Memorials*, p. 191 (Northumberland's confession). Northumberland was probably correct: Alba persistently refused to provide aid, and nothing was forthcoming from Phillip himself until February of 1570. The ambassador may, however, have made such a promise and certainly did his best to convince Alba to comply.
130. SP 15/15, no. 65.
131. SP 15/15, no. 86; BL Cotton Caligula B.IX vol. 2, fol. 434.
132. BL Cotton Caligula B.IX vol. 2, fol. 474.
133. *HMC Salisbury* I, no. 1490.
134. BL Cotton Caligula B.IX, fol. 361.
135. DDCL Raine MS 124, fols. 98–99.
136. SP 15/15, no. 76.
137. E 178/746.
138. SP 15/15, no. 81.
139. BL Add MS 40746 f. 21.
140. SP 15/15, nos. 88, 91.
141. BL Harleian 6991 fol. 67.

142. Durham County Record Office D/St/C1/2/4(6); Glamis Castle, Bowes MS vol. 11 no. 30.
143. See, for instance, *Sadler Papers*, II, p. 67.
144. Sharp, *Memorials*, pp. 103–4.
145. *Sadler Papers*, II, pp. 48, 64.
146. SP 15/15, nos. 89, 89i, 90.
147. SP 15/15, nos. 93 and 94.
148. SP 15/15, nos. 109, 111, 115.
149. BL Cotton Caligula B.IX vol. 2, fol. 492.

3 The Rebels in Scotland

1. For this and other cross-border marriages, see Berwick-upon-Tweed Record Office, Enrolment Books B 6/1 (1570–1636) and Bailiff's Court Book, 1568–1603.
2. For recent attempts to rescue the borderers' reputation and to document the variety of non-violent cross-border ties, see Meikle, *A British Frontier?* and Newton, *North-East England*. On the development of the Borders as a distinctive political and legal space, see Neville, *Violence, Custom and Law*. For Border identities, see also: Stringer, "Frontier Society," pp. 28–66 and King, "Thomas Gray's *Scalacronica*," pp. 217–31.
3. *CSP Foreign Elizabeth*, VIII, no. 2524; Tough, *Last Years*, p. 179.
4. Thomas Musgrave, quoted in Fraser, *Steel Bonnets*, p. 65.
5. Ronald Pollitt has previously examined the English rebels' flight to Scotland and its significance for subsequent Anglo-Scottish policy: "Defeat of the Northern Rebellion," pp. 1–21.
6. Pastor, *Popes*, pp. 210, 410 (Sander to Graziani from Louvain, February 14, 1570).
7. *HMC Salisbury* I, no. 1463.
8. Lee, *Earl of Moray*, pp. 257–61.
9. SP 52/16, no. 74.
10. *Register of the Privy Council of Scotland*, vol. 2, pp. 66–73.
11. SP 15/15, nos. 115, 117.
12. *Sadler Papers*, II, p. 117.
13. Lee, *Earl of Moray*, p. 270. On the long tradition of fugitives receiving welcome on either side of the border, see Merriman, "Home Thoughts," pp. 90–117.
14. SP 15/17, no. 27, also, no. 37 for Forster; SP 59/16, fols. 122, 124.
15. *Sadler Papers*, II, pp. 118–19.
16. Cody, *Leslie's Historie of Scotland*, pp. 97–101. On the Scottish borderers, see also: Fraser, *Steel Bonnets* and Rae, *Scottish Frontier*. For their English counterparts, see Robson, *English Highland Clans*.
17. *Sadler Papers*, II, p. 102.
18. SP 15/17, no. 20 (3).
19. McInnes, *Accounts of the Treasurer of Scotland*, vol. 12, pp. 185–6.
20. *Sadler Papers*, II, p. 136.
21. *Sadler Papers*, II, p. 123.
22. *Sadler Papers*, II, pp. 110–25, 127–9, 133–40, 144–5.

23. Potter, *Bloodfeud*.
24. SP 15/17, no. 69.
25. SP 15/17, no. 81; SP 59/16, fols. 171, 186–189, 222; SP 59/20, fols. 92–110; Strathmore Estates, Glamis Castle Bowes MS vol. 18, p. 13.
26. *CSP Foreign*, vol. 9, no. 701.
27. SP 15/17, nos. 72, 76; SP 59/16, fol. 186.
28. SP 15/17, nos. 38 (ii) and 75.
29. SP 15/15, no. 121.
30. SP 15/17, no. 46.
31. SP 15/17, no. 56 (iii).
32. SP 12/68, no. 23.
33. SP 15/18, no. 11 (ii.i).
34. SP 15/17, no. 107.
35. *Holinshed's Chronicle*, IV, p. 237.
36. SP 15/17, nos. 97, 107, 110; SP 15/18, nos. 4, 20; SP 59/16, f. 210.
37. Dawson, *Earl of Argyll*, p. 182.
38. Cowan, "Marian Civil War," p. 98 (95–112).
39. Wormald, *Mary, Queen of Scots*, p. 127.
40. Blake, *William Maitland of Lethington*.
41. Dawson, *Earl of Argyll*, pp. 81, 84, 121.
42. Donaldson, *All the Queen's Men*, pp. 8, 51, 91–108, 151.
43. Palmer, "Gender, Violence, and Rebellion," p. 702; Thomson, *Diurnal*, p. 170.
44. Binchy, "Irish Ambassador," pp. 575–6.
45. SP 59/16, f. 272; SP 52/19 no. 27 (i).
46. Thomson, *Diurnal*, p. 162. In the English civil wars of the early 1130s, Scots King David I ruled northern England for a time. In the early 1200s, rebel lords in these counties turned to the Scots King for protection. Only in 1237 did Alexander II relinquish claims to Northumberland, Cumberland, and Westmorland.
47. Bannatyne, *Transactions in Scotland*, pp. 18–19.
48. SP 52/17, no. 59.
49. *Sadler Papers*, II, p. 147.
50. See Guy, *Queen of Scots* for the differences between Elizabeth and Cecil on approaches to Mary. On Leicester, see MacCaffrey, *Elizabethan Regime*, p. 384.
51. See especially the *Diurnal*, pp. 161–9.
52. SP 52/18, no. 2.
53. SP 52/17, no. 41.
54. SP 52/17, nos. 54, 54(i)–(iv).
55. SP 70/111, fols. 3, 16.
56. BL Cotton Caligula C.I, fols. 76v, 98 r; see Alford, *Succession*, pp. 59, 163–7.
57. *CSP Spanish*, II, p. 244.
58. *By the Queene: A declaration of the just, honourable, and necessarie causes …* TRP, II, no. 571.
59. SP 70/112, fols. 4–6; SP 52/17, no. 69; SP 52/18, nos. 22 (i) and (ii).
60. National Archives of Scotland SP 6/61; also printed in *Foedera*, vol. 6, pp. 120–22. Also, Hunsdon warned in early January that he thought the treaty irrelevant in this case. He believed it applied only to those that "inhabit upon the borders which are meant to answer to prince and warden," not to noblemen and those living in the interior. SP 59/16, fol. 155.

61. SP 52/17, no. 49.
62. SP 52/17, no. 60.
63. SP 59/16, fols. 287–90.
64. *Holinshed's Chronicles*, IV, pp. 238–42.
65. SP 59/17, fols. 12–13, 93.
66. SP 52/17, no. 59; SP 59/16, fol. 296.
67. SP 53/5, no. 36.
68. SP 59/17, fol. 12.
69. SP 59/17, fols. 21–23.
70. Donaldson, *Sir James Melville*, pp. 86–7.
71. Bannatyne, *Transactions in Scotland*, pp. 41, 53.
72. SP 59/17, f. 58.
73. SP 52/18, no. 94.
74. SP 59/17, f. 81; *CSP Foreign*, vol. 9, no. 1175.
75. SP 52/19, no. 6 (iii), SP 52/18, no. 80 (i).
76. SP 52/19, no. 10.
77. SP 59/17, fols. 91, 93–4.
78. SP 52/19, no. 30(i).
79. *CSP Foreign*, vol. 9, no. 1014.
80. *CSP Foreign*, vol. 9, nos. 2059, 2065; vol. 10, nos. 98, 99.
81. SP 59/17, fol. 104.
82. See, for instance, the detailed report in SP 12/105, no. 10, and also *CSP Foreign*, vol. 9, nos. 1261, 1296. See also Lechat, *Réfugiés Anglais*, pp. 44–7.
83. *CPR Elizabeth I*, vol. IV., nos. 455 and 457. See also, N. Jones, "Defining Superstitions," pp. 187–203.
84. *CSP Foreign, Elizabeth*, vol. 9, no. 1232.
85. Anonymous, *A Copie of a Letter…concernying Dr Story* (London, 1571), sig. C2r. See Ronald Pollitt's suggestion that Prestall was involved in the plot to kidnap Dr Story and return him to England for execution: "Doctor John Story," p. 142.
86. SP 15/19, nos. 75, 78, 79, 85.
87. For the latter groups, see for instance, Trim, "Protestant Refugees," pp. 68–79.
88. *CSP Foreign*, vol. 9, no. 2171. For the longstanding animosities, see Neville, "Local Sentiment," pp. 419–37.
89. SP 52/18 no 3.
90. HMC, vol. 45, *Duke of Buccleuch, Montagu House* (I), p. 23.
91. *CSP Foreign*, vol. 9, nos. 1715, 1720; *By the Queene: A Proclamation declaring the untruth…*; for the Earl of Huntley, see *CSP Foreign*, vol. 9, nos. 1001, 1244.
92. *Ane Discourse tuiching the estait present in October anno Domini 1571* (St Andrews, 1572), sigs. B4v–B5r.
93. See Dawson, "Anglo-Scottish Protestant Culture," pp. 87–114; Alford, *Succession*; Mason, "Scottish Reformation," pp. 161–86; and Morgan, "British Policies." For the ties even before 1560, see Kellar, *Scotland, England, and the Reformation*. Lisa McClain is currently working on the Anglo-Scottish Catholic connections and identities, thus far largely ignored; I would like to thank her for sharing a copy of her unpublished paper, "Border Crossings: Reconsidering the Boundaries of 'English' Catholicism, 1559–1642."

94. See Alford for Cecil's providential views on international politics, and also Thorp's essays: "Catholic Conspiracy," pp. 431–8 and "William Cecil," pp. 289–304, esp. p. 291.
95. Quoted in Donaldson, *All the Queen's Men*, p. 115.
96. Robinson, *Zurich Letters*, I, p. 228.
97. Buchanan, *An Admonition*, sigs. A4r, B1r. See also BL Add MS 48049 for a treatise attacking recent works that supported Mary's claim to the English succession. The author sought to demonstrate that the tracts "had a uniformity" with the English rebels' proclamations, the papal bull, and other such links in the "chain of treasons."
98. Bannatyne, *Transactions in Scotland*, pp. 18–19.
99. SP 59/17, fol. 269; *CSP Foreign*, vol. 9, nos. 1680, 1745; vol. 10, no. 186.
100. Lechat, *Réfugiés Anglais*, p. 44. See also de Lettenhove, *Relations politiques des Pays-Bas et d'Angleterre*, VI, p. 11.
101. *Registrum Honoris de Morton*, pp. 75–6.
102. *CSP Foreign*, vol. 10, nos. 200, 226, 232.
103. National Archives of Scotland, GD149/265, Miscellaneous state papers, 1565–1628, fol. 3.
104. *CSP Foreign*, vol. 10, nos. 327, 356, 364, 367, 414.
105. *Diurnal*, p. 298.
106. See Holmes, *Resistance and Compromise*.
107. Milton, *Kings and Magistrates*, p. 31. On Protestant theories of resistance, see Danner, "Christopher Goodman," pp. 60–73; Greaves, "John Knox," pp. 1–36; and Skinner, "Calvinist Theory," pp. 309–30.

4 The Aftermath

1. STAC 5/K11/18.
2. See for example, Norton, *Poor Deceyued Subiectes*, sigs. E2v-E3r; "Cold Pye," no. 68.
3. Norton, *A Warning Against the Dangerous Practices of Papists*, sigs. B3r-v, D1r-v, L3v, N2v.
4. Drant, *Two Sermons Preached . . . at Windsor*, sigs. I8r, K4r.
5. For the Pilgrimage tallies, see Bush and Bownes, *Defeat of the Pilgrimage*, pp. 73, 314, 364, 411–12. As the authors note, some seven or eight of these men had not actually participated in the postpardon revolts, but were nonetheless convicted and sentenced on evidence (however tenuous) that they had.
6. Fletcher and MacCulloch, *Tudor Rebellions*, p. 98.
7. On attainder, see Lehmberg, "Parliamentary Attainder," pp. 675–702; Hicks, "Attainder, Resumption and Coercion," pp. 15–31; Lander, "Attainder and Forfeiture," pp. 119–49; Simpson, *Land Law*, pp. 20–1; Coke, *First Part of the . . . Laws of England*, fols. 8, 13, 41; Coke, *Third Part of the . . . Laws of England*, fols. 19, 227.
8. SP 15/15, no. 95.
9. SP 15/15, no. 125. For the financial aspects of the rebellion's suppression, see also Kesselring, "Mercy and Liberality," pp. 213–35. Much of its discussion is included here, but the article explores some financial aspects in greater depth.

10. SP 15/15, no. 132.
11. BL Lansdowne MS 115, fols. 123–124d; SP 15/15, no. 139. For an earlier example of the removal of church bells that had been used to raise revolt, see Duffy, *Voices of Morebath*, p. 145.
12. AO 1/284, no. 1070; E 351/ 34, 227, 228, 229. See also Dietz, *Public Finance*, ii.16.
13. Sharp, *Memorials*, pp. 130–1; BL Cotton Caligula C.I, fol. 499.
14. SP 15/17, nos. 3, 9; SP 15/18, no. 26.
15. SP 15/15, no. 125.
16. *The English Reports*, 73. pp. 644–5. On the disputes with the bishop of Durham, see Bellamy, *Tudor Law of Treason*, pp. 214–15.
17. SP 15/17, no. 100; SP 15/18, no. 26.
18. SP 15/15, no. 132.
19. SP 15/15, no. 139.
20. *TRP*, II, nos. 438, 441, 443, 571, 598, 699, 704, 716, 728, 740, 769, 796, 809.
21. Smith, *De Respublica Anglorum*, p. 59.
22. Edwards, "Beyond Reform," p. 18. See also Edwards, "Ideology and Experience," pp. 127–57; Holdsworth, "Martial Law," pp. 117–32; Christianson, "Billeting and Martial Law," pp. 539–67; Boynton, "Tudor Provost-Marshal," pp. 437–55.
23. Edwards, "Beyond Reform," p. 18. In subsequent years in England, when martial law was used against vagrants, pay was offered the marshals.
24. Langbein, *Torture*, calls 1540–1640 the "century of torture" in English law. Its use never became regularized, but it certainly became more common. Torture here is meant as a method of obtaining information, as an "aid to fact-finding," rather than simple cruelty or "afflictive sanctions" such as quartering traitors or slitting the noses of petty offenders.
25. SP 15/15, no. 138.
26. SP 12/59, no. 43; see also SP 15/21, no. 67, where Hunsdon asks permission to rack a messenger arrived from the rebels in exile.
27. Coke, *Third Part of the . . . Laws of England*, p. 25 (Rolston's Case, 1571).
28. Strathmore Estates (Glamis Castle), Bowes MS, vol. 13, pp. 4, 33, 34.
29. Strathmore Estates (Glamis Castle), Bowes MS, vol. 14, no. 7.
30. BL Harleian MS 6991, fol. 68.
31. Sharp, *Memorials*, pp. 133, 188; Bodleian Library Tanner MS 50 no. 19. Most reports told of the execution of "aldermen," but a few suggested only the singular.
32. DUL MS 534 (Bowes Papers), nos. 2, 6, 7, 18.
33. Strathmore Estates (Glamis Castle), Bowes MS, vol. 14, nos. 3, 13, 48.
34. Strathmore Estates (Glamis Castle), Bowes MS, vol. 14, p. 40.
35. DUL MS 534 (Bowes Papers), nos. 2,6, 7, 18; Bowes Museum, Bowes MS vol. 2, no. 18. There was some dispute whether the goods of men executed at martial law in this particular case belonged to the crown or to the marshal. (Sharp, *Memorials*, p. 173.)
36. Durham County Record Office, D/St/C1/2/4 (9).
37. Strathmore Estates (Glamis Castle), Bowes MS, vol. 14, no. 41. Sharp, *Memorials*, p. 141.
38. Bowes Museum, Bowes MS, item no. 17; Sharp, *Memorials*, pp. 140–2, 151–2, 162–3, 187–8; BL Harleian 6991, fols. 63, 68. See also McCall, "Rising in

the North," pp. 74–87, which correctly argues that fewer men were executed than had been appointed to die. How many fewer, though, is unclear. McCall provides no specific estimates, but concludes that the final number "fell very considerably short" of the number appointed. In one case, he is misled into thinking that a list "of such as be executed by martial law whose goods be not inventoried in Darnetone Ward" is likely a complete list of executions for that area, when it seems quite clearly what it claims to be: a list of those whose goods were not yet inventoried. Other lists used by McCall to tally the dead lack such explicit labels, but seem similarly intended to account for goods catalogued and received, rather than to list the names of all the executed. McCall believes that Bowes's statement on the numbers killed was in error and was the number "to be" executed. Having read through the same lists and correspondence, I agree that Bowes did not kill as many as first appointed but see no reason to doubt his verb tense when he writes that roughly 600 had been killed. This claim was, furthermore, in a letter to a family member and not to the Queen or Council, so there seems no need for him to exaggerate his efforts to prove his ardour. Thomas Gargrave, intimately familiar with the proceedings, also estimated that "there is by martial law already executed above 500 of the poor sort." It should also be noted that Bowes disavowed any knowledge of the numbers of executions further to the north, where Sir John Forster took charge. How many Forster executed is unknown.

39. Sharp, *Memorials*, p. 172.
40. SP 15/17, no. 64.
41. SP 15/17, no. 68.
42. *TRP*, III, no. 569. See also PRO 30/26/116, fol. 205.
43. SP 15/17, no. 110.
44. *TRP*, III, no. 570.
45. *TRP*, III, no. 568. See also the draft in BL Lansdowne 12, 20, fols. 45d–50, which shows the later insertion of the striking phrase "as the minister of Almighty God."
46. *TRP*, III, no. 568.
47. See for example Raine, *York Civic Records*, vii. 6.
48. BL Harleain MS 6991, fol. 67.
49. This sermon was most likely the "Homily Against Disobedience and Wilful Rebellion," which was written during the rebellion and later added to the second book of homilies. See Bond, *Homily*.
50. SP 15/18, nos. 6, 7; *TRP*, III, no. 569.
51. For a discussion of the role of pardons in the suppression of other protests and as propaganda, see Kesselring, *Mercy and Authority*, esp. pp. 163–99.
52. SP 15/18, no. 7.
53. E 137/133/1.
54. SP 15/18, no. 75 (i).
55. One might also note here the use of 3000 marks worth of timber from the estate of one attainted rebel to repair northern fortifications: SP 59/17, fol. 37.
56. C 66/ 1066, mm. 15–38; *CPR Elizabeth I*, vol. V, nos. 585–1019. This number refers to the people included on the mass pardon list, not those pardoned

individually over coming weeks. The £600 total assumes a fee of 26s 8d per charter, the same as that charged for Elizabeth's coronation pardon. See also SP 1/121, f. 203; when discussing the pardon for the Pilgrims of Grace, the councilors noted that "the benefit of the seal" would compensate for any forfeited forfeitures.

57. SP 15/17, no. 13
58. SP 15/18, no. 17 (i).
59. SP 15/18, no. 16. The nature of Cleasby's relationship with the Conyers daughters is unclear, but as Cuthbert Sharp notes, it continued throughout Cleasby's life: at his death, he held a tenancy from Katherine Conyers, and left his eldest daughter in her care. Sharp, *Memorials*, p. 227.
60. Simpson, *Land Law*, p. 90; Spring, *Law, Land, and Family*, pp. 27–8.
61. SP 15/18, no. 17.
62. SP 15/18, no. 21.
63. *CPR Elizabeth I*, vol. V, p. 268: Leonard Metcalf, pardoned September 1, 1571 at the suit of Anthony Mildmay; p. 163: Robert Lambert, pardoned March 20, 1571, pp. 271, 388 land grants; p. 375: Robert Claxton, pardoned March 12, 1572 at the suit of Robert, earl of Leicester, p. 464 land grant; p. 341: Ralph Conyers, pardoned November 22, 1571, p. 213, land grant.
64. SP 15/17, no. 13.
65. SP 15/15, nos. 80, 95.
66. 73 *English Reports* 644; 13 Elizabeth I c. 16.
67. See SP 15/15, no. 125; 15/17, no. 100; 15/18, no. 26; 73 *English Reports* 644–5; 13 Elizabeth I c. 16.
68. BL Lansdowne 12, fols. 197–199.
69. Thomas Percy, the seventh earl, had been the nephew and heir of the childless sixth earl, but did not succeed upon his uncle's death due in part to his own father's attainder for participating in the Pilgrimage of Grace. Queen Mary restored Thomas to the title and estates in 1557 with a grant in tail to his male heirs.
70. Dietz, *Public Finance*, p. 28.
71. Reid, *Durham Crown Lordships*, p. 3.
72. Dietz, *Public Finance*, p. 298.; *CPR Elizabeth I*, v, no. 1715; vi, no. 974; LR 2/66, f. 174. On the sales and management of crown lands, see Hoyle, *Estates of the English Crown*; Outhwaite, "Who Bought Crown Lands?," pp. 18–33; Habakkuk, "Monastic Property," pp. 362–80.
73. *CPR Elizabeth I*, vols. V–VII.
74. Hurstfield, "Fiscal Feudalism," pp. 53–61.
75. MacCaffrey, "Place and Patronage," pp. 95–126; MacCaffrey, "Patronage and Politics," pp. 21–35. See also Peck, "For a King," pp. 31–61.
76. Brodie, *Tree of the Commonwealth*, pp. 28, 61.
77. SP 15/15, no. 114.
78. See, for instance, SP 15/18, nos. 22 and 57.
79. SP 15/18, no. 24.
80. *CPR Elizabeth I*, vol V, nos. 3094, 3095.
81. SP 15/21, no. 39. See also Meikle, "Godly Rogue," pp. 126–63.
82. Marcombe, "Dean and Chapter," p. 177.
83. Marcombe, *The Last Principality*, p. 131.

84. See Jones, *The English Reformation*, pp. 61–70, esp. p. 66.
85. Freeman, "Ecclesiastical Patronage," p. 156. For livings on the Dacre estates that passed into the Queen's gift, see also E 164/42, p. 8, 11, 15, 29, 67. On the importance of ecclesiastical patronage to the crown, see also Heal, *Of Prelates and Princes* and O'Day, *English Clergy*.
86. Collinson describes the dramatic changes post-1570, as "effective protest-antization began in earnest" with the impetus of the rebellion and the appointment of Grindal: *Archbishop Grindal*, p. 188.
87. Ellis, "Tudor State Formation," pp. 40–63; Ellis, *Tudor Frontiers*.
88. Hoyle, "Faction, Feud and Reconciliation," pp. 590–613; Marcombe, *The Last Principality*, pp. 117–51.
89. Historical Manuscripts Commission, Salisbury I, 536.
90. BL Lansdowne MS 12, f. 70.
91. SP 15/17, no. 13.
92. Rowse, *Tudor Cornwall*, pp. 137–8. See also Arthurson, "The Rising of 1497," p. 13.
93. Bush and Bownes, *Defeat of the Pilgrimage*, p. 380; see also Hoyle, *Pilgrimage of Grace*, p. 405.
94. See works in footnote 6. Wyndham also gives a few examples of land grants made on special terms offered in reward for service against the Western rebels of 1549; "Crown Lands and Royal Patronage," p. 26.
95. SP 15/15, nos. 30, 49, 54.
96. See 13 Elizabeth I c. 5 and especially 18 Elizabeth I c. 4. As a result of the latter, any conveyance of property once owned by the 1569 rebels made within the two years preceding the rising had to be specially enrolled and examined, or else considered void. These statutes have been considered foundational for the development of modern laws of fraudulent conveyance. See Ross, *Elizabethan Literature*, ch. 2.
97. Bacon, *King Henry the Seventh*, p. 164.
98. SP 59/20, fols. 98, 122.
99. See, for example, E 178/576, 737, 742, 2572.
100. See James, *Family, Lineage, and Civil Society*, pp. 64, 80, 147; "Concept of Order," pp. 70–5.
101. For a discussion of the fines due on transfers of property, see Appleby, "Agrarian Capitalism," p. 584 and Hoyle, "Lords, Tenants, and Tenant Right," p. 40.
102. *CPR Elizabeth I*, vol. VI, nos. 482, 971.
103. James, "Concept of Order," pp. 63–4.
104. See Thorne, *Inns of Court*, p. 41; Coke, *First Part of the … Laws of England* (1670), fol. 8; St. German, *Doctor and Student*, p. 61, 71; Lander, "Attainder and Forfeiture," p. 119, citing Bracton, *De Legibus et Consuetudinubus Anglie*, ii. 335.
105. 13 Elizabeth I c. 27. For comparison, see Neville's discussion of the wives of an earlier group of "rebels": "Widows of War," pp. 109–39.
106. Lander, "Attainder and Forfeiture," 119; Ross, "Forfeiture for Treason," pp. 561, 566–8.
107. 1 Edward VI c. 12; 5&6 Edward VI c. 11; 5 Elizabeth I cc. 1, 11; 18 Elizabeth I c. 1. See Bellamy, *Tudor Law of Treason*, p. 216.
108. E 310/12/34, m. 38.

109. *CPR Elizabeth I*, vol. V, no. 2653.
110. See, for example, *CPR Elizabeth I*, vol. V, no. 2653; Vi, nos. 36, 934.
111. 13 Elizabeth I c. 3. See the *Journals of the House of Commons*, i. pp. 85–7, 92–3, and the *Journals of the House of Lords*, i. pp. 679, 690; for a draft of the act, see SP 12/77, fols. 206–35.
112. *CPR Elizabeth I*, vol. V, no. 2156; SP 15/21, no. 9.
113. Bowes would find, however, that the queen and her commissioners rather thought that they were now owed the repayment of his debt to Norton. SP 46/31, fols. 82, 352; E 134/19 Eliz/East 3; E 134/18 & 19 Eliz/Mich 5; Strathmore Estates (Glamis Castle) Bowes MS vol. 11 no. 30.
114. E 112/50/32.
115. *CPR Elizabeth I*, vol. V, no. 2684.
116. BL Add MS 40746, f. 60.
117. E 123/1A fols. pp. 120, 121, 126.
118. *CPR Elizabeth I*, vol. VI, no. 423.
119. 13 Elizabeth I, OA 29.
120. See Bellamy, *Tudor Law of Treason*, p. 217. For women's property rights more generally, see Erickson, *Women and Property* and Spring, *Law, Land, and Family*.
121. Thomas, in Hoyle, *Estates of the English Crown*, p. 169. Thomas was not referring specifically to the aftermath of the 1569 rebellion, but to the general policy of using crown revenue as reward in diminishing the financial resources of Elizabeth's successors. Of course, as Hoyle noted in the same volume, the argument can be taken a step further: while such a policy eventually weakened "the crown", it ultimately strengthened "the state" by forcing a shift from the financial basis of medieval monarchy to government supported by parliamentary taxation (p. 432).
122. Howell, *State Trials*, I, pp. 1083–6; this reprints a contemporary pamphlet, How, *The several confessions of . . . two of the Northern Rebels*. See also: Davie, *T. Norton and C. Norton, rebels* (London, 1570).
123. SP 15/17, no. 72.
124. SP 15/17, no. 89.
125. Sharp, *Memorials*, pp. 212–13 (Northumberland's confession).
126. BL Cotton Caligula C.III, f. 381 (Sharp, *Memorials*, p. 335).
127. BIHR HC.AB 7, fol. 40.

5   Meanings and Memories

1. Robinson, *Zurich Letters*, pp. 222–3, 246–7.
2. Thornton, "Blessed Thomas Percy," p. 32.
3. Sharp, *Memorials*, p. 8; SP 15/96, no. 6; BL Salisbury MS 158, 101.
4. SP 12/59, nos. 20, 25, 36; Salisbury MS 156, 70.
5. Raine, *York Civic Records*, p. 160.
6. C 66/1073, m. 30
7. SP 12/60, nos. 48, 49, 54.
8. C 66/1112, m.1 (*CPR Elizabeth I*, vol. VI, no. 1230).
9. Williams, "Risings in Norfolk," 73–5; *CSP Spanish, 1568–79*, p. 225.

10. STAC 5/K11/18.

11. SP 15/15, nos. 64, 79.

12. SP 15/15, no. 113.

13. BL Lansdowne MS 11, f. 156.

14. See Cust, "News and Politics," pp. 60–90; Fox, "Rumour, News, and Popular Political Opinion," pp. 597–620; Walker, "Rumour, Sedition, and Popular Protest," pp. 31–65; Shagan, "Rumours and Popular Politics," 30–66; Walter, "Public Transcripts," pp. 123–48; Cooper, *Propaganda and the Tudor State*, pp. 93–107; Mears, *Queenship and Political Discourse*. Much of this work addresses to one degree or another Jürgen Habermas's influential but problematic notion of the "public sphere," as presented in *The Structural Transformation of the Public Sphere*. For an older but still valuable treatment of the subject, see Samaha, "Gleanings from Local Criminal-Court Records," pp. 61–79.

15. Cooper, *Propaganda and the Tudor State*, pp. 96–101.

16. See for example, SP 12/60/27. As Adam Fox and others note, surely the best evidence of the importance of plebeian politics and communications networks is the amount of official attention paid to policing them. See Fox, "Rumour, News, and Popular Political Opinion," p. 599. See also Manning, "Doctrine of Sedition," pp. 99–121.

17. Raine, *York Civic Records*, VI, p. 160.

18. SP 15/15, nos. 30.I, 39.I; Raine, ed., *York Civic Records*, VI, p. 170.

19. Waddington, "Order of the Garter," p. 106. On the importance of the Order in Elizabethan politics, see Strong, *The Cult of Elizabeth*, pp. 164–85.

20. SP 12/59, no. 40. See Keen, *Laws of War*, pp. 54–5, 173–4.

21. Hayward, *First Fours Years*, p. 15.

22. STC # 12779; *TRP*, III, no. 567.

23. Haynes, *State Papers*, pp. 558–9.

24. Haynes, *State Papers*, p. 556.

25. Raine, *York Civic Records*, VI, pp. 175–7, quote on p. 176.

26. Collins, *Queen Elizabeth's Defence*, pp. 37, 39–40. Drafts survive with emendations in the hands of both Elizabeth and Cecil. See SP 12/66, no. 54 and Haynes, *State Papers*, pp. 589–93. A copy is also in the National Library of Scotland, Adv. MS. 34.1.11, fols. 77–80d, a volume of papers collected by Walsingham later in the century to help defend the Queen against foreign libels.

27. *Queen Elizabeth's Defence*, p. 34. For churchwardens' accounts, see for instance, Williams, *Churchwardens' Accounts of Hampshire*, pp. 126, 214; Guildhall Library, City of London, MS. 5090, fols. 6–6d; MS 645, fols. 87–87d. I have not checked every surviving set of churchwardens' accounts, but the thirty or so that were checked had no reference to this *Defence*.

28. Bond, *Homily*. Cooper provides an extended discussion of the use of the earlier Homily on Obedience and the new 1570 homily as propaganda to inculcate the Tudor doctrine of absolute non-resistance; *Propaganda and the Tudor State*, pp. 221–31.

29. Bond, *Homily*, pp. 209, 214.

30. Bond, *Homily*, pp. 227, 229, 234.

31. Bond, *Homily*, pp. 225, 233.

32. Bond, *Homily*, pp. 234–5.

33. On this literature, see Lowers, *Mirrors for Rebels*, and Busse, "Anti-Catholic Polemical Writing," pp. 11–30. On Cecil's efforts and ties, see Read, "Public Relations," pp. 21–55.

34. Norton, "A warning against the dangerous practices of papists," sigs. G1r-v; G2r, H3r.

35. Phillips, *A Frendly Larum*, sigs. A4r, C9r.

36. Norton, "Deceived Subiectes," sig. B5v. Notably, while Norton did also address the issue of tenant loyalty, he gave it small consideration compared to his other rebuttals (sig. D1).

37. Norton, "Deceived Subjects," sigs. A3v, B1r, B6v, C8r.

38. Elvidian, *New Years Gift*, sig. A3r, C1r.

39. Seres, *Answer to the Proclamation*, sig. B2r.

40. Elderton, *Northumberland News*.

41. Preston, *Lamentation from Rome*.

42. See, for example, Norton, "A warning against the dangerous practices of papists," sig. L1v. Norton was a lawyer, MP, son-in-law of Thomas Cranmer, and friend of John Foxe. Perhaps best known now for *Gordobuc* and his translation of Calvin's *Institutes*, he attained sixteenth-century notoriety as a "rackmaster" of Catholics. For his own providential history of England, see Marten, "Thomas Norton's 'v periodes,'" pp. 37–53. See also: Graves, *Thomas Norton*, esp. pp. 112–18, 147–70 and Freeman, "Thomas Norton, John Foxe, and the Parliament of 1571," pp. 131–47.

43. Norton, "A warning against the dangerous practices of papists," sigs. A4v, B4r.

44. Norton, "A warning against the dangerous practices of papists," sig. H2v.

45. Norton, "A warning against the dangerous practices of papists," sigs. B5r-v; see also sig. M4r.

46. Drant, "A sermon preached at the Court at Windsor, 8 January 1569 [ie: 1570]," sig. G4v.

47. Collman, *Ballads And Broadsides*, pp. 209–11.

48. For this anti-Catholic rhetoric and its uses, see Lake, "Anti-popery," pp. 72–106; Weiner, "Beleaguered Isle," pp. 27–62; Clifton, "Popular Fear of Catholics," pp. 23–55; Walter, *Understanding Popular Violence*; Haydon, *Anti-Catholicism*.

49. Laderchi, *Annales Ecclesiastici*, 1570, nos. 332–345; Pastor, *Popes*, vol. 18, pp. 212–13.

50. Norton, *An Addition Declaratorie to the Bulles*, sigs. A2v–A3r; also reprinted in his *Disclosing of the Great Bull and Certain Calves that he hath gotten, and especially the monster bull that roared at my Lord Byshops Gate* (London, 1570).

51. Even Laderchi, the annalist of the Catholic church, admits some confusion on this question and suggests (based on Sander and later English writers) that there might, in fact, have been an earlier bull of excommunication prepared in 1569. See: Laderchi, *Annales Ecclesiastici*, 1570, no. 365; Cecil, *Execution of Justice*, pp. 13–17.

52. Norton, "To The Quenes Maiesties Poore Deceived Subiectes of the Northe Country," sigs. A6r, A7v.

53. Norton, "A warning against the dangerous practices of papistes," sigs. E1v, I4r; "All such treatises," title page.

54. For details on these measures, see Neale, *Elizabeth I and Her Parliaments*, I, pp. 177–312.
55. Hartley, *Proceedings in Parliament*, I, p. 186. This was also the first parliament in which all members of the Commons had to take the oath of supremacy, and thus the first that included no declared Catholics.
56. For the rebellion-as-punishment, see for example the prayer of thanksgiving published at the end of the rebellion, Clay, "A thanksgiving for the suppression," pp. 538–9.
57. 13 Elizabeth I c. 1; also, 13 Elizabeth I, cc. 2, 3, 12, 16. See also Graves, *Norton*, pp. 172ff, and Freeman, "The reformation of the church...," passim.
58. SP 12/59, no. 19; Read, *Mr Secretary Walsingham*, I, pp. 67–8. On Ridolfi's "turning", see Parker, "Messianic Vision," 167–221, esp. 215–17.
59. Edwards, *Marvellous Chance* goes further in suggesting that Norfolk and Mary (via Ross) never actually committed themselves to such a plot, that the entire thing was a fabrication. His argument is interesting and certainly answers "qui bono?," but as he acknowledges, remains conjectural.
60. Pastor, *Popes*, vol. 18, pp. 229–30; Maltby, *Alba*, p. 201.
61. Quoted in Parker, "Messianic Vision," p. 204.
62. See also the account of the plot, trial, and execution in Williams, *Duke of Norfolk*, pp. 189–254 and the transcript of his trial in Howell, *State Trials*, vol. 1, pp. 958–1042.
63. Catena, *Vita del Gloriosissimo*, pp. 112–18. For English use of Catena to brand the papacy and the Spanish, see, for instance, National Library of Scotland, Adv. MS 34.1.11, a dossier of Walsingham's papers that includes one to prove Spanish involvement in causing the rebellion, which notes as evidence "the book of the life of Pius printed at Rome declareth the King to have been a chief actor in the rebellions of Westmorland and Northumberland" (fol. 12d). In the same volume, "Mr Robert Beale's Collection of the King of Spain's injuries to the Queen of England made 30 May 1591" similarly refers to evidence "published to the whole world by foreign historiographers" (fol. 29d).
64. Hartley, *Proceedings in Parliament* I, pp. 270–2.
65. Hartley, *Proceedings in Parliament*, I, pp. 276, 374; Neale, *Elizabeth I and her Parliaments*, I, p. 289. For the ways in which these discussions drew upon Protestant resistance theory, not just against Mary but also against Elizabeth, see Bowler, "Axe or an Acte," pp. 349–59 and Collinson, "Monarchical Republic," pp. 45–6.
66. Hartley, *Proceedings in Parliament*, I, p. 298.
67. On this point, see Walsham, "'A Very Deborah?'," p. 151. Walsham asks why Protestants' grumbling about Elizabeth's lukewarm reformation did not prompt more open opposition, and argues that "it is not an exaggeration to say that she largely had the Roman Catholics to thank for her elevation to the status of a Protestant icon."
68. On Accession Day, see: Neale, "November 17th"; Strong, "Popular Celebration," pp. 86–103; Cressy, *Bonfires and Bells*, chapter 4; Mears, *Queenship and Political Discourse*, p. 250.
69. Quoted in Cressy, *Bonfires and Bells*, p. 52.
70. Clay, *Liturgical Services*, pp. 548–58.

71. Ayre, *The Sermons of Edwin Sandys*, pp. 65, 75. See also Walsham, "'A Very Deborah?'," pp. 143–70 for a discussion of how this sermon, and other texts, used flattery to exhort and admonish the queen with the thinly veiled proviso that she ruled safely only so long as she ruled according to God's commands.

72. See: Allestree, *A New Almanacke and Prognostication* and those of Jonathan Dove.

73. Burgess, *Another Sermon Preached to the Honorable House of Commons*, p. 22.

74. Taylor, "God's Manifold Mercies," vol. 2, pp. 142–3.

75. Carleton, *A Thankfull Remembrance of God's Mercie*, pp. 13–26.

76. Walsham, *Providence*, pp. 258–60.

77. Walsham, *Providence*, pp. 225, 245, 248, 249–50.

78. Anonymous, *Loyalty's Speech to Englands Subjects*, pp. 4–5. See Brand, "British Debate," p. 105.

79. Walter, *Understanding Popular Violence*, p. 18.

80. Interestingly, M.M. Merrick, a modern hagiographer of the earl of Northumberland, states that the countess wrote a tract after the rebellion defending her husband. He identifies it as *The troubles of the Count of Northumberland*. [See Merrick, *Thomas Percy, Seventh Earl*, p. 123.] I have been unable to locate a copy of this work. The work with which it is sometimes identified, Anonymous, *Discours des Troubles nouvellement advenuz au Royaume d'Angleterre* (Paris, 1570) and subsequent editions from Paris and Lyon, is unlikely to have been written by the countess, considering its idiosyncratic identification of participants. On this point, see also Busse, "Anti-Catholic Polemical Writings," p. 25.

81. For this and much of what follows, see Dillon, *Construction of Martyrdom*, p. 13 and passim.

82. The work was finished and edited by Edward Rishton. See: Sander, *Rise and Growth of the Anglican Schism*; Highley, "Nicholas Sander's *Schismatis Anglicani*," pp. 151–71.

83. Bristow, *A brief treatise of diverse plaine and sure wayes to finde out the truthe*, pp. 69–73v.

84. See, for example, Foxe's *Acts and Monuments*, also known as the *Book of Martyrs*, and various works of John Bale, especially the *Examinations of Anne Askew*.

85. Munday, *The English Romayne Life*, p. 27.

86. Dillon, *Construction of Martyrdom*, pp. 172–5, 275.

87. For discussions of the divisions among Catholics and their attitudes to opposition, see Vidmar, *English Catholic Historians*; and Questier, "Elizabeth and the Catholics," pp. 69–94, McCoog, "Construing Martyrdom," pp. 95–12, and Sommerville, "Papalist Political Thought," pp. 162–84.

88. Leslie, *Treatise of Treasons*; R.G., *Salutem in Christo*. It should be noted that while Leslie is commonly assumed to be the author of the *Treatise*, this attribution remains somewhat uncertain. The style and some of the claims do seem quite consistent with other works known to be by Leslie, and the work clearly emerged from his circle if not from Leslie himself.

89. Watson (attr. Thomas Bluet), *Important Considerations*, pp. 2, 10–13.

90. Anonymous, *A Brief Historical Account of the Behaviour of the Jesuits*.

91. Wooding, *Rethinking Catholicism*, p. 6.

92. Davies, *Owain Glyn Dŵr*, p. 338.
93. Greenwell, ed., *Wills and Inventories from the Registry at Durham*, pt. 2, p. 285.
94. Durham County Record Office, D/Sa/L59.
95. SP 12/175, no. 89. I am not sufficiently attuned to the details of early modern magic to know what this man hoped to do with the earl's head. He did have some precedent, however: see the yearbook report of 1371 which relates the case of man who was arrested with the head of a corpse and a book of sorcery: Baker, *Dyer's Reports*, p. lxix; 82 Selden Society 162, no. 111. Also of some interest, Gregson was arrested along with one "Old Birtles, the great devil": Keith Thomas has speculated that this might be the same "Mr. Bircles" wanted for his involvement with the Derbyshire rioters in 1569. See Thomas, *Religion and the Decline of Magic*, p. 404.
96. Child, *The English and Scottish Popular Ballads*, pt. VI, pp. 401–23.
97. See, for instance, Colin Haydon's catalogue of instances of popular belief in a papal "bogeyman" throughout the eighteenth century; Haydon, *Anti-Catholicism*, pp. 28–70.
98. Cockburn, *Calendar of Assize Records, Elizabeth I: Essex*, no. 1233.
99. Cockburn, *Calendar of Assize Records, Elizabeth I: Essex*, no. 1624.
100. See Mears, *Queenship and Political Discourse*, pp. 196–8.

Conclusion

1. Wordsworth, *The White Doe*, ll.344–6, 570–1, 628–40, 664–9.
2. Wordsworth, *The White Doe*, p. 7.
3. See Norman, *Anti-Catholicism in Victorian England*.
4. Pollen, "English Confessors and Martyrs," vol. 5.
5. Housley, "Insurrection as Religious War," pp. 141–54, quote at 154.
6. Clifton, *Last Popular Rebellion*.
7. On the latter, see Hosford, *Nottingham, Nobles and the North*.
8. See, for instance, Tilly, *The Contentious French*.
9. From the commission for Warwick and Clinton, the commanders of the southern army: PRO 30/26/116, fol. 202.
10. Fletcher and MacCulloch, *Tudor Rebellions*, pp. 123, 136–8.

Bibliography

Manuscript sources

Berwick-upon-Tweed Record Office
Enrolment Books
Bailiff's Court Books

British Library
Additional MS vols. 40746, 48049.
Cotton Caligula B.IX vols. 1 and 2, C.I., CIII, CIV.
Cotton Titus B. II, F. III.
Harleian MS vols. 6990, 6991.
Lansdowne MS vols. 11, 12, 15, 20, 102, 115.
Salisbury MS [Microfilm] vols. 5, 70, 156, 158.
Stowe MS 145.

Bodleian Library, Oxford
Tanner MS [Microfilm] vol. 50.
MS Eng Hist e. 198.

Borthwick Institute of Historical Research
HC.CP 1569, 1570, High Commission Cause Papers.
HC.AB vols. 3–7, High Commission Act Books.
V. 1567–68, CB1 and CB2, Visitation Court Books.

Bowes Museum, Barnard Castle
Bowes MS.

Cheshire and Chester Record Office
EDA 12/2, Commissioners for Ecclesiastical Causes.

Corporation of London Record Office
Repertories of the Court of Aldermen, vol. 16.
Journals of the Court of Common Council, vol. 19.

Durham County Record Office
D/St/C1/2/4, Strathmore Estate, Estate and Family Records.
D/Sa/L59, Salvin Family of Croxdale, Estate and Family Records.

Durham Dean and Chapter Library
Raine MS 124.

Durham University Library, Palace Green, Archives and Special Collections
DDR/EJ/CCD/1, Consistory Court Deposition Books.
MS 534 Bowes Papers.

Guildhall Library, City of London
MS 649, 5090, Churchwardens' Accounts.

National Archives, Public Record Office, Kew
  AO 1, Auditors of the Imprest . . . Declared Accounts.
  C 66, Chancery: Patent Rolls.
  E 112, Exchequer: King's Remembrancer: Bills and Answers.
  E 123, Exchequer: King's Remembrancer: Entry Books of Decrees and Orders.
  E 134, Exchequer: King's Remembrancer: Depositions Taken By Commission.
  E 137, Exchequer: Lord Treasurer's and King's Remembrancer: Estreats.
  E 164, Exchequer: King's Remembrancer: Miscellaneous Books, Series 1.
  E 178, Exchequer: King's Remembrancer: Special Commissions of Enquiry.
  E 310, Exchequer: Particulars for Crown Leases.
  E 351, Exchequer: Pipe Office: Declared Accounts.
  LR 2, Officers of the Auditors of Land Revenue . . . : Miscellaneous Books.
  PRO 30/26/116, Chancery, Crown Office, Precedent Book.
  SP 12, Secretaries of State: State Papers Domestic, Elizabeth I.
  SP 15, Secretaries of State: State Papers Domestic, Edward VI–James I: Addenda.
  SP 46, Secretaries of State: State Papers Domestic Supplementary.
  SP 52, Secretaries of State: State Papers Scotland, Series I, Elizabeth I.
  SP 53, Secretaries of State: State Papers Scotland, Series I, Mary Queen of Scots.
  SP 59, Secretaries of State: State Papers Scotland, Border Papers.
  SP 63, State Papers Office: State Papers Ireland, Elizabeth I–George III.
  SP 70, Secretaries of State: State Papers Foreign, Elizabeth I.
  STAC 5, Court of Star Chamber, Proceedings, Elizabeth I.

National Archives Scotland
  GD149/265, Miscellaneous State Papers, 1565–1628.

National Library of Scotland
  Adv. MS 34.1.11 and 35.4.1.

North Yorkshire Record Office
  DC/RMB, Richmond Urban District Council Records.

Strathmore Estates, Glamis Castle
  Bowes MS.

Printed primary sources

Allestree, Richard. *A New Almanacke and Prognostication*. London, various editions.
Anonymous. *The Forme and Shape of a Monstrous Child born at Maydstone in Kent, the xxiiii of October*. London, 1568.
Anonymous. *Ballad Against Rebellious and False Rumours*. London, 1570.
Anonymous. *Discours des Troubles nouvellement advenuz au Royaume d'Angleterre*. Paris, 1570.
Anonymous. *A Meruaylous Straunge Deformed Swine*. London, 1570.
Anonymous. *Ane Discourse tuiching the estait present in October anno Domini 1571*. St Andrews, 1572.
Anonymous. *Loyalty's Speech to Englands Subjects*. London, 1639.
Anonymous. *A Brief Historical Account of the Behaviour of the Jesuits . . . with an Epistle of W. Watson, a secular priest, showing how they were thought of by the other Romanists of the time*. London, 1689.

Bristow, Richard. *A Brief Treatise of Diverse Plaine and Sure Wayes to Finde out the Truthe.* Antwerp, 1574.

Buchanan, George. *An Admonition Direct to the Trew Lordis Mantenaris of the Kingis Graces Authoritie.* 2d edn. London, 1571.

Bullein, William. *A Dialogue . . . Against the Fever Pestilence.* London, 1573.

Burgess, Cornelius. *Another Sermon Preached to the Honorable House of Commons.* London, 1641.

By the Queene: A declaration of the just, honourable, and necessarie causes, that move the Queenes Maiestie to leuie and send an armie to the borders of Scotland. London, 1570.

By the Queene: A Proclamation declaring the untruth of certain malitious reportes deuised and published in the Realm of Scotland. London, 1569.

Carleton, George. *A Thankfull Remembrance of God's Mercie.* London, 1624.

Catena, Girolamo. *Vita del Gloriosissimo Papa Pio Quinto.* Rome, 1587.

Churchyard, Thomas. *General Rehersall of Warres.* London, 1579.

Coke, Sir Edward. *The First Part of the Institutes of the Laws of England.* London, 1670.

Coke, Sir Edward. *The Third Part of the Institutes of the Laws of England.* London, 1644.

Drant, Thomas. "A Sermon preached at the Court at Windsor, 8 January 1569 [ie: 1570]." *Three Godly Learned Sermons.* London, 1584.

Drant, Thomas. *Two Sermons Preached . . . at Windsor.* London, 1570.

Elderton, William. *A Ballad Entitled Northumberland News, Wherein you may see what rebels do use.* London, 1570.

Elvidian, Edmund. *A New Years Gift to the Rebellious Persons in the North Parts of England.* London, 1570.

G., R. *Salutem in Christo.* London, 1571.

How, William. *The Several Confessions of Thomas Norton and Christopher Norton, Two of the Northern Rebels.* London, 1570.

Leslie, John. *Treatise of Treasons.* Louvain, 1572.

Milton, John. *The Tenure of Kings and Magistrates.* London, 1649.

Munday, Anthony. *The English Romayne Life.* London, 1582.

Norton, Thomas. *To the Queenes Maiesties Poor Deceyued Subiectes of the North Country.* London, 1569.

Norton, Thomas. "A Warning Against the Dangerous Practises of Papists, and Especially the Partners of the Late Rebellion." Reprinted in *All Such Treatises as have been Lately Published by Thomas Norton.* London, 1570.

Norton, Thomas. *A Warning Agaynst the Dangerous Practises of Papistes.* London, 1570.

Norton, Thomas. *An Addition Declaratorie to the Bulles.* London, 1570.

Norton, Thomas. *Disclosing of the Great Bull and Certain Calves that He hath Gotten, and Especially the Monster Bull that Roared at my Lord Byshops Gate.* London, 1570.

Norton, Thomas. "To The Quenes Maiesties Poore Deceived Subiectes of the Northe Country." Reprinted in *All Such Treatises as have lately been published by Thomas Norton.* London, 1570.

Phillips, John. *A Frendly Larum, or Faythful Warning to the True Harted Subiectes of England.* London, 1570.

Plowden, Edmund. *Commentaries*. London, 1761.

Preston, Thomas. *A Lamentation from Rome, How the Pope Doth Bewail that the Rebels in England can not Prevail*. London, 1570.

Seres, William. *An Answer to the Proclamation of the Rebels in the North*. London, 1569.

Taylor, John. "God's Manifold Mercies in these Miraculous Deliverances of our Church of England," In *All the Works of John Taylor*. vol. 2. London, 1630.

Taylor, John. *The Old, Old, Very Old Man: Or, the Age and Long Life of Thomas Par*. London, 1635.

Watson, William (attr. Thomas Bluet). *Important Considerations*. London, 1601.

Edited primary sources

"A thanksgiving for the suppression of the last rebellion." In *Liturgical Services of the Reign of Queen Elizabeth*, edited by William Keatinge Clay. Parker Society. Cambridge, 1847.

"An Exhortation to Obedience." In *Certain Sermons or Homilies (1547) and A Homily against Disobedience and Wilful Rebellion (1570): A Critical Edition*, edited by Ronald Bond. Toronto, 1987.

Ayre, John, ed. *The Sermons of Edwin Sandys*. Parker Society. Cambridge, 1842.

Bacon, Francis. *The History of the Reign of King Henry the Seventh*, edited by J. Weinberger. Ithaca, 1996.

Bannatyne, Richard. *Memorials of Transactions in Scotland*. Edinburgh, 1836.

Baskerville, E.J. "A Religious Disturbance in Canterbury: John Bale's Unpublished Account." *Historical Research* 65 (1992): 340–48.

Bateson, Mary. "A Collection of Original Letters for the Bishops to the Privy Council, 1564." *Camden Miscellany* 9 (1895).

Bracton. *De Legibus et Consuetudinubus Anglie*, edited by G.E. Woodbine. 4 vols. 1915–42.

Burton, J.H. and D. Mason, eds, *Register of the Privy Council of Scotland*. 14 vols. Edinburgh, 1877–98.

Calendar of the Patent Rolls... Elizabeth I, vols 5–7, London, 1939–86.

Cecil, William. *The Execution of Justice in England*, edited by Robert M. Kingdon. Ithaca, 1965.

Clifford, A. *The State Papers... of Sir Ralph Sadler*. 2 vols. Edinburgh, 1809.

Cockburn, J.S., ed. *Calendar of Assize Records, Essex Indictments, Elizabeth I*. 1978.

Collman, Herbert L., ed. *Ballads And Broadsides Chiefly of the Elizabethan Period*. 1912. Reprint, New York, 1971.

Calendar of State Papers, Foreign Series, of the Reign of Elizabeth, vols 8–10. London, 1863–1929.

Calendar of Letters and State Papers... Preserved Principally in the Archives of Simancas, vol. 2. London, 1892–1999.

Calendar of State Papers relating to Scotland and Mary Queen of Scots, vols 2–4. Edinburgh, 1898–1999.

Drew, Charles, ed. *Lambeth Churchwardens Accounts*. vol. 1. Surrey Record Society vol. 18. 1841.

Foley, H. *Records of the English Province of the Society of Jesus*. 7 vols in 8. London, 1875–83.

Foster, J.E., ed. *Churchwardens' Accounts of St Mary the Great, Cambridge.* Cambridge, 1905.

Fowler, A., ed. *The Rites of Durham.* Surtees Society, vol. 15. 1842.

Green, M.A.E., ed. "The Life and Death of Mr. William Whittingham deane of Durham." *Camden Miscellany* 6 (1871).

Greenwell, William, ed. *Wills and Inventories from the Registry at Durham*, pt. 2. Surtees Society, vol. 38. 1860.

Hartley, T.E., ed. *Proceedings in the Parliaments of Elizabeth I.* vol. I. Leicester, 1981.

Haynes, Samuel, ed. *Collection of State Papers ... From the Year 1540 to 1570 ... left by William Cecil, Lord Burghley.* London, 1740.

Hayward, John. *Annals of the First Fours Years of the Reign of Queen Elizabeth*, edited by J. Bruce. Camden Society, vol. 7. London, 1840.

Holinshed, Raphael, et al., *Holinshed's Chronicles of England, Scotland, and Ireland.* 6 vols., edited by John Hooker et al. London, 1587. Reprint edited by Sir Henry Ellis, London, 1807–08.

Howell, T.B. *A Complete Collection of State Trials and Proceedings for High Treason.* 21 vols. London, 1816–26.

Hughes, P.L. and J.F. Larkin, eds, *Tudor Royal Proclamations.* 3 vols. New Haven, 1964–69.

Hussey, Arthur, ed. "Archbishop Parker's Visitation, 1569." *Home Counties Magazine* 5 (1903): 8–16, 113–19, 208–12, 285–9.

Kitching, C.J., ed. *The Royal Visitation of 1559: Act Book for the Northern Province.* Surtees Society, vol. 187. 1975.

Laderchi, James. *Annales Ecclesiastici.* 37 vols. Guerin, 1864.

Leslie's Historie of Scotland, ed. E.G. Cody. 2 vols. Scottish Text Society. Edinburgh, 1888.

Lettenhove, Kervyn de. *Relations Politiques des Pays-Bas et de l'Angleterre sous le Règne de Philippe II.* Vol. V. Bruxelles, 1886.

McInnes, Charles Thorpe, ed. *Accounts of the Treasurer of Scotland.* Vol. 12. Edinburgh, 1970.

Murdin, William. *A Collection of State Papers Relating to Affairs in the Reign of Queen Elizabeth From the Year 1571 to 1596 Transcribed from Original Papers ... Left by William Cecill.* London, 1759.

Ormsby, G., ed. *Selections from the Household Book of Lord William Howard of Naworth*, Surtees Society 68. 1877.

Pollard, A.J., ed. *Tudor Tracts, 1532–1588.* New York, 1964.

Queen Elizabeth's Defence of Her Proceedings in Church and State, edited by W.E. Collins. 1899. Reprint, London, 1958.

Raine, J., ed. *Depositions and other Ecclesiastical Proceedings from the Courts of Durham.* Surtees Society, vol. 21. London, 1845.

Raine, J., ed. *The Correspondence of Dr. Matthew Hutton.* Surtees Society, vol. 17. London, 1843.

Raine, A. et al., eds, *York Civic Records.* 9 vols. Yorkshire Archaeological Society Record Series, 1938–78.

Rigg, J.M., ed. *Calendar of State Papers relating to English Affairs preserved Principally at Rome.* Vol. 1, 1558–71. London, 1916.

Registrum Honoris de Morton. Edinburgh, 1853; Bannatyne Club.

Robinson, Hastings, ed. *Zurich Letters, 1558–1579.* Parker Society. Cambridge, 1845.

Salignac de la Mothe Fénélon, Bertrand de. *Correspondance Diplomatique du Salignac de la Mothe Fénélon.* 7 vols. Paris, 1838–40.

Sander, Nicholas. *Rise and Growth of the Anglican Schism.* Translated by David Lewis. London, 1877.

Sharp, Cuthbert, ed., *Memorials of the Rebellion of the Earls of Northumberland and Westmorland,*1840. Reprint, Shotton, 1975, as *The Rising in the North: The 1569 Rebellion* with a new introduction by Robert Wood.

Smith, Thomas. *De Respublica Anglorum,* edited by L. Alston. Cambridge, 1906.

Statutes of the Realm. 11 vols in 12. London, 1810–28.

St German, Christopher. *Doctor and Student.,* edited by T.F.T. Plucknett and J.L. Barton. Selden Society, vol. 91. 1974.

Strype, John. *Annals of the Reformation.*1824. Reprint, 4 vols in 7. New York, 1968.

Tawney, R.H. and E. Power, eds, *Tudor Economic Documents.* 3 vols. London, 1924.

The English Reports. 175 vols. Edinburgh, 1900–32.

The Memoirs of Sir James Melville of Halhill, ed. Gordon Donaldson. London, 1969.

The Tree of the Commonwealth: A Treatise by Edmund Dudley, edited by D.M. Brodie. Cambridge, 1948.

Thomson, Thomas, ed. *A Diurnal of Remarkable Occurrents that Have Passed within the Country of Scotland.* Edinburgh, 1883; Bannatyne Club no. 43.

Thorne, S.E., ed. *Readings and Moots at the Inns of Court.* Selden Society, vol. 71. 1954.

Williams, John Foster, ed. *The Early Churchwardens' Accounts of Hampshire.* Winchester, 1913.

Wordsworth, William. *The White Doe of Rylstone; or, The Fate of the Nortons,* edited by Kristine Dugas. Ithaca, 1988.

Secondary sources

Abrams, Philip. *Historical Sociology.* Somerset, 1982.

Adams, Simon. "Eliza Enthroned? The Court and its Politics." In *The Reign of Elizabeth I,* edited by Chistopher Haigh, 55–77. Basingstoke, 1984.

Adams, Simon. "Favourites and Factions at the Elizabethan Court." Reprinted with postscript in *Tudor Monarchy,* edited by John Guy, 253–74. London, 1997.

Alford, Stephen. *The Early Elizabethan Polity: William Cecil and the British Succession Crisis, 1558–1569.* Cambridge, 1998.

Appleby, A. "Agrarian Capitalism or Seigneurial Reaction? The Northwest of England, 1500–1700." *American Historical Review* 80 (1975): 574–94.

Arthurson, Ian. "The Rising of 1497: A Revolt of the Peasantry?" In *People, Politics and Community in the Later Middle Ages,* edited by J. Rosenthal and C. Richmond. Gloucester, 1987.

Aston, Margaret. *England's Iconoclasts.* Vol. 1. Oxford, 1988.

Bagwell, Richard. *Ireland Under the Tudors.* 3 vols. London, 1885–90.

Beier, A.L. "Vagrancy and the Social Order in Elizabethan England." *Past and Present* 64 (1974): 3–29.

Bellamy, J.G. *The Tudor Law of Treason: An Introduction.* London, 1979.

Bernard, G.W. *The King's Reformation: Henry VIII and the Remaking of the English Church.* New Haven, 2005.

Binchy, Daniel A. "An Irish Ambassador at the Spanish Court, 1569–1574." *Studies* 10 (1921): 353–74, 573–84.

Blake, William. *William Maitland of Lethington, 1528–1573: A Study of the Policy of Moderation in the Scottish Reformation.* Studies in British History, vol. 17. Lewiston, 1990.

Bowler, David. "'An Axe or an Acte': The Parliament of 1572 and Resistance Theory in Early Elizabethan England." *Canadian Journal of History* 19 (1984): 349–59.

Boynton, Lindsay. "The Tudor Provost-Marshal." *English Historical Review* 77 (1962): 437–55.

Braddick, M.J. and John Walter, eds, *Negotiating Power in Early Modern Society: Order, Hierarchy and Subordination in Britain and Ireland.* Cambridge, 2001.

Brady, Ciaran. *Chief Governors: The Rise and Fall of Reform Government in Tudor Ireland, 1536–1588.* Cambridge, 1994.

Brammall, Kathryn. "Monstrous Metamorphosis: Nature, Morality, and the Rhetoric of Monstrosity in Tudor England." *Sixteenth Century Journal* 27 (1996): 3–21.

Brand, Sarah. "The Performance of a British Debate for an English Audience: Public Discourses about the Bishops' Wars, 1638–1640." M.A. Thesis, Dalhousie University, 2005.

Bush, Michael. *The Pilgrimage of Grace: A Study of the Rebel Armies of October 1536.* Manchester, 1996.

Bush, Michael. "The Pilgrimage of Grace and the Pilgrim Tradition of Holy War." In *Pilgrimage: The English Experience from Becket to Bunyan*, edited by Colin Morris and Peter Roberts, 178–98. Cambridge, 2002.

Bush, M.L. and D. Bownes. *The Defeat of the Pilgrimage of Grace: A Study of the Postpardon Revolts of December 1536 to March 1537.* Hull, 1999.

Busse, Daniela. "Anti-Catholic Polemical Writing on the 'Rising of the North' (1569) and the Catholic Reaction." *Recusant History* 27 (2004): 11–30.

Calder, Angus. *Revolutionary Empire: The Rise of the English-Speaking Empires from the Fifteenth Century to the 1780s.* New York, 1981.

Canny, Nicholas. *The Elizabethan Conquest of Ireland: A Pattern Established, 1565–1576.* Hassocks 1976.

Carlson, Eric. "Clerical Marriage and the English Reformation." *Journal of British Studies* 31 (1992): 1–31.

Christianson, Paul. "Arguments on Billeting and Martial Law in the Parliament of 1628." *Historical Journal* 37 (1994): 539–67.

Clifton, Robin. *The Last Popular Rebellion: The Western Rising of 1685.* London, 1984.

Clifton, Robin. "The Popular Fear of Catholics during the English Revolution." *Past and Present* 52 (1972): 23–55.

Collinson, Patrick. *Archbishop Grindal, 1519–1583: The Struggle for a Reformed Church.* Berkeley, 1979.

Collinson, Patrick. "The Monarchical Republic of Queen Elizabeth I." In Collinson, *Elizabethan Essays.* London, 1994.

Cooper, J.P.D. *Propaganda and the Tudor State.* Oxford, 2003.

Cowan, Ian B. "The Marian Civil War, 1567–1573." In *Scotland and War, AD 79–1918*, edited by Forman MacDougall, 95–112. Edinburgh, 1991.

Cressy, David. *Agnes Bowker's Cat: Travesties and Transgressions in Tudor and Stuart England.* Oxford, 2001.

Cressy, David. *Bonfires and Bells: National Memory and the Protestant Calendar in Elizabethan and Stuart England.* London, 1989.

Crouzet, Denis. *Les Guerriers de Dieu: la Violence au Temps des Troubles de Religion.* 2 vols. Seyssel, 1990.

Cust, Richard. "News and Politics in Early Seventeenth-Century England." *Past and Present* 112 (1986): 60–90.

Danner, Dan G. "Christopher Goodman and the English Protestant Tradition of Civil Disobedience." *Sixteenth Century Journal* 8 (1977): 60–73.

Davies, C.S.L. "The Pilgrimage of Grace Reconsidered," *Past and Present* 41 (1968): 39–64.

Davies, C.S.L. "Popular Religion and the Pilgrimage of Grace." In *Order and Disorder in Early Modern England,* edited by A. Fletcher and J. Stevenson, 58–91. Cambridge, 1986.

Davies, R.R. *The Revolt of Owain Glyn Dŵr.* Oxford: 1995.

Davis, N.Z. "The Rites of Violence: Religious Riot in Sixteenth-Century France." *Past and Present* 59 (1973): 51–91.

Dawson, Jane E.A. "Anglo-Scottish Protestant Culture and Integration in Sixteenth-Century Britain." In *Conquest and Union: Fashioning a British State, 1485–1725,* edited by Steven G. Ellis and Sarah Barber, 87–114. London, 1995.

Dawson, Jane E.A. *The Politics of Religion in the Age of Mary, Queen of Scots: The Earl of Argyll and the Struggle for Britain and Ireland.* Cambridge, 2002.

Dietz, Frederick C. *English Public Finance, 1485–1641.* 2 vols. New York, 1932.

Dillon, Anne. *The Construction of Martyrdom in the English Catholic Community, 1535–1603.* Aldershot, 2002.

Donaldson, Gordon. *All the Queen's Men: Power and Politics in Mary Stewart's Scotland.* London, 1983.

Donaldson, Gordon. *The First Trial of Mary, Queen of Scots.* Westport, Connecticut, 1983.

Duffy, Eamon. *The Voices of Morebath: Reformation and Rebellion in an English Village.* New Haven, 2001.

Edwards, David. "Beyond Reform: Martial Law and the Tudor Reconquest of Ireland." *History Ireland* 5.2 (1997): 16–21.

Edwards, David. "Ideology and Experience: Spenser's *View* and martial law in Ireland." In *Political Ideology in Ireland, 1541–1641,* edited by Hiram Morgan, 127–57. Dublin, 1999.

Edwards, David. "The Butler Revolt of 1569." *Irish Historical Studies* 28 (1993): 228–55.

Edwards, Francis. *The Marvellous Chance: Thomas Howard, Fourth Duke of Norfolk, and the Ridolphi Plot, 1570–1572.* London, 1968.

Edwards, R. Dudley. "Ireland, Elizabeth I and the Counter-Reformation." In *Elizabethan Government and Society,* edited by S.T. Bindoff et al., 315–39. London, 1961.

Ellis, Steven. *Ireland in the Age of the Tudors, 1447–1603.* London, 1998.

Ellis, Steven. *Tudor Frontiers and Noble Power: The Making of the British State.* Oxford, 1995.

Ellis, Steven. "Tudor State Formation and the Shaping of the British Isles." In *Conquest and Union: Fashioning a British State, 1485–1725,* edited by Steven Ellis and Sarah Barber, 40–63. London, 1995.

Elton, G.R. "Politics and the Pilgrimage of Grace." In *After the Reformation,* edited by B. Malament, 25–56. London, 1979.

Elton, G.R. *Reform and Reformation: England, 1509–1558.* London, 1977.

"Enclosure Riots at Chinley, AD 1569." *Journal of the Derbyshire Archaeological and Natural History Society* 21 (1899): 61–8.

Erickson, Amy L. *Women and Property in Early Modern England.* London, 1993.

Fisher, R.M. "Privy Council Coercion and Religious Conformity at the Inns of Court, 1569–84." *Recusant History* 15 (1979–81): 305–24.

Fissel, Mark Charles. *English Warfare, 1511–1642.* London, 2001.

Fox, Adam. "Rumour, News, and Popular Political Opinion in Elizabethan and Early Stuart England." *Historical Journal* 40 (1997): 597–620.

Fraser, George MacDonald. *The Steel Bonnets: The Story of the Anglo-Scottish Border Reivers.* London, 1971.

Freeman, Jane. "The Distribution and Use of Ecclesiastical Patronage in the Diocese of Durham, 1558–1640." In *The Last Principality: Politics, Religion, and Society in the Bishopric of Durham, 1494–1660,* edited by David Marcombe, 152–75. Nottingham, 1987.

Freeman, Thomas S. " 'The reformation of the church in this parliament': Thomas Norton, John Foxe, and the Parliament of 1571." *Parliamentary History* 16 (1997): 131–47.

Graves, Michael A.R. *Thomas Norton: The Parliament Man.* Oxford, 1994.

Greaves, Richard L. "John Knox, the Reformed Tradition, and the Development of Resistance Theory." *Journal of Modern History* 48 (1976): 1–36.

Guy, John. *Queen of Scots: The True Life of Mary Stuart.* Boston, 2004.

Habakkuk, H.J. "The Market for Monastic Property, 1539–1603." *Economic History Review,* 2d ser., 10 (1957–8): 362–80.

Habermas, Jürgen. *The Structural Transformation of the Public Sphere.* Translated by T. Burger with F. Lawrence. Cambridge, Massachusetts, 1989.

Haigh, Christopher. *Reformation and Resistance in Tudor Lancashire.* Cambridge, 1975.

Haigh, Christopher. *English Reformations: Religion, Politics, and Society under the Tudors.* Oxford, 1993.

Haugaard, William P. *Elizabeth and the English Reformation.* Cambridge, 1968.

Haydon, Colin. *Anti-Catholicism in Eighteenth-Century England, c. 1714–80.* Manchester, 1993.

Heal, Felicity. *Of Prelates and Princes: A Study of the Economic and Social Position of the Tudor Episcopate.* Cambridge, 1980.

Hicks, Michael. "Attainder, Resumption and Coercion, 1461–1529." *Parliamentary History* 3 (1984): 15–31.

Highley, Christopher. " 'A Pestilent and Seditious Book': Nicholas Sander's *Schismatis Anglicani* and Catholic Histories of the Reformation." *Huntington Library Quarterly* 68 (2005): 151–71.

Holdsworth, William. "Martial Law Historically Considered." *Law Quarterly Review* 18 (1902): 117–32.

Holmes, Peter. *Resistance and Compromise: The Political Thought of the Elizabethan Catholics.* Cambridge, 1982.

Hosford, David. *Nottingham, Nobles and the North: Aspects of the Revolution of 1688.* Hamden, Connecticut, 1976.

Housley, Norman. "Insurrection as Religious War, 1400–1536." *Journal of Medieval History* 25 (1999): 141–54.

Hoyle, R.W., ed. *The Estates of the English Crown, 1558–1640.* Cambridge, 1992.

Hoyle, R.W. "Faction, Feud, and Reconciliation amongst the Northern English Nobility, 1535–1659." *History* 84 (1999): 590–613.

Hoyle, R.W. "Lords, Tenants, and Tenant Right in the Sixteenth Century: Four Studies." *Northern History* 20 (1984): 38–63.

Hoyle, R.W. *The Pilgrimage of Grace and the Politics of the 1530s*. Oxford, 2001.

Hurstfield, Joel. "The Profits of Fiscal Feudalism, 1541–1602." *Economic History Review*, 2d ser., 8 (1955): 53–61.

James, Mervyn. *Family, Lineage and Civil Society: A Study of Society, Politics, and Mentality in the Durham Region, 1500–1640*. Oxford, 1974.

James, M.E. *Society, Politics, and Culture*. Cambridge, 1986.

James, M.E. "The Concept of Order and the Northern Rising of 1569." *Past and Present* 60 (1973): 49–83.

Jones, Norman. *The Birth of the Elizabethan Age: England in the 1560s*. Oxford, 1993.

Jones, Norman. "Defining Superstitions: Treasonous Catholics and the Act against Witchcraft, 1563." In *State, Sovereigns, and Society in Early Modern England*, edited by Charles Carlton et al., 187–203. Stroud, 1998.

Jones, Norman. "Living the Reformation: Generational Experience and Political Perception in Early Modern England." *Huntington Library Quarterly* 60 (1999): 273–88.

Jones, Norman. *The English Reformation: Religion and Cultural Adaptation*. Oxford, 2002.

Jones, Ann Rosalind and Peter Stallybrass. *Renaissance Clothing and the Materials of Memory*. Cambridge, 2000.

Keen, Maurice. *The Laws of War in the Late Middle Ages*. Toronto, 1965.

Kellar, Clare. *Scotland, England, and the Reformation, 1534–1561*. Oxford, 2003.

Kent, Joan R. *The English Village Constable, 1580–1642: A Social and Administrative History*. Oxford, 1986.

Kesselring, K.J. *Mercy and Authority in the Tudor State*. Cambridge, 2003.

Kesselring, K.J. "Deference and Dissent in Tudor England: Reflections on Sixteenth-Century Protest." *History Compass* 3 (2005): 1–16.

Kesselring, K.J. "Mercy and Liberality: The Aftermath of the 1569 Northern Rebellion." *History* 90 (2005): 213–35.

King, A. "Englishmen, Scots and Marchers: National and Local Identities in Thomas Gray's *Scalacronica*." *Northern History* 36.2 (2000): 217–31.

Lake, Peter. "Anti-popery: The Structure of a Prejudice." In *Conflict in Early Stuart England*, edited by Richard Cust and Ann Hughes, 72–106. London, 1989.

Lander, J.R. "Attainder and Forfeiture, 1453–1509." *Historical Journal* 4 (1961): 119–49.

Langbein, John. *Torture and the Law of Proof: Europe and England in the Ancien Régime*. Chicago, 1977.

Lechat, Robert. *Les Réfugiés Anglais dans les Pays-Bas espagnole Durant le règne d'Elisabeth, 1558–1603*. Louvain, 1914.

Lee, Maurice, Jr. *James Stewart, Earl of Moray: A Political Study of the Reformation in Scotland*. 1953. Reprint, Westport, Connecticut, 1971.

Lehmberg, Stanford E. "Parliamentary Attainder in the Reign of Henry VIII." *Historical Journal* 18 (1975): 675–702.

Lemaitre, Nicole. *Saint Pie V*. Paris, 1994.

Litzenberger, Caroline. *The English Reformation and the Laity: Gloucestershire, 1540–1580*. Cambridge, 1997.

Loades, D.M. *Two Tudor Conspiracies*. Cambridge, 1965.

Lock, Julian. "Percy, Thomas, seventh earl of Northumberland (1528–1572)." *Oxford Dictionary of National Biography*. Oxford University Press, 2004.

Lowers, J.K. *Mirrors for Rebels: A Study of Polemical Literature Relating to the Northern Rebellion, 1569*. Berkeley, 1953.

Lyons, Mary Ann. *Franco-Irish Relations, 1500–1610: Politics, Migration, and Trade*. Woodbridge, 2003.

MacCaffrey, Wallace. "Place and Patronage in Elizabethan Politics." In *Elizabethan Government and Society*, edited by S.T. Bindoff, J. Hurstfield, and C.H. Williams, 95–126. London, 1961.

MacCaffrey, Wallace. *The Shaping of the Elizabethan Regime*. Princeton, 1986.

MacCaffrey, Wallace. "Patronage and Politics under the Tudors," in *The Mental World of the Jacobean Court*, edited by Linda Levy Peck, 21–35. Cambridge, 1991.

Maltby, Judith. *Prayer Book and People in Elizabethan and Early Stuart England*. Cambridge, 1998.

Maltby, William S. *Alba: A Biography of Fernando Alvarez de Toledo, Third Duke of Alba 1507–1582*. Berkeley, 1983.

Manning, R.B. "Patterns of Violence in Early Tudor Enclosure Riots." *Albion* 6 (1974): 120–33.

Manning, R.B. "Violence and Social Conflict in Mid-Tudor Rebellions." *Journal of British Studies* 16 (1977): 18–40.

Manning, R.B. "The Origins of the Doctrine of Sedition." *Albion* 12 (1980): 99–121.

Marcombe, David. "The Dean and Chapter of Durham, 1558–1603." Ph.D. diss., Durham University, 1973.

Marcombe, David. "'A Rude and Heady People': The Local Community and the Rebellion of the Northern Earls." In *The Last Principality: Politics, Religion, and Society in the Bishopric of Durham, 1494–1660*, edited by David Marcombe, 117–51. Nottingham, 1987.

Marsh, Christopher. "Order and Place in England, 1580–1640: The View from the Pew." *Journal of British Studies* 44 (2005): 3–26.

Marten, Anthony. "The End of History: Thomas Norton's 'v periodes' and the Pattern of English Protestant Historiography." In *John Foxe and His World*, edited by Christopher Highley and John N. King, 37–53. Aldershot, 2002.

Mason, Roger A. "The Scottish Reformation and the Origins of Anglo-British Imperialism." In *Scots and Britons: Scottish Political Thought and the Union of 1603*, edited by Roger A. Mason, 161–86. Cambridge, 1994.

McCall, H.B. "The Rising in the North: A New Light Upon One Aspect of It." *Yorkshire Archaeological Journal* 18 (1905): 74–87.

McCoog, Thomas. "Construing Martyrdom in the English Catholic Community, 1582–1602." In *Catholics and the 'Protestant Nation'*, edited by Ethan Shagan, 95–127. Manchester, 2005.

McLaren, Anne. "Gender, Religion, and Early Modern Nationalism: Elizabeth I, Mary Queen of Scots, and the Genesis of English Anti-Catholicism." *American Historical Review* 107 (2002): 739–69.

Mears, Natalie. *Queenship and Political Discourse in the Elizabethan Realms*. Cambridge, 2005.

Meikle, Maureen. "A Godly Rogue: The Career of Sir John Forster, An Elizabethan Border Warden." *Northern History* 28 (1992): 126–63.

Meikle, Maureen. *A British Frontier? Lairds and Gentlemen in the Eastern Borders, 1540–1605*. East Linton, 2004.

Menmuir, Charles. *The Rising of the North.* Newcastle, 1907.

Merrick, M.M. *Thomas Percy, Seventh Earl.* Duckett, 1949.

Merriman, Marcus. "Home Thoughts from Abroad: National Consciousness and Scottish Exiles in the Mid-Sixteenth Century." In *Social and Political Identities in Western History*, edited by Claue Bjørn et al., 90–117. Copenhagen, 1994.

Meyer, Arnold Oskar. *England and the Catholic Church under Queen Elizabeth.* Translated by J.R. McKee. London, 1967.

Morgan, Hiram. "British Policies before the British State." In *The British Problem, c. 1534–1707: State Formation in the Atlantic Archipelago*, edited by Brendan Bradshaw and John Morrill, 66–88. London, 1996.

Neale, J.E. *Elizabeth I and Her Parliaments.* 2 vols. London, 1953–57.

Neville, C.J. "Widows of War: Edward I and the Women of Scotland During the War of Independence." In *Wife and Widow in Medieval England*, edited by Sue Sheridan Walker, 109–39. Ann Arbor, 1993.

Neville, C.J. "Local Sentiment and the 'National' Enemy: Northern English Communities in the Later Middle Ages." *Journal of British Studies* 35 (1996): 419–37.

Neville, Cynthia. *Violence, Custom and Law: The Anglo-Scottish Borderlands in the Later Middle Ages.* Edinburgh, 1998.

Newton, Diana. *North-East England, 1569–1625: Governance, Culture, and Identity.* Woodbridge, Suffolk, 2006.

Norman, E.R. *Anti-Catholicism in Victorian England.* London, 1968.

O'Day, Rosemary. *The English Clergy: The Emergence and Consolidation of a Profession, 1558–1642.* Leicester, 1979.

Outhwaite, R.B. "Who Bought Crown Lands? The Pattern of Purchases, 1589–1603." *Bulletin of the Institute of Historical Research* 44 (1971): 18–33.

Palmer, William. "Gender, Violence, and Rebellion in Tudor and Early Stuart Ireland." *Sixteenth Century Journal* 23 (1992): 699–712.

Parish, Helen. *Clerical Marriage and the English Reformation: Precedent, Policy and Practice.* Aldershot, 2000.

Parker, Geoffrey. *The Grand Strategy of Philip II.* New Haven, 1998.

Parker, Geoffrey. "The Place of Tudor England in the Messianic Vision of Philip II of Spain." *Transactions of the Royal Historical Society* 12 (2002): 167–221.

Pastor, Ludwig. *History of the Popes.* 40 vols., edited by Ralph Kerr. St Louis, 1923–53.

Peck, Linda Levy. "'For a King not to be bountiful were a fault': Perspectives on Court Patronage in Early Stuart England." *Journal of British Studies* 25 (1986): 31–61.

Peters, Christine. *Patterns of Piety: Women, Gender and Religion in Late Medieval and Reformation England.* Cambridge, 2003.

Pittock, Murray. *Jacobitism.* New York, 1998.

Pollen, J.H. *The English Catholics in the Reign of Queen Elizabeth.* London, 1920.

Pollen, J.H. "English Confessors and Martyrs, 1534–1729." *Catholic Encyclopedia.* Vol. 5. 1909. Online edition, 2003.

Pollitt, R. "An 'Old Practizer' at Bay: Thomas Bishop and the Northern Rebellion." *Northern History* 16 (1980): 59–84.

Pollitt, Ronald. "The Defeat of the Northern Rebellion and the Shaping of Anglo-Scottish Relations." *Scottish Historical Review* 64 (1985): 1–21.

Potter, Harry. *Bloodfeud: The Stewarts and Gordons at War in the Age of Mary Queen of Scots.* Stroud, 2002.

Prior, M. "Reviled and Crucified Marriages: The Position of Tudor Bishops' Wives." In *Women in English Society 1500–1800*, edited by M. Prior, 118–48. London, 1985.

Pucci, Michael S. "Reforming Roman Emperors: John Foxe's Characterization of Constantine in the *Acts and Monuments*." In *John Foxe: An Historical Perspective*, edited by D.M. Loades, 29–51. Aldershot, 1999.

Questier, Michael. "Elizabeth and the Catholics." In *Catholics and the 'Protestant Nation'*, edited by Ethan Shagan, 69–94. Manchester, 2005.

Rae, Thomas I. *The Administration of the Scottish Frontier, 1513–1603*. Edinburgh, 1966.

Read, Conyers. *Mr Secretary Walsingham and the Policy of Queen Elizabeth*. 2 vols. Oxford, 1967.

Read, Conyers. "Queen Elizabeth's Seizure of the Duke of Alva's Pay-Ships." *The Journal of Modern History*, 5 (1933): 443–64.

Ramsay, G.D. *The Queen's Merchants and the Revolt of the Netherlands*. Manchester, 1986.

Read, Conyers. "William Cecil and Elizabethan Public Relations." In *Elizabethan Government and Society*, edited by S.T. Bindoff et al., 21–55. London, 1961.

Reid, D.S. *The Durham Crown Lordships in the Sixteenth and Seventeenth Centuries*. Durham, 1990.

Reid, R.R. "The Rebellion of the Earls, 1569." *Transactions of the Royal Historical Society*, 2d ser., 20 (1906): 171–203.

Reid, R.R. *The King's Council in the North*. London, 1921.

Robison, W. "The National and Local Significance of Wyatt's Rebellion in Surrey." *Historical Journal* 30 (1987): 769–90.

Robson, Ralph. *The English Highland Clans: Tudor Responses to a Medieval Problem*. Edinburgh, 1989.

Ross, Charles. *Elizabethan Literature and the Law of Fraudulent Conveyance*. Aldershot, 2003.

Ross, C.D. "Forfeiture for Treason in the Reign of Richard II." *English Historical Review* 71 (1956): 560–75.

Rowse, A.L. *Tudor Cornwall*. London, 1941.

Samaha, J. "Gleanings from Local Criminal-Court Records: Sedition amongst the 'Inarticulate' in Elizabethan Essex." *Journal of Social History* 8 (1975): 61–79.

Sasso, C.R. "The Desmond Rebellions, 1569–1573 and 1579–1583." Ph.D. diss., Loyola University of Chicago, 1980.

Shagan, Ethan. "Rumours and Popular Politics in the Reign of Henry VIII." In *The Politics of the Excluded, c. 1500–1850*, edited by Tim Harris, 30–66. Basingstoke, 2001.

Shagan, Ethan. *Popular Politics and the English Reformation*. Cambridge, 2002.

Simpson, A.W.B. *A History of the Land Law*. 2nd edn. Oxford, 1986.

Skinner, Quentin. "The Origins of the Calvinist Theory of Revolution." In *After the Reformation*, edited by B.C. Malament, 309–30. Manchester, 1980.

Slack, Paul. "Vagrants and Vagrancy in England, 1598–1664." *Economic History Review*, 2d ser., 27 (1974): 360–79.

Sommerville, Johann P. "Papalist Political Thought and the Controversy over the Jacbobean Oath of Allegiance." In *Catholics and the 'Protestant Nation'*, edited by Ethan Shagan, 162–184. Manchester, 2005.

Spring, Eileen. *Law, Land, and Family: Aristocratic Inheritance in England, 1300 to 1800*. Chapel Hill, 1993.

Stringer, Keith. "Identities in Thirteenth-Century England: Frontier Society in the Far North." In *Social and Political Identities in Western History*, edited by Claus Bjørn et al., 28–66. Copenhagen, 1994.

Strong, Roy. "The Popular Celebration of the Accession Day of Queen Elizabeth I." *Journal of the Warburg and Courtauld Institutes* 21 (1958): 86–103.

Strong, Roy. *The Cult of Elizabeth*. London, 1977.

Tawney, R.H. *The Agrarian Problem in the Sixteenth Century*. London, 1912.

Taylor, S.E. "The Crown and the North of England, 1559–70." Ph.D. thesis, Manchester, 1981.

Thomas, Keith. *Religion and the Decline of Magic*. London, 1971. Reprint, 1997.

Thornton, George. "Blessed Thomas Percy (1528–1572)." *Northern Catholic History* 45 (2004).

Thorp, M. "Religion and the Wyatt Rebellion of 1554." *Church History* 47 (1978): 363–80.

Thorp, Malcolm R. "Catholic Conspiracy in Early Elizabethan Foreign Policy." *Sixteenth Century Journal* 15 (1984): 431–48.

Thorp, Malcolm R. "William Cecil and the anti-christ: A Study in Anti-Catholic Ideology." In *Politics, Religion and Diplomacy*, edited by Malcolm R. Thorp and Arthur J. Slavin, 289–304. Kirksville, Missouri, 1994.

Tilly, Charles. *The Contentious French*. Cambridge, Massachusetts, 1986.

Todd, Margo. *The Culture of Protestantism in Early Modern Scotland*. New Haven, 2002.

Tough, D.L. *The Last Years of a Frontier: A History of the Borders during the Reign of Elizabeth*. Oxford, 1928.

Trim, David. "Protestant Refugees in Elizabethan England and Confessional Conflict in France and the Netherlands, 1562–c.1610." In *From Strangers to Citizens: The Integration of Immigrant Communities in Britain, Ireland, and Colonial America, 1550–1750*, edited by Randolph Vigne and Charles Littleton, 68–79. Brighton, 2001.

Tyerman, Christopher. *England and the Crusades, 1095–1588*. Chicago, 1988.

Usher, Brett. "Queen Elizabeth and Mrs Bishop." In *The Myth of Elizabeth*, edited by Susan Doran and Thomas S. Freeman, 200–20. Basingstoke, 2003.

Van Patten, J.K. "Magic, Prophecy, and the Law of Treason in Reformation England." *American Journal of Legal History* 27 (1983): 1–32.

Vidmar, John. *English Catholic Historians and the English Reformation, 1585–1954*. Brighton, 2005.

Waddington, Raymond B. "Elizabeth I and the Order of the Garter." *Sixteenth Century Journal* 24 (1993): 97–113.

Walker, Simon "Rumour, Sedition, and Popular Protest in the Reign of Henry IV." *Past and Present 166* (2000): 31–65.

Wall, Alison. *Power and Protest in England, 1525–1640*. London, 2000.

Walsham, Alexandra. *Providence in Early Modern England*. Oxford, 1999.

Walsham, Alexandra. " 'A Very Deborah?': The Myth of Elizabeth I as a Providential Monarch" In *The Myth of Elizabeth*, edited by Susan Doran and Thomas S. Freeman, 143–70. Basingstoke, 2003.

Walter, John. *Understanding Popular Violence in the English Revolution: The Colchester Plunderers*. Cambridge, 1999.

Walter, John. "Public Transcripts, Popular Agency and the Politics of Subsistence." In *Negotiating Power in Early Modern Society: Order Hierarchy and Subordination in Britain and Ireland,* edited by Michael J. Braddick and John Walter, 123–48. Cambridge, 2001.

Wark, K.R. *Elizabethan Recusancy in Cheshire.* Chetham Society. 3d ser., vol. 19. Manchester, 1971.

Warnicke, Retha M. *Mary Queen of Scots.* London, 2006.

Weiner, Carol. "The Beleaguered Isle. A Study of Elizabethan and Early Jacobean Anti-Catholicism." *Past and Present* 51 (1971): 27–62.

Wenham, Leslie P. "The Chantries, Guilds, Obits and Lights of Richmond, Yorkshire." *Yorkshire Archaeological Journal* 38 (1952–54): 96–111, 185–214, 310–32.

Wernham, R.B. *The Making of Elizabethan Foreign Policy, 1558–1603.* Berkeley, 1980.

Whiting, Robert. "Abominable Idols: Images and Image-Breaking under Henry VIII." *Journal of Ecclesiastical History* 33 (1982): 30–47.

Whiting, Robert. *The Blind Devotion of the People: Popular Religion and the English Reformation.* Cambridge, 1989.

Williams, Neville. "The Risings in Norfolk, 1569 and 1570." *Norfolk Archaeology* 32 (1959): 73–5.

Williams, Neville. *Thomas Howard, Fourth Duke of Norfolk.* London, 1964.

Wood, Andy. *Riot, Rebellion and Popular Politics in Early Modern England.* New York, 2002.

Wooding, Lucy. *Rethinking Catholicism in Reformation England.* Oxford, 2000.

Wormald, Jenny. *Mary Queen of Scots: A Study in Failure.* London, 1988.

Wormald, Jenny. "Politics and Government of Scotland." In *A Companion to Tudor Britain,* edited by Robert Tittler and Norman Jones, 151–66. Oxford, 2004.

Wyndham, K.S.H. "Crown land and royal patronage in mid-sixteenth century England." *Journal of British Studies* 19(2) (1980): 18–34.

Index